The Bride's Choice Cook Book

D1608631

By Emma Sanders

Canadian Cataloguing in Publication Data

Sanders, Emma, 1928-
The bride's choice

ISBN 0-88925-897-X

1. Cookery. I. Title.
TX715.S35 1988   641.5   C88-091573-0

Registered Trade Marks:
Jell-o, Kool-Aid, Pam.
Miracle Whip is a product of Kraft Ltd.

Photos by F22 Photography, Surrey, B.C.

© 1988
Kountry Koop Kitchen Ltd.
21314 - 80th Avenue, R.R. #11
Langley, B.C.
V3A 6Y3

PRINTED IN CANADA
By D.W. Friesen
Cloverdale, B.C.

A Toast
to
"The Bride's Choice Cook Book"

My book is written, there ain't no more
I've scraped the dough, up off the floor.
The recipes down, on paper by quill
Now wipe up the flour, from the window sill.
The mess of papers, piled so high
Upon my table, I hardly got by.
The company came, the company went
Thanks for the help, with my experiment
The hours I worked was labour well spent
With the help of my friends, their prize recipes lent
Jot down the ingredients, that went into that cake
My only hope is, I made no mistake.
I'll pass on to you, this recipe collection
With practice I know, you'll have them down to perfection.
On your recipe search, you'll find in these pages
The pleasures we've had, down through the ages.

Composed in celebration on the completion of her cookbook.
Authored by: Emma (Quickstad) Sanders, 1988.

Acknowledgements

A special thank you to my relatives and friends who over the years have shared their favorite recipes to add to my collection.

Donna Moore for making the album cover.

Thanks for articles loaned for pictures go to Sharen Hamm, Langley, B.C.; Lovin Spoonfull, Langley, B.C.; Classic Rattan, Langley, B.C.; Village Antiques, Ft. Langley, B.C.; Florist Hills Florist, Langley, B.C.; Silver Service, Surrey, B.C.; Sharen Hamm, pottery pork & beans; Linda Sanders, potato salad bowl; Kathleen Sanders, kitchen curtain.

Bride pictured on front cover, Barbara Sanders (nee Berg).

Two Young Hearts

Fifty years ago today
They knelt before the Lord to pray
They prayed for guidance from above
These two young hearts so much in love.

A golden ring on her left hand
He promised then to be her man
A promise he has kept so well
We who have witnessed all can tell.

She wore her ring with special care
Her body, heart and soul to share
Undying love none can compare
This maiden pure with auburn hair.

The years have passed they've stood the test
A family strong, four of the best
With music rich in country style
They entertained us all this while.

Their hair has changed, their steps have slown
But their true love has only grown
To have and hold with all their heart
Forever love till death they part.

Today we kneel in special prayer
And we give thanks to God up there
For a helping hand from up above
For two young hearts so much in love.

This poem was written for my oldest sister and her husband, Bertha and Chester Botting, on the celebration of their 50th Wedding Anniversary in the year of 1985. By Emma (Quickstad) Sanders.

Table of Contents

Reflections of My Mama

I often think of Mama, I see her working there,
Her cotton dress fit snugly, her kerchief tamed her hair.
I remember looking at her, how pretty that she was!
Her face was never painted, her hair was never fuzzed.

With fourteen kids and Daddy, her load was quite a task.
She always seemed so cheerful, and for nothing did she ask.
And Mama I remember, when Daddy went to town,
You kept the home fires burning, us kids all gathered round.

And Mama I remember, the songs you sang back then.
Oh, Mama, could I hear you sing those songs again.
The many loaves of bread she baked, for a family of our size.
The doughnuts heaped upon the plate, the cookies, cakes and pies.

And on those chilly mornings, when we fussed o'er our clothes,
The porridge pot stood waiting, to ward off the wind that blows.
And Mama I remember, when we hurried home from school,
Those buns you made so often, in a cinnamon buttery pool.

She cooked our meals, she washed our clothes,
These things we took for granted;
And all the time she did her work, those precious seeds she planted.
She taught us how to rightly live, and how to love so deeply.
A gift from God through Mama, that she conveyed discreetly.

And Mama, I remember, your every word was true.
But of all things I remember, I remember, always loving you.

This poem was written for my mother, Julienne Quickstad, with much love and admiration by her daughter, Emma (Quickstad) Sanders in the year of 1986.

Dedication

To my Mama who let me make a mess in her kitchen,
At the age of twelve. Trying to make bread just
like her. Also dedicated to my husband, Wilmer,
without his loyal support this book would not have
become a reality.

Salads

Orange Jello with Shrimp

Very good served with Chinese food...

170g.....1-6 oz. pkg. orange jello
500mL...2 cups boiling water
45mL....3 Tbsp. salad dressing
1........1 can small shrimp
       (drained)*
390mL...1-14 oz. can cubed pine-
      apple (drained)
****

(1) Rinse bowl with cold water.
(2) Place jello into bowl, add boiling water. Stir until jello is dissolved (about 3 minutes).
(3) Chill until heavy syrup stage.
(4) Add salad dressing, beat very well, chill until a little firmer.

(5) Drain and rinse shrimp in cold water.*
(6) Add shrimp and pineapple. Stir well.
(7) Place into prepared mould, chill until firm.

* Rinsing bowl with cold water prevents jello from sticking to the bowl.
* If mould is used, rub salad dressing inside mould, to prevent it from sticking.

Marinated Bean Salad

This is a very tasty salad...

2........2 cans waxed beans
2........2 cans green beans
500mL...2 cups kidney beans
500mL...2 cups lima beans
2........2 cans garbanzo beans
500mL...2 cups chopped celery
250mL...1 cup green peppers
250mL...1 cup onions
****

(1) Drain liquid from beans.
(2) In a bowl combine beans, celery, onions and green peppers, sliced into rings.

Marinade

250mL...1 cup salad oil
175mL...3/4 cup vinegar
5mL.....1 tsp. salt
5mL.....1 tsp. celery seed
175mL...3/4 cup sugar
****

(1) In a jar with tight fitting lid combine all marinade ingredients.
(2) Shake well, pour over bean salad and marinate overnight.

7

Potato Salad (Large)**

Party Size...

11.25kg..25 lbs. cooked, cooled,
    diced potatoes
7........7 dozen cooked, cooled
    eggs
3........3 chopped green onions
3........3 large chopped cooking
    onions
2........2 stalks finely chopped
    parsley
2........2 heads chopped celery
    (not really large)
2L......2-32 oz. jars miracle whip
    salad dressing
385mL...1-14 oz. can evaporated
    milk
30mL....2 Tbsp. dry mustard
125mL...1/2 cup sugar
30mL....2 Tbsp. salt
5mL.....1 tsp. pepper
........Sprinkle paprika
****

(1) Cook, cool and dice potatoes.
(2) Cook eggs, see about cooking hard boiled eggs p. 232. Cool thoroughly preferably overnight.
(3) In a large bowl combine potatoes, green onions, parsley, (remove tough stems from parsley) onions and celery. Stir well.
(4) In a medium bowl combine salad dressing, milk (replace about 1/3 of milk with vinegar, if desired), mustard, sugar, salt & pepper.
(5) Pour dressing over potato mixture. Stir together well.
(6) Slice 6 boiled eggs, reserve for top of salad.
(7) Chop remaining eggs and add to salad. Stir well.

(8) Arrange sliced eggs on top of salad.
(9) Sprinkle with paprika. Garnish with parsley sprigs.

*   Cover and refrigerate until served.
*   Serves 75.

Mini Lettuce Salads

........Romaine lettuce
........Prepared mustard
........Strips of onion
........Shoestring potatoes
........Strips of sliced cheese
****

(1) Use smaller inside ribs of Romaine lettuce.
(2) Spread inside with mustard.
(3) In the centre of lettuce leaf place strips of onion and shoestring potatoes.

(4) Top with strip of cheese.
(5) Roll up and place close together on platter.
(6) Serve before potatoes have a chance to become soggy.

Macaroni Salad

2L . . . . . . 8 cups water
5mL . . . . . 1 tsp. salt
10mL . . . . 2 tsp. margarine
500mL . . . 2 cups uncooked elbow
          macaroni
3 . . . . 3 chopped green onions
10mL . . . . 2 tsp. minced parsley
250mL . . . 1 cup chopped celery
250mL . . . 1 cup whipped salad dress-
          ing (divided) p. 15
1mL . . . . . 1/4 tsp. oregano
. . . . Salt & pepper to taste
          (sprinkled)
****

(1) In a large saucepan bring water to a boil, add salt, margarine and macaroni.
(2) Boil continuously for 8 minutes.
(3) Stir gently 3 or 4 times.
(4) Place colander in sink.
(5) Drain macaroni, rinse with cold water. Drain again.
(6) Place macaroni in mixing bowl, stir in 125mL (1/2 cup) of the measured salad dressing to keep it from sticking together.

(7) Add onions, parsley, celery, 125mL (1/2 cup) salad dressing and oregano.
(8) Mix together well, add salt & pepper.
(9) Chill before serving.

* Serves 6 to 8.

Lime Jello with Cottage Cheese

170g . . . . . 1-6 oz. pkg. lime jello
500mL . . . 2 cups boiling water
45mL . . . . 3 Tbsp. salad dressing
125mL . . . 1/2 cup dry cottage cheese
250mL . . . 1 cup miniature marshmal-
          lows
398mL . . . 1-14 oz. can drained
          crushed pineapple
****

(1) Rinse bowl with cold water.
(2) Place jello into bowl, add boiling water.
(3) Stir well until dissolved. (Approx. 3 minutes). Chill until heavy syrup stage.
(4) Add salad dressing, beat very well, chill until a little firmer.

(5) Add cottage cheese, marshmallows and pineapple. Stir well.
(6) Place into prepared mould, chill until firm.

* Rinsing bowl with cold water prevents jello from sticking.
* If you are using a mould, rub a small amount of salad dressing inside the mould to prevent jello from sticking.

Fresh Vegetable Salad

1........1 head lettuce
3........3 large tomatoes
5........5 green onions
2........2 stalks celery
1/2......1/2 cucumber
.........Radish, mushrooms, bean
        sprouts, alfalfa sprouts
****

(1) Choose fresh crisp lettuce as head lettuce or romaine. Tear into bite size pieces.
(2) Chop remaining vegetable, add to lettuce.
(3) Radish, mushrooms and sprouts may be added as desired.

(4) Toss all vegetables together. Keep chilled until served. Serve dressings of your choice as Italian Dressing p. 15 or French Dressing p. 14.

Sprout Salad

1L ......4 cups salad greens
6........6 radishes
1/2......1/2 cucumber
250mL...1 cup alfalfa or bean
        sprouts
125mL...1/2 cup toasted sunflower
        seeds
****

(1) Tear salad greens into bite size pieces. Slice radishes and cucumber.
(2) Combine with sprouts and sunflower seeds; toss well.
(3) Cover with the following dressing.

Dressing

50mL....1/4 cup salad oil
30mL....2 Tbsp. vinegar
1/2mL...1/8 tsp. salt
.........Dash pepper
1/2mL...1/8 tsp. garlic powder
2........2 sliced hard boiled eggs
****

(1) Put all ingredients except eggs into a jar with tight fitting lid.
(2) Shake well. Pour over salad and toss.
(3) Garnish with eggs.

Cucumber-Sour Cream Salad

2........2 medium cucumbers
2mL.....1/2 tsp. salt
45mL....3 Tbsp. sour cream
15mL....1 Tbsp. vinegar
2mL.....1/2 tsp. sugar
1/2mL...1/8 tsp. pepper
.........Dill, if desired
****

(1) Peel then slice cucumbers into thin slices. Sprinkle with salt and let set 30 minutes.
(2) Drain well and discard juice.
(3) Combine sour cream, vinegar, sugar, pepper and sprinkling of dill, if desired, pour over cucumbers. Toss well.

(4) Serve chilled. Toss before serving.

10

Luscious Fruit Salad

500mL...2 cups canned pears
500mL...2 cups canned peaches
250mL...1 cup green seedless grapes
250mL...1 cup or more cottage
　　　　cheese
.........Ice-cream
****

(1) Drain pears and peaches, re-serve pear juice.
(2) Dice fruit and combine with grapes.
(3) Spoon into stemmed goblets, add 30mL (2 Tbsp.) cottage cheese.

(4) Pour in pear juice, covering 3/4 of fruit or more.
(5) Top with vanilla ice-cream, if desired.

Gelatin Fruit Salad

15mL....1 Tbsp. unflavoured
　　　　gelatin
125mL...1/2 cup cold juice or
　　　　water
375mL...1 1/2 cups fruit juice
****

(1) In a saucepan put 125mL (1/2 cup) cold water, sprinkle gelatin over top.

(2) Stir constantly over low heat until gelatin is dissolved.
(3) Combine with 375mL (1 1/2 cups) fruit juice.
(4) Add fruit immediately and stir again when slightly set, or add fruit after prepared gelatin has thickened.
(5) Serve in large stemmed goblets. Top with whipped cream.

* Serves 4.

Jello and Fruit Salad

85g......3 oz. pkg. raspberry jello
　　　　powder
85g......3 oz. pkg. lime or lemon
　　　　jello powder
1........1 of each peeled, cored
　　　　chunked apple, orange
　　　　banana
.........Whipped cream or ice-cream
****

(1) Prepare jello following instruc-tions on pkg. When set, cut in-to 1.5cm. (1/2-inch) cubes.
(2) In a large bowl gently combine the two jellos and the fruit.
(3) Spoon into stemmed goblets.
(4) Top with whipped cream.

* Rinse bowl with water to prevent jello from sticking to it.
* Very pretty.
* Makes 10 servings.

11

24 Hour Salad

An easy make ahead salad...to help you on a busy day...

2........2 beaten eggs
50mL....1/4 cup vinegar
50mL....1/4 cup sugar
30mL....2 Tbsp. butter
568mL...1-20 oz. can crushed pine-
        apple (drained)
568mL...1-20 oz. can fruit cocktail
        (drained)
250mL...1 cup whipping cream
500mL...2 cups miniature marsh-
        mallows

(1) In a saucepan, beat together eggs, vinegar, sugar and butter.
(2) Cook until smooth and thick. Cool.
(3) Whip cream, add marsh-mallows.
(4) Fold in fruit and dressing.
(5) Let set 24 hours.

****

Cabbage Salad

Just a good tasting salad...you will probably make it time and time again...

1L ......4 cups thinly sliced
        cabbage
4........4 chopped green onions
2........2 large grated carrots
175mL...3/4 cup whipped salad
        dressing
50mL....1/4 cup vinegar
15mL....1 Tbsp. sugar
........Dash salt, pepper &
        paprika
........Parsley sprigs

(1) In a mixing bowl combine cabbage, onions and carrots.
(2) In a small bowl combine salad dressing, vinegar and sugar.
(3) Pour dressing over vegetables.
(4) Sprinkle with salt & pepper.
(5) Blend well. Sprinkle with paprika.
(6) Garnish with parsley.
(7) Chill thoroughly.

****

* Makes 1L (1 Qt.).

Potato Salad

No picnic would be the same without it...not to mention lunch...
at 12:00 A.M. or 12:00 P.M....

2.25kg...5 lbs. cooked potatoes
7........7 hard boiled eggs
4........4 green onions
125mL...1/2 cup diced celery
30mL....2 Tbsp. chopped cooking
           onions
250mL...1 cup salad dressing
5mL.....1 tsp. prepared mustard
30mL....2 Tbsp. vinegar
5mL.....1 tsp. sugar
........Salt & pepper to taste
........Sprinkle of paprika
........Garnish with parsley
           sprigs
            ****

(1) Cook, cool and dice potatoes or mash potatoes while warm, then cool.
(2) Cook eggs, see hard boiled eggs p. 232. Set aside. Cool.
(3) Combine potatoes, green onions, celery and cooking onions.
(4) In a separate bowl, combine salad dressing, mustard, vinegar, sugar, salt & pepper.
(5) Pour dressing over potato mixture. Stir well.
(6) Slice two boiled eggs, reserve for top of salad.
(7) Chop remaining eggs and add to salad. Stir well.
(8) Arrange sliced eggs on top of salad.
(9) Sprinkle with paprika. Garnish with parsley sprigs.

* Cover and refrigerate until ready to serve.
* Makes 7-175mL (3/4 cup servings).

Heritage Salad Dressing

This is a boiled salad dressing from yester-year...still requested today...

175mL...3/4 cup sugar
2mL.....1/2 tsp. salt
5mL.....1 tsp. dry mustard
10mL....2 tsp. cornstarch
2........2 well beaten eggs
125mL...1/2 cup vinegar
125mL...1/2 cup water

            ****

(1) In a saucepan mix sugar, salt, mustard and cornstarch together.
(2) Add eggs and beat until smooth.
(3) Add vinegar and water, cook over medium heat until thick, stir constantly.
(4) Thin with cream for use.

* Makes 375mL (1 1/2 cups).

Blender Mayonnaise

1........1 whole egg
2mL......1/2 tsp. salt
1/2mL...1/8 tsp. cayenne pepper
2mL......1/2 tsp. prepared or dry
        mustard
5mL......1 tsp. honey
30mL....2 Tbsp. lemon juice or
        apple cider vinegar
250ml ...1 cup olive oil
****

(1) In a blender combine egg, salt, cayenne pepper, mustard, honey and 50ml (1/4 cup) of the measured oil.
(2) Cover and on low speed, blend until well mixed.
(3) If you have no opening in the blender lid, take off the cover and in a thin steady stream add half of the remaining oil.

(4) Only when the mixture thickens, add the lemon juice and blend.
(5) Continue slowly pouring in the rest of the oil.

* **Important:** For best results have all the ingredients at room temperature.
* For creamier mayonnaise add 30mL (2 Tbsp.) of boiling water after it is finished. If you should use cold eggs and oil the mayonnaise could suddenly turn. If this happens, clean blender. Add an egg yolk. Gradually add the turned mixture. You can still save your mayonnaise. Blend until smooth.
* Do not over blend.
* Makes 300mL (1 1/4 cups).

Dip

125mL...1/2 cup blender mayon-
        naise
30mL....2 Tbsp. vinegar
2mL......1/2 tsp. garlic powder
****

(1) Mix mayonnaise with vinegar and garlic powder.
(2) Serve with potato chips.

* For coleslaw dressing add 2mL (1/2 tsp.) sugar to above dip ingredients. Pour over coleslaw.

French Dressing

50mL....1/4 cup oil
50mL....1/4 cup vinegar
50mL....1/4 cup chili sauce
50mL....1/4 cup ketchup
5mL......1 tsp. worcestershire sauce
1........1 small minced garlic clove
50mL....1/4 cup firmly packed
        brown sugar
1mL......1/4 tsp. salt
.........Dash hot pepper sauce
****

(1) In a 250mL to 500mL (1 to 2 cup) jar with a tight fitting lid combine all ingredients.
(2) Shake until smooth.
(3) Cover and refrigerate.
(4) Shake well before serving

* Makes 250mL (1 cup).

14

Whipped Salad Dressing

Kountry Koop Favorite...

50mL....3 1/2 Tbsp. sugar
50mL....1/4 cup cornstarch
5mL.....1 tsp. salt
1/2mL...1/8 tsp. white pepper
1/2mL...1/8 tsp. cayenne pepper
1/2mL...1/8 tsp. paprika
125mL...1/2 cup white vinegar
75mL....1/3 cup water
      (full measure)
3........3 beaten egg yolks
150mL...2/3 cup salad oil
****

(1) In a medium saucepan, stir together sugar, cornstarch, salt, white pepper, cayenne pepper and paprika.
(2) Gradually add water, and white vinegar.
(3) Beat egg yolks until foamy, add to mixture, stir well.
(4) Bring to boil over medium heat, stirring vigorously. Mixture will become very lumpy, not to worry, it will stir smooth.
(5) When mixture becomes smooth, reduce heat to medium low; stir gently and cook 2 minutes.
(6) Transfer hot mixture into blender, turn blender on; add salad oil very slowly while blending.
(7) Blend one minute more after adding oil.
(8) Pour into sterilized jar. Cool uncovered. Cover and refrigerate.

* Makes 375mL (1 1/2 cups).

Italian Dressing

50mL....1/4 cup water
175mL...3/4 cup oil
125mL...1/2 cup vinegar
5mL.....1 tsp. salt
2mL.....1/2 tsp. celery salt
1mL.....1/4 tsp. cayenne pepper
1mL.....1/4 tsp. dry mustard
1........1 large or 2 small cloves
      of garlic (crushed) **or**
1mL.....1/4 tsp. garlic powder
........Dash of hot pepper sauce
****

(1) Put all ingredients into blender, cover and mix until well blended.
(2) Store in a jar with a tight fitting lid.
(3) Shake well before using.

* Makes 375mL (1 1/2 cups).

Caesar Salad

1........1 egg
250mL...1 cup oil
30mL....2 Tbsp. red wine vinegar
3........3 cloves garlic (crushed)
15mL....1 Tbsp. Dijon mustard
15mL....1 Tbsp. lemon juice
5mL.....1 tsp. worcestershire
       sauce
.........Pepper to taste
30mL....2 Tbsp. anchovy paste
       (Opt.)
1 head...Romaine lettuce
.........Croutons, parmesan
       cheese
       ****

(1) Blend in blender one egg, add oil very, very slowly. (Remove opening lid of blender, and add oil in a slow steady stream).
(2) Add remaining ingredients, blend well.
(3) Let sit overnight.
(4) Pour over *romaine lettuce, sprinkle with parmesan cheese, add croutons.

* Tear lettuce into bite size pieces.

Pickled Cabbage Salad

1........1 large head cabbage
       (sliced fine)
1........1 large grated carrot
1........1 large onion (sliced)
1/2......1/2 head celery (sliced
       thinly)
175mL...3/4 cup sugar
5mL.....1 tsp. salt
       ****

(1) After all vegetables are cut up, put them in a large dish.
(2) Sprinkle with 175mL (3/4 cup) sugar and 5mL (1 tsp.) salt, mix well.
(3) Let set until you bring the next seven ingredients to a boil.
(4) Pour hot over vegetables.
(5) Put into jars, cool.

Boil:

175mL...3/4 cup sugar
5mL.....1 tsp. salt
250mL...1 cup vinegar
175mL...3/4 cup oil
30mL....2 Tbsp. prepared mustard
30mL....2 Tbsp. celery seed
30mL....2 Tbsp. mustard seed
       ****

(6) Store in refrigerator for at least 3 days before serving.
(7) Makes approx. 3L (3 Qts.).
(8) Will keep for 5 to 6 weeks.

* Other vegetables of your choice may be added.

16

Jellied Cabbage Salad

170g.....1-6 oz. pkg. lemon jelly
       powder
375mL...1 1/2 cups boiling water
125mL...1/2 cup vinegar
375mL...1 1/2 cups chopped cab-
       bage
75mL....1/3 cup chopped celery
30mL....2 Tbsp. minced onion
1mL.....1/4 tsp. salt
........Dash pepper and paprika
        ****

(1) Dissolve jelly powder in boiling water.
(2) Cool to lukewarm, add vinegar.
(3) When mixture begins to thicken, add remaining ingredients.
(4) Mix well and pour into prepared mould, chill until firm.
(5) Unmould and serve on lettuce or cabbage leaves.

* Rub inside of mould with salad dressing to prevent jello from sticking.

Jellied Turkey Salad

375mL...1 1/2 cups water divided
1........1 pkg. unflavoured gelatin
2mL.....1/2 tsp. salt
75mL....1/3 cup diced onion
250mL...1 cup cranberry sauce
       p. 49
500mL...2 cups diced, roasted tur-
       key or chicken breast
       meat
5mL.....1 tsp. poultry seasoning
        ****

(1) In a mixing bowl sprinkle gelatin over 50mL (1/4 cup) cold water. Allow to stand 1 minute.
(2) Stir in 300mL (1 1/4 cups) boiling water, add salt, stir to dissolve.
(3) Refrigerate. When mixture is cold and is beginning to thicken, add onions, cranberry sauce and turkey meat. Add poultry seasoning.

(4) Mix well and pour into slightly oiled straight sided container about 10x13cm (4x5-inches) may be used. Large enough to hold 550mL (2 1/4 cups).
(5) Unmould on crisp lettuce.

Cranberry Salad

4........4 tart apples
500mL...2 cups cranberries
2........2 oranges
250mL...1 cup sugar or less
1mL.....1/4 tsp. salt
        ****

(1) Remove core from apples. Cut into pieces. *Do not peel.
(2) Seed and quarter unpeeled oranges.
(3) Combine apples, cranberries and oranges. Chop.

(4) In a bowl combine fruit, sugar and salt. Mix well. Cover.
(5) Chill for 4 hours.

* Makes 750mL (3 cups).

Wilted Lettuce Salad

1........1 head lettuce
6........6 slices side bacon
4........4 chopped green onions
45mL....3 Tbsp. vinegar
45mL....3 Tbsp. water
30mL....2 Tbsp. brown sugar
2mL.....1/2 tsp. salt
1mL.....1/4 tsp. pepper
2mL.....1/2 tsp. oregano
****

(1) Tear lettuce into large bowl.
(2) In a frying pan fry bacon until crisp. Remove bacon onto paper towel.
(3) Pour all fat from pan except 30mL (2 Tbsp.).
(4) Add onions, vinegar, water, brown sugar, salt, pepper and oregano.

(5) Bring to a boil. Pour over lettuce.
(6) Toss well. Crumble bacon over salad. Toss slightly.

* Serve immediately.

Tomato-Onion Salad

The addition of wheat germ changes the flavour of this salad...
Try a small amount...for taste test...

6........6 large peeled and diced ripe tomatoes
250mL...1 cup finely chopped onion
2mL.....1/2 tsp. pepper
5mL.....1 tsp. salt
50mL....1/4 cup salad oil
7mL.....1 1/2 tsp. vinegar
30mL....2 Tbsp. chopped parsley
50mL....1/4 cup wheat germ (Opt.)
.........Lettuce leaves
****

(1) Mix first seven ingredients together well.
(2) Add wheat germ, mix lightly. Chill.
(3) Serve on lettuce leaves.

* Pour boiling water over tomatoes, skins will peel off easily.

Thousand Island Dressing

250mL...1 cup whipped salad dress-
        ing
50mL....1/4 cup chili sauce
125mL...1/2 cup tomato paste
50mL....1/4 cup *sweet pickle
        relish
30mL....2 Tbsp. minced green
        onions
50mL....1/4 cup vinegar
5mL.....1 tsp. worcestershire sauce
15mL....1 Tbsp. lemon juice
1/2mL...1/8 tsp. cayenne pepper
           ****

(1) In a mixing bowl combine salad dressing, chili sauce, tomato paste, and relish.

(2) Add onions, vinegar, worcestershire sauce, lemon juice and cayenne pepper.

(3) Blend all ingredients together very well.

(4) Pour into sterilized jar and chill. Makes 425mL (1 3/4 cups).

* Thousand Island Relish, p. 212 is excellent to use here.

Pineapple-Carrot Salad

398mL...1-14 oz. can crushed pine-
        apple
85g......1-3 oz. pkg. lemon Jello
        powder
1mL.....1/4 tsp. salt
15mL....1 Tbsp. sugar
30mL....2 Tbsp. lemon juice
250mL...1 cup shredded carrots
250mL...1 cup whipping cream
75mL....1/3 cup maraschino
        cherries drained and
        quartered
           ****

(1) Drain pineapple, measure pineapple juice and add water to make 375mL (1 1/2 cups). Heat to boiling.

(2) In a mixing bowl stir Jello powder, salt and sugar together. Pour hot juice over Jello powder, stir until dissolved. Stir in lemon juice, chill until unbeaten egg white consistency. (Set in bowl of ice and stir constantly to hurry setting).

(3) Stir in pineapple, carrots and cherries. Whip cream until it softly mounds. Fold into fruit mixture.

(4) Rub inside of mould with salad dressing. Pour mixture into mould, refrigerate over night.

Ambrosia Salad

250mL...1 cup drained, pineapple
        chunks
398mL...1-14 oz. can fruit cocktail
125mL...1/2 cup medium sweeten-
        ed coconut
250mL...1 cup miniature marsh-
        mallows
125mL...1/2 cup drained, mara-
        schino cherries (cut in
        halves)
125mL...1/2 cup whipping cream
15mL....1 Tbsp. sugar
50mL....1/4 cup sour cream
****

(1) In a medium serving bowl combine first 5 ingredients.
(2) Whip cream until it softly
mounds, adding sugar. Stir in
sour cream.
(3) Fold cream into fruit mixture.
Refrigerate 4 hours.

*   Serves 6.

Waldorf Salad

75mL....1/3 cup mayonnaise
15mL....1 Tbsp. lemon juice
5mL.....1 tsp. sugar
250mL...1 cup grated cabbage
250mL...1 cup chopped unpeeled
        red apple
50mL....1/4 cup chopped walnuts
30mL....2 Tbsp. chopped celery
****

(1) In a small bowl combine mayonnaise, lemon juice and sugar
together, set aside.
(2) In a separate bowl combine
cabbage and apple; quickly stir
in mayonnaise mixture to prevent apple from discolouring.
Add walnuts and celery. Chill
thoroughly.

Soups

Spinach Zucchini Soup

1L ......4 cups water
2 2/3L ..12 cups chicken soup
        stock p. 24 (divided)
500mL...2 cups soup mix
125mL...1/2 cup diced onion
250mL...1 cup diced celery
10mL....2 tsp. salt
2mL.....1/2 tsp. pepper
1L ......4 cups spinach (divided)
1L ......4 cups carrots (divided)
2........2 large grated potatoes
500mL...2 cups grated zucchini
      ****

(1) In a large kettle place water, and half of chicken soup stock. *Soup mix. Onions, celery, salt & pepper.

(2) Bring to a boil and boil gently for 2 hours or until soup mix is cooked through.

(3) Stir occasionally to keep from sticking to the bottom.

(4) Finely dice half of the spinach and the carrots, put the other half of spinach and carrots in the blender. Chop until very fine.

(5) Add to soup mixture. Add potato, zucchini and remaining 1 1/3L (6 cups) of chicken broth.

(6) Bring to a boil and boil gently for 2 hours.

* Soup mix may contain a mixture of barley, lentils, split peas, rice and a small amount of alphabet noodles.
* Approx. 4 1/2L (5 Qts.).

Bean Soup

500g.....1 lb. beans (2 1/4 cups)
2L ......2 quarts water
1........1 ham bone
30mL....2 Tbsp. butter or margar-
        ine
1........1 medium diced onion
15mL....1 Tbsp. flour
10mL....2 tsp. brown sugar
.........Salt to taste
      ****

(1) Soak beans overnight in 2 litres (2 quarts) water. Add hambone or bacon strips, cut in cubes.

(2) Saute onions in butter, add to bean pot.

(3) Cover, cook slowly until skins pop. Add more water if needed.

(4) Blend flour with 30mL (2 Tbsp.) cold water. Add to bean pot along with sugar. Simmer until beans are soft.

(5) Adjust seasoning. Add salt, if necessary.

Borscht Soup (Canned)

That good beet soup we love so much...

4L ......4 quarts finely diced beets
50mL....1/4 cup sugar
2mL.....1/2 tsp. salt
250mL...1 cup vinegar or lemon
juice
1L ......1 quart finely diced
carrots
1L ......1 quart finely diced green
beans
3........3 large finely diced
parsnips
500mL...2 cups chopped beet tops
30mL....2 Tbsp. chopped green dill
****

(1) In a large kettle bring beets to a boil. Add sugar, salt, vinegar and enough water to just cover. Boil 1/2 hour.
(2) Add remaining vegetables. Boil an additional 1/2 hour.
(3) Pour into sterilized jars and process for 2 hours.

* To serve heat thoroughly.
* Pass sour cream or sweet cream.
* Makes approx. 6 1/2L (7 Qts.).

Vegetable Beef Soup

This is definitely a first class soup. It takes extra time to prepare but the end results are well worth it...

2 1/2L ..10 cups beef stock
750mL...3 cups V8 juice or tomato
juice
45mL....3 Tbsp. pearl barley
5mL.....1 tsp. salt
1mL.....1/4 tsp. pepper
250mL...1 cup diced carrots
125mL...1/2 cup of each turnip,
potato, onion and celery
(diced).
1mL.....1/4 tsp. bouquet garni
(scant)
****

(1) In a pot combine beef stock, V8 juice, barley, salt & pepper.
(2) Bring to a boil, reduce heat to simmer and cook 2 hours.
(3) Add *chopped vegetables and *bouquet garni.
(4) Simmer slowly for an additional 2 hours. Stir occasionally.

* Chop vegetables 2.5cm (1/3-inch) square for appearance. Husbands can tell if they are being served soup, not stew.
* Makes approx. 2 1/3L (2 1/2 Qts.).
* Bouquet garni is a blend of herbs minced together. Usually 4 to 6 different kinds. Use fresh or dried. If fresh, tie in a bundle for easy removal.
* Caution. The addition of bouquet garni makes this soup extraordinary, but too much will ruin your soup. Use sparingly.

Minestrone Soup

Very thick... very delicious...

1L ......4 cups water	(1)	In a large kettle slowly simmer beef shanks, tomato soup and the water for 2 hours.
1kg .....2 lbs. beef shanks		
540mL...1-19 oz. can tomato soup		
340g.....12 oz. package frozen mixed vegetables, thawed	(2)	Add vegetables and spices. Simmer 4 hours.
2........2 medium diced onions	(3)	Remove bones from soup.
2........2 stalks diced celery	(4)	With fingers remove meat from bones. Dice and return to kettle. Discard gristle, fat particles and bones.
2........2 small diced zucchini		
2........2 medium diced carrots		
15mL....1 Tbsp. salt	(5)	Add cabbage and noodles, simmer 2 hours.
15mL....1 Tbsp. basil		
15mL....1 Tbsp. worcestershire sauce	(6)	*Add small amounts of water, if needed. Keep soup at a good thick consistency.
15mL....1 Tbsp. oregano		
15mL....1 Tbsp. pepper	(7)	*Pass parmesan cheese.
250mL...1 cup grated cabbage		
125mL...1/2 cup fine vermicelli noodles		
1........1 clove minced garlic		
........Parmesan cheese (Opt.)		

****

Beef Soup Stock

Any amount of beef bones...

(1) In a large kettle place soup bones, add cold water to almost cover. Bring to a boil. Reduce heat.

(2) Cook slowly for 5 to 6 hours, stirring bones twice.

(3) When cooled but not cold remove bones from kettle; with fingers remove meat from bones, dice and return to stock. Discard gristle, fat particles and bones. Inspect stock; remove bone chips, if any.

(4) Measure stock and record.

(5) Reheat until hot; this will assure that all the fat will be melted and will come to the surface when chilled.

(6) Cool uncovered; cover and refrigerate overnight.

(7) Skim fat from stock. Reserve 30mL (2 Tbsp.) of fat to 2 1/2L (10 cups) of soup stock; discard the rest of the fat.

* Freezes well.

Mushroom Soup

If you want good soup, then this one is a must...

250g.....8-12 oz. fresh mushrooms,
      cut-up
75mL....1/3 cup or 1 small diced
      onion
50mL....1/4 cup butter
875mL...3 1/2 cups milk, (divided)
75mL....1/3 cup flour
50mL....1/4 cup milk
4.......4 chicken bouillon cubes
........Pinch of thyme
........Pinch of salt & pepper
125mL...1/2 cup plain yogurt
      (Opt.)
****

(1) In a medium saucepan brown onions and mushrooms in hot butter. 5 min.
(2) Make paste with flour and 50mL (1/4 cup) milk.
(3) Add flour paste, milk, bouillon cubes and thyme.
(4) Heat over moderate heat stirring frequently until thickened and begins to boil.
(5) Remove from heat, add salt & pepper.
(6) Stir 250mL (1 cup) of hot mixture into yogurt. Return back to saucepan.

(7) Heat slightly (do not boil). Serve at once.

* Garnish with fresh dill.
* Serves 4.

Chicken Soup Stock

Handy to have on hand, canned or frozen...

2 1/2 kg .6 lbs. stewing fowl
........Water
1........1 medium onion
1........1 medium carrot
1........1 stock celery
50mL....1/4 cup tomato paste
5mL.....1 tsp. salt
1mL.....1/4 tsp. each pepper, sage
      and rosemary
****

(1) Cut up stewing fowl and place in large kettle.
(2) Add cold water to almost cover.
(3) Bring slowly to a boil uncovered, for 30 minutes, skim.
(4) Remove foam from surface.
(5) Add onions, carrots, celery, salt, pepper, tomato paste, sage and rosemary.

(6) Continue to simmer partially covered, until liquid is slightly reduced, approx. 3-3 1/2 hours.
(7) Strain, cool uncovered, cover to store. Refrigerate overnight.
(8) Reserve 30mL (2 Tbsp.) of fat for 2 1/2L (10 cups) soup stock. Discard the rest of the fat.

Potato Soup

1L ......4 cups peeled and diced potatoes
250mL...1 cup diced onions
5mL.....1 tsp. salt
.........Dash of pepper
875mL...3 1/2 cups water
30mL....2 Tbsp. butter (divided)
15mL....1 Tbsp. flour
****

(1) In a saucepan combine potatoes, onions, salt, pepper and water.
(2) Cook until potatoes are tender. Drain and reserve liquid.
(3) In a second saucepan slightly brown 15mL (1 Tbsp.) butter and flour while stirring constantly.

(4) Add 750mL (3 cups) reserved liquid; cook and stir until smooth.
(5) Add cooked potatoes and onions, heat through.
(6) Add additional 15mL (1 Tbsp.) of butter.
(7) Sprinkle with parsley.

Beet Soup (Borscht)

A favorite superb soup...

1L ......4 cups shredded beets
125mL...1/2 cup shredded onion
1 1/2L ..6 cups water
10mL....2 tsp. vinegar
5mL.....1 tsp. salt
500mL...2 cups shredded cabbage
15mL....1 Tbsp. sugar
.........*cream
****

(1) In a large sauce pan bring beets, onions, vinegar, salt and water to a boil. Boil gently 15 minutes.
(2) Add cabbage and sugar.
(3) Reduce heat and simmer 40 minutes.

* Pass sweet cream or sour cream.
* 10mL (2 tsp.) cream per 300mL (1 1/4 cup) serving.
* Makes 2 1/3L or 10 cups.

Tomato Soup

This is delicious...

500mL...2 cups canned or stewed tomatoes
2mL.....1/2 tsp. baking soda
500mL...2 cups milk
5mL.....1 tsp. butter or margarine
.........Salt & pepper to taste
****

(1) Bring tomatoes to a boil, stirring in baking soda until dissolved.
(2) Add milk and heat thoroughly. Do not boil after milk is added.
(3) Add butter, if desired.
(4) Sprinkle with salt & pepper.

* Care must be taken not to boil after milk is added.

Barley Soup

1L ......4 cups soup stock, beef, chicken or ham
75mL....1/3 cup barley
50mL....1/4 cup yellow split peas
125mL...1/2 cup grated carrot
45mL....3 Tbsp. chopped onions
2mL.....1/2 tsp. salt
1/2mL...1/8 tsp. pepper
****

(1) In a medium saucepan, combine all ingredients.
(2) Bring to boil, reduce heat to low.
(3) Cover and simmer until barley and peas are tender. 2 1/2-3 hours.

Clam Chowder

2........2 strips fried crumbled bacon or 50mL (1/4 cup) cooked diced ham
375mL...1 1/2 cups water
625mL...2 1/2 cups cubed potatoes
125mL...1/2 cup shredded carrots
50mL....1/4 cup butter or margarine
125mL...1/2 cup flour
500mL...2 cups milk
3........3 chopped green onions
5mL.....1 tsp. salt
1mL.....1/4 tsp. pepper
142mL...1-5 oz. can baby clams
****

(1) Prepare bacon or ham, set aside.
(2) In a saucepan boil potatoes in water for 10 minutes. Add carrots; cook 10 minutes more (do not drain).
(3) In another saucepan heat butter until very hot, add flour, cook for 3 minutes, stirring constantly. Slowly stir in milk.
(4) Cook until thickened, stirring constantly. Add onions, parsley, salt, pepper, clams, bacon, cooked potatoes and carrots, including the water they were cooked in.

(5) Simmer slowly for 30 minutes to 1 hour. Stir occasionally.

* Keep heat low.

Split Pea Soup

250mL...1 cup diced ham
2 1/2L ..10 cups water
1........1 hambone
250mL...1 cup diced onion
500mL...2 cups split green peas
1mL.....1/4 tsp. pepper
****

(1) In a large pot combine all ingredients. Simmer slowly 3-4 hours or until peas are tender. Stir occasionally.
(2) Remove hambone, cut off all the meat, put meat into soup pot, discard the bone, fat and gristle.

(3) Adjust seasoning, salt may be needed.

Cream of Tomato Soup

500mL...2 cups tomatoes
2mL.....1/2 tsp. onion powder
37mL....2 1/2 Tbsp. flour
37mL....2 1/2 Tbsp. melted butter
2mL.....1/2 tsp. sugar
1/2mL...1/8 tsp. baking soda
500mL...2 cups milk
2mL.....1/2 tsp. salt
1mL.....1/4 tsp. pepper
15mL....1 Tbsp. chopped chives
****

(1) In a saucepan cook tomatoes 10 minutes.
(2) Press tomatoes through sieve then discard peels.
(3) In a saucepan combine tomatoes, onion powder, butter, flour and sugar.
(4) Stir in baking soda until dissolved.
(5) Gradually add milk, salt & pepper.

(6) Cook until heated through (do not boil).
(7) Garnish with chopped chives or green onions.

French Onion Soup

50mL....1/4 cup margarine
500mL...2 cups thinly sliced onions
2mL.....1/2 tsp. salt
30mL....2 Tbsp. flour
1L ......4 cups beef or chicken stock
4........4 slices french bread, toasted
125g.....4 oz. shredded mozzarella cheese
125g.....4 oz. grated parmesan cheese (Opt.)
****

(1) In a frying pan melt margarine until bubbly, add onions. Cover and cook for 15 minutes.
(2) Blend in salt and flour. Add beef or chicken stock. Heat to boiling, stirring constantly. Reduce heat and simmer 20 min.
(3) Toast french bread in the oven until dry and crisp.

(4) In each of 4 ovenproof soup crocks place one slice of the toasted bread, then pour 1/4 of the soup into each crock. Sprinkle each portion with 30g (1 oz.) mozzarella cheese and 30g (1 oz.) parmesan cheese. Broil until cheese melts and is lightly browned. About 5 minutes.

* This soup will be extraordinary if beef or chicken stock is of good flavour.
* Some enjoy the taste of the packaged broth (to each his own I say unto that).
* If you do not enjoy cheese or if health forbids cheese, it is very good without it.
* Serve hot. Makes 4 servings.

Cauliflower or Broccoli Soup

1........1 head cooked cauliflower
75mL....1/3 cup butter
125mL...1/2 cup minced celery
50mL....1/4 cup minced onion
75mL....1/3 cup flour
500mL...2 cups chicken broth
500mL...2 cups milk
2mL.....1/2 tsp. salt
1mL.....1/4 tsp. paprika
.........Grated cheese, if desired
****

(1) Remove tough stems from cauliflower. Boil gently in 250mL (1 cup) salted water until tender.
(2) Drain and reserve liquid and 375mL (1 1/2 cups) of florets (diced).
(3) Mash remaining florets until smooth (blender works well).
(4) In a 4L (4 Qt.) saucepan melt butter until bubbling.

(5) Saute celery and onions until tender. Add flour and stir.
(6) Gradually stir in 500mL (2 cups) broth and reserved cauliflower liquid.
(7) Add milk, diced florets, salt and paprika.

* Heat thoroughly but do not boil.
* Pass grated cheese.
* This soup freezes well.
* Do not add cheese before freezing.
* Makes 2L (2 Qts.).

Celery Soup

30mL....2 Tbsp. butter or margarine
500mL...2 cups finely chopped celery
125mL...1/2 cup finely chopped onion (less may be desired)
500mL...2 cups chicken broth
22mL....1 1/2 Tbsp. cornstarch
500mL...2 cups milk
30mL....2 Tbsp. chopped parsley
****

(1) In a medium saucepan saute celery and onion in hot butter until limp (do not brown).
(2) Add chicken broth, simmer 10 minutes.
(3) Mix cornstarch with 50mL (1/4 cup) milk and add to remaining milk. Stir milk into hot soup.
(4) Bring to a boil (do not boil) stirring constantly. Cook 1 min.

* Sprinkle with parsley.
* Makes 1L (4 cups).

Croutons

1 1/2L ..6 cups cubed fresh bread
125mL...1/2 cup butter or margarine
2.......2 cloves garlic
5mL.....1 tsp. Italian herb seasoning
........Sprinkle with dried parsley
****

(1) Cut bread into 1.5cm. (1/2-inch) cubes. Spread on a large cookie sheet.
(2) In frying pan heat butter, cut garlic into slices and add to hot butter.

(3) Stir garlic around so butter will have a good garlic flavour. Lift out and discard garlic pieces.
(4) Spoon hot butter evenly over bread cubes, turning cubes over a few times as butter is added.
(5) Sprinkle with herb seasoning and parsley, turning as before.
(6) Place cookie sheet just above centre in 150°C (300°F) oven for 25-30 minutes, turning once. Cool completely before storing.

* Use white or whole wheat bread, cracked wheat bread is delicious also.
* Other herbs and spices of your choice can be used. Mix spices to equal 5mL (1 tsp.). Celery salt, paprika and sage go well together; sprinkle with all purpose seasoning salt. Bake as above.
* These croutons are excellent made into dressing (stuffing) for meats. Just add small amount of hot water to hold dressing together. Too much water will make dressing undesirable. Add chopped raw onion for desired taste.

Corn Chowder

5........5 slices bacon
30mL....2 Tbsp. bacon drippings
125mL...1/2 cup chopped onion
375mL...1 1/2 cups diced raw potatoes
125mL...1/2 cup water
389mL...1-14 oz. can cream corn
175mL...3/4 cup milk
30mL....2 Tbsp. parsley (chop fine)
........Dash EACH salt & pepper
****

(1) In a frying pan fry bacon until crisp, set aside. Drain, leave 30mL (2 Tbsp.) drippings in pan.
(2) Add onions and fry until limp. Add water and potatoes. Simmer until potatoes are tender.
(3) Stir in corn, bring to a boil. Add milk, parsley, salt & pepper. Heat thoroughly, do not boil.

* Makes 1L (4 cups).

Chicken Noodle Soup

2 1/2kg..1-5 lb. stewing fowl
........Water
8........8 peppercorns
10mL....1 tsp. salt
1........1 small piece star anise
125mL...1/2 cup sliced carrots
125mL...1/2 cup sliced celery
125mL...1/2 cup sliced onion
250mL...1 cup fine noodles **or**
125mL...1 cup small bows
****

(1) Cut up chicken and place in a large saucepan. Add cold water to barely cover. Bring to a boil uncovered, skim and discard foam.

(2) Add peppercorns, salt, pepper, star anise, carrots, celery and onion. Cover and simmer two hours.

(3) Lift chicken out with slotted spoon. Remove bones, fat and gristle, discard. Strain soup, reserve vegetables except spices.Refrigerate overnight. Remove fat and discard.

(4) Bring noodles to a boil in plenty of salted water. Cook 15 minutes. Drain, add desired amount of noodles and meat to rewarmed stock.

(5) Add reserved vegetables. Simmer 20-30 minutes.

* A small piece of star anise is about the size of the finger nail on your index finger.

* If star anise is not available, add anise seed to desired taste.

Ham Chowder

284mL...1-10 oz. can green pea soup
45mL....3 Tbsp. margarine
50mL....1/4 cup fresh chopped mushrooms
30mL....2 Tbsp. flour
500mL...2 cups milk
45mL....3 Tbsp. chopped green onions (include tops)
250mL...1 cup diced cooked ham
........Dash EACH salt & pepper
****

(1) In a small saucepan over low heat, warm undiluted pea soup.

(2) In a separate saucepan, heat margarine until bubbling. Saute mushrooms 2 minutes.

(3) Stir in flour, cook 3 minutes, do not brown.

(4) Gradually add milk. Stir constantly and cook until mixture is smooth.

(5) Add pea soup, stir until smooth (use wire whip). Add ham, green onions, salt & pepper. Heat thoroughly, do not boil

* Makes 3 cups.

Vegetables

Chow Mein

30mL....2 Tbsp. oil
500mL...2 cups celery, diagonally
         sliced
500mL...2 cups halved onion rings
500mL...2 cups chopped chinese
         cabbage*
500mL...2 cups broccoli floweretts
500mL...2 cups fresh bean sprouts
         or one can drained
........Add small amount sugar
         or honey
500mL...2 cups fresh mushrooms
         or canned (drain) re-
         serve liquid
175mL...3/4 cup hot water, or re-
         served liquid
30mL....2 Tbsp. light soy sauce
5mL.....1 tsp. salt
........pepper to taste
30mL....2 Tbsp. cornstarch
340g.....12 oz. pkg. chinese steam
         fried noodles
        ****

(1) In a wok or large frypan heat oil, add celery, onion, cabbage, and broccoli.
(2) Cover and steam 2 min.
(3) Add bean sprouts and mushrooms stirring lightly to combine.
(4) Sprinkle cornstarch over vegetables and mix lightly.
(5) Add hot water, soy sauce, salt & pepper to taste. Cook a little longer.
(6) Cook noodles as instructed. Starting the same time as starting vegetables. Drain, rinse under hot water. Drain well. Stir in 30mL (2 Tbsp.) butter. Sprinkle with salt.

* Shui Choy.
* Garnish with toasted almonds or sesame seeds.
* Serves 6.

Fried Rice

50mL....1/4 cup salad oil
500mL...2 cups cooked rice
3........3 beaten eggs
4........4 slices cooked crumbled
        bacon
30mL....2 Tbsp. soy sauce
1/2mL...1/8 tsp. pepper
3........3 sliced green onions
        ****

(1) In a frying pan heat oil until hot.
(2) Add rice and cook slowly 5 minutes.
(3) Stir eggs into rice.
(4) Cook over medium heat 3 minutes, stirring constantly.
(5) Add crumbled bacon, soy sauce and pepper. Combine well.

(6) Garnish with green onions.

Honeyed Baked Acorn Squash

This is an economical oven meal...Rich in Vitamin A...

4........4 acorn squash about 170g (3/4 lb.) each
50mL....1/4 cup butter (softened)
50mL....1/4 cup honey
2mL.....1/2 tsp. salt
1/2mL...1/8 tsp. pepper
2mL.....1/2 tsp. nutmeg
2mL.....1/2 tsp. grated lemon rind
****

(1) Wash squash, cut in half lengthwise. Remove seeds and stringy portions.
(2) Place cut side down in a shallow baking pan. Add a very little water to pan.
(3) Bake just below centre in 180°C (350°F) oven until tender, about 45 minutes.

(4) Carefully scoop out pulp with a spoon, leaving four of the shells in tact.
(5) Mash pulp with remaining ingredients, spoon back into the four shells.

* This may be prepared ahead.

(6) Bake just below centre in 180°C (350°F) oven until thoroughly hot. About 30 minutes.

* Serves 4.

Baked Squash

1........1 squash
5mL.....1 tsp. butter or margarine
15mL....1 Tbsp. brown sugar
****

(1) Wash squash, cut in half lengthwise. Remove seeds and stringy portions.

(2) Rub inside squash with butter, and sprinkle with brown sugar.
(3) Place cut side up in shallow pan.
(4) Add a very little water to pan.
(5) Bake just below centre in 180°C (350°F) oven for 45 min. or until tender.
(6) To serve slice diagonally with a sharp knife.

Baked Corn

50mL....1/4 cup butter
1........1 large onion chopped fine
625mL...1-20 oz. can creamed corn
1........1 beaten egg
15mL....1 Tbsp. flour
250mL...1 cup milk
125mL...1/2 cup bread crumbs
2mL.....1/2 tsp. salt
1mL.....1/4 tsp. pepper
4........4 precooked bacon strips
****

(1) In frying pan fry onions in butter until clear (do not brown). Stir in creamed corn.
(2) Add egg, flour, milk, bread crumbs, salt & pepper.
(3) Mix well. Pour into a buttered casserole dish.
(4) Break bacon into pieces. Add to top of casserole.
(5) Bake just below centre in a 160°C (325°F) oven for 30-45 minutes.

Baked Potatoes

| 4.......4 medium size potatoes | (1) Scrub potatoes with a brush. |
| ....Salt, pepper & butter | (2) Pierce skins with a fork. |

****

(3) Bake in a 220°C (425°F) oven for 1 hour until soft. Remove from oven.
(4) Cut a cross in the top of each potato.
(5) Force the soft portion up through opening to let steam escape.
(6) Sprinkle with salt & pepper.
(7) Place butter in opening. Serve immediately. Serves 4.

Variation:
* Remove potato from oven. Wrap in towel until time to serve.
* Serve with sour cream.
* Yams and sweet potatoes are baked as above.

Potatoes in Foil

For the Bar-B-Q or oven...

4.......4 medium size potatoes	(1) Scrub potatoes with a brush.
20mL....4 tsp. butter	(2) Slit potatoes almost in half
.........Salt & pepper	lengthwise.
********	(3) Place 5mL (1 tsp.) butter in
	each potato.

(4) Sprinkle with salt & pepper. Close potato together.
(5) Wrap in aluminum foil.
(6) Bake in 200°C (400°F) oven for 1 hour or place over hot coals until tender.
(7) Test for doneness with a fork.

Mashed Potatoes

6.......6 medium potatoes	(1) In a saucepan place peeled, cut-
75mL....1/3 cup butter	up potatoes. Add water & salt.
125mL...1/2 cup hot milk	(2) Cook until tender. Drain.
2mL.....1/2 tsp. salt	(3) Transfer potatoes to large mix-
1/2mL...1/8 tsp. pepper	ing bowl, add butter.
********	

(4) Mash vigorously until smooth.
(5) Add hot milk, salt & pepper. Mash again vigorously until well whipped.
(6) Serve immediately or return to buttered saucepan.
(7) Leave lid ajar, as potatoes take on an odour if covered.
(8) Saucepan may be set in pan of hot water to keep warm.

* Any vegetable may be mashed as above. eg., turnips, parsnips, etc.

Scalloped Potatoes with Mushroom Sauce

284mL...1-10 oz. can mushroom soup

250mL...1 cup milk

6........6 medium peeled, thinly sliced potatoes

1/2......1/2 medium thinly sliced onion

.........salt & pepper

30mL....2 Tbsp. butter

.........Parsley flakes

****

(1) Mix mushroom soup and milk together. Set aside.

(2) In a 2L (2 Qt.) casserole place 1/3 of the potatoes and 1/3 of the onions.

(3) Pour over 1/3 of the mushroom soup, sprinkle lightly with salt & pepper.

(4) Add remaining ingredients in layers ending with the mushroom soup.

(5) Dot with butter. Sprinkle with parsley and cover.

(6) Bake just below centre of 180°C (350°F) oven for 1 hour or until potatoes are cooked through.

Scalloped Potatoes #2

90mL....6 Tbsp. butter

50mL....1/4 cup flour

750mL...3 cups milk

6........6 medium potatoes

1/2......1/2 medium thinly sliced onion

.........Salt & pepper

.........Parsley flakes

****

(1) In a saucepan heat butter until hot and bubbling.

(2) Add flour, stir vigorously.

(3) Cook for 3 minutes.

(4) While stirring briskly gradually add milk. Cook 3 minutes more. Set aside.

(5) In a 2L (2 Qt.) casserole place 1/3 of the potatoes and 1/3 of the onions.

(6) Pour over 1/3 of the milk mixture.

(7) Sprinkle lightly with salt & pepper.

(8) Add remaining ingredients in layers ending with the milk mixture.

(9) Sprinkle with parsley. Cover.

* Bake just below centre in 180°C (350°F) oven for 1 hour or until the potatoes are cooked through.

Fried Potatoes with Bacon

6........6 slices bacon

1L ......4 1/2 cups raw potato slices

1mL.....1/4 tsp. salt

1/2mL...1/8 tsp. pepper

****

(1) In a frying pan cook bacon until crisp.

(2) Remove bacon, dry on paper towel.

(3) Boil potatoes for 5 min., drain.

(4) Cook potatoes in bacon fat until lightly browned.

(5) Sprinkle with salt, pepper and crumbled bacon.

34

Hash Brown Potatoes

A favorite with eggs and bacon...

45mL....3 Tbsp. butter
45mL....3 Tbsp. finely chopped
        onions
750mL...3 cups diced, cooked
        potatoes
2mL.....1/2 tsp. salt
1/2mL...1/8 tsp. pepper.
****

(1) In frying pan saute onions in butter until limp.
(2) Add potatoes, salt & pepper.
(3) Over moderately high heat cook potatoes until browned and somewhat crisp.
(4) Stir often. Serve hot...serves 5.

* Potatoes may be coarsely grated or mashed. Onions may be omitted.

New Potatoes with Dill

1kg .....2 lbs. new potatoes
2mL.....1/2 tsp. salt
50mL....1/4 cup melted butter
30mL....2 Tbsp. fresh dill
........Dash paprika
****

(1) Scrub skins off new potatoes.
(2) In a saucepan boil potatoes in boiling salted water until tender. Drain.
(3) Place in serving bowl, drizzle butter over potatoes.

(4) Sprinkle with fresh dill, stir gently to cover all potatoes with dill.
(5) Sprinkle with paprika.

* Serve hot...serves 4.

Skillet Fried Potatoes

45mL....3 Tbsp. butter or margarine
4........4 potatoes
30mL....2 Tbsp. minced onions
30mL....2 Tbsp. finely chopped
        celery
30mL....2 Tbsp. snipped parsley
2mL.....1/2 tsp. oregano (Opt.)
........Salt & pepper to taste
****

(1) Peel potatoes and slice in 1/2 cm. (1/8-inch) slices. About 750mL (3 cups).
(2) In a heavy frying pan melt butter. Add potato slices.
(3) Cover and cook over medium heat for 10 minutes.
(4) Turn potatoes carefully.

(5) Cook uncovered for 10 minutes more, turning occasionally to brown all sides.
(6) For the last 5 minutes of cooking sprinkle with onions, celery, parsley, oregano, salt & pepper.
(7) Turn carefully to distribute flavour.

French Fried Potatoes

1kg ..... 2 lbs. potatoes
.... Oil for deep frying
.... Salt
****

(1) Wash and peel potatoes.
(2) Cut into 6cm. (1/4-inch) thick by 6cm. (1/4-inch) wide strips.

(3) Place in a bowl, cover with cold water.
(4) Let stand 15 minutes. Drain, dry with paper towel (dry well).
(5) In a heavy pot heat 5cm. (2-inches) oil.
(6) Cook potatoes until cooked through (about 6 minutes); turn to brown all sides.
(7) Remove. Drain on paper towel.
(8) Sprinkle with salt. Serve immediately.

* Serves 4.
* For shoestring potatoes, slice peeled potatoes into long thin strips. Follow instructions above.

Cabbage

1 .... 1 cabbage
2mL ..... 1/2 tsp. salt
15mL .... 1 Tbsp. butter
15mL .... 1 Tbsp. vinegar
1/2mL ... 1/8 tsp. pepper
****

(1) Wash cabbage, remove core, slice into serving pieces.
(2) In a saucepan steam cabbage in a small amount of salted water until tender. Drain.

(3) Drizzle with butter and vinegar. Sprinkle with pepper.

* Serves 6.

Red Cabbage

22mL .... 1 1/2 Tbsp. butter
50mL .... 1/4 cup finely chopped green onions
1L ...... 4 1/2 cups shredded red cabbage
150mL ... 2/3 cup water
30mL .... 2 Tbsp. vinegar
7mL ..... 1 1/2 tsp. sugar
2mL ..... 1/2 tsp. salt
1/2mL ... 1/8 tsp. pepper
****

(1) In a saucepan saute onions in butter until tender.
(2) Add cabbage, cover, cook slowly for 5 minutes.
(3) Add water, vinegar, sugar, salt & pepper.
(4) Cover, cook slowly for 30 minutes. Stir often.
(5) Serve hot...serves 4.

Harvard Beets

10.......10 small cooked, cubed
       beets
125mL...1/2 cup sugar
15mL....1 Tbsp. cornstarch
50mL....1/4 cup vinegar
50mL....1/4 cup water
30mL....2 Tbsp. butter or margar-
       ine
****

(1) In a saucepan combine sugar
     and cornstarch.
(2) Add vinegar and water, boil
     and stir until mixture thickens
     (about 5 minutes).
(3) Add beets and butter.
(4) Reheat until butter melts and
     beets are heated through.

*   Serves 4.

Sauerkraut

4 1/2kg..10 lbs. cabbage
105mL...7 Tbsp. coarse pickling
       salt
1........1 handful pickling spices
2........2 finely shredded carrots
****

(1) Remove outer leaves from cab-
     bage, cut into quarters.
(2) Remove core.
(3) Shred cabbage very fine.

(4) Mix shredded cabbage, pickling salt, spices, and carrots together. Place
     in a crock or non-metal container. Press down firmly.
(5) Cover with a triple layer of cheesecloth.
(6) Set in a warm place to ferment (12 days).
(7) Each day check sauerkraut, remove scum as it forms. Wash and scald
     cloth often to keep it free from scum and mold. As soon as curing is
     through, pack into sterilized jars. Fill 2/3 full.
(8) Fill to 4cm. (1 1/2-inches) from the top with juice. If there isn't
     enough, make a brine of 30mL (2 Tbsp.) salt to 1L (1 Qt.) water and
     add to jars that need it.
(9) Seal jars according to manufacturers instructions.
(10) Process 15 minutes in boiling water bath, or package and freeze in
     freezer containers (covered in own juice).

Hot Potato Salad

1kg .....2 lb. pkg. of frozen hash
         browns or shoestring
         potatoes
175mL...3/4 cup grated onion
250mL...1 cup sour cream
284mL...1-10 oz. can cream of
         celery or cream of
         chicken soup
250mL...1 cup grated cheese
........Bread crumbs
........Salt & pepper
........Butter
****

(1) Mix potatoes, onion, sour cream and celery soup together.
(2) Spread evenly into a 22x33cm. (9x13-inch) baking dish.
(3) Sprinkle with grated cheese then bread crumbs.
(4) Sprinkle with salt & pepper. Dot with butter.
(5) Bake just above center in a 200°C (400°F) oven for 40 minutes.

* Serves 8.
* Soup should be undiluted.

Canned Mixed Vegetables

Ready and waiting, at any time needed...

500mL...2 cups peas
500mL...2 cups corn
500mL...2 cups chopped celery
500mL...2 cups chopped carrots
500mL...2 cups chopped potato
500mL...2 cups chopped green
         beans
500mL...2 cups chopped onion
150mL...2/3 cup pearl barley
1........1 large chopped red
         pepper
1........1 large chopped green
         pepper
15mL....1 Tbsp. white or black
         pepper corns
375mL...1 1/2 cups garbanzo beans
250mL...1 cup small broad beans
****

(1) While chopping vegetables, boil barley with some water until soft.
(2) In a large kettle mix all ingredients together, barely covering with water. Boil 20 minutes.
(3) Put into sterilized jars and process for 3 hours in quart jars, 2 hours in pint jars.

* Makes approx. 6 1/2L (7 Qts.).
* Serve hot as a vegetable or make into soup.
* Make sure vegetables are covered with water when packed in jars.

Pyrogies

Dough

1L . . . . . . 4 cups flour
2mL . . . . . 1/2 tsp. cream of tartar
30mL . . . . 2 Tbsp. oil
250mL . . . 1 cup lukewarm water or
            skimmed milk
****

(1) In a bowl combine flour and cream of tartar.
(2) Add oil with enough water or milk to make a soft dough. Set aside for 30 minutes.

Filling

75mL . . . . 1/3 cup finely chopped
            onion
15mL . . . . 1 Tbsp. butter or margar-
            ine.
175mL . . . 3/4 cup mashed potatoes
125mL . . . 1/2 cup cheez whiz **or**
            175mL (3/4 cup) cottage
            cheese
. . . . Salt & pepper to taste
****

(1) Saute 75mL (1/3 cup) onion in butter until soft, do not brown.
(2) Combine with mashed potatoes, cheez whiz, salt & pepper.

To assemble:

(1) On a floured surface roll dough out thinly (half at a time).
(2) Cut into circles with cookie cutter.
(3) Place 5ml. (1 tsp.) of filling in centre of each circle.
(4) Fold in half and press edges together to seal securely.
(5) Lay on a dry towel, keep covered while preparing remaining pyrogies.

To cook:

(1) Drop pyrogies into a large pot of boiling, salted water. Boil 12-15 min. after water starts to boil again.
(2) Lift out into a colander, rinse with hot water, drain.
(3) Coat with melted butter, cover and keep hot until all are cooked and ready to serve.

To serve:

Saute 1 large sliced onion in 125mL (1/2 cup) butter (do not brown). Pour over pyrogies.

Vegetable Soup

Vegetable soup from canned vegetables. Ref. page 38...

1L ......1 quart canned vegetables
750mL...3 cups V8 juice or tomato
        juice
50mL....1/4 cup ketchup
50mL....1/4 cup water
      ****

(1) In a medium saucepan combine ingredients.
(2) Place over medium heat and simmer slowly until heated through.

* Makes 1 3/4L (7 cups).

Boiled Vegetables

A basic method for boiling all vegetables is used. Use as little water as you need to keep from burning. Keep heat at a low temperature.
* Vegetables that take longer to cook should be boiled in salted water.
* More tender vegetables are delicious when steamed.
* Vegetables like cauliflower, broccoli, etc., should be steamed; where potatoes, turnips, etc., should be cooked in water.
* Wash and scrub vegetables in cold water. Boil, steam or bake unpeeled, if desired.
  — If peeling, peel off a very thin layer as many nutrients lie just under the skin. Do not over cook vegetables.
  — Scrape vegetables such as carrots, parsnips and new potatoes.
  — Remove strings from beans and shell peas.
* Broccoli: Choose heads that are all green. Skin outer surface of stems. Cut deep gashes in stems.
* Remove excess core and outer leaves from cauliflower. Remove core and any wilted leaves from cabbage. Brussel sprouts: choose small green heads; remove any wilted leaves, cut off excess stem. Make crosswise gashes in stems.
* Choose green asparagus, tie in bundles with string; place upright in a deep kettle with 125mL (1/2 cup) of salted water. Cover and steam just until tender.
* Beet greens, spinach and swiss chard must be washed very well to rid it of any sand or soil. Cut off tough stems. Boil for 10-12 minutes in boiling, salted water until tender. Drain well.
* Beets are at their best if boiled unpeeled. Cut off tops, leaving 2.5cm. (1-inch) of the stem. This will prevent them from bleeding or losing their colour. Half cover with water, cover and cook until tender. Approx. 1 hour, 2-2 1/2 hours for large beets. When beets are done, slip peel off. Running water is helpful at this point to keep hands cool while slipping skins off the hot beets. Place in serving dish, drizzle with butter.
* Husk corn and remove all silk.

Steaming Vegetables

Place salted water in saucepan, set the steamer in place; add vegetables and cover. Bring water to boiling point.
* Some prefer the addition of sugar to peas and corn while they are cooking. However, do not omit salt if sugar is used.
* To preserve the fresh texture and set the green colour in beans, broccoli and peas, boil in salted water until crisp tender. Immediately drain and plunge into ice cold water for several minutes and drain. This may be done in advance. Cover and refrigerate. Shortly before serving, vegetables may be tossed back into boiling, salted water until heated through. Drain and serve immediately or reheat in buttered frying pan until heated through.

Sour Head Cabbage

1........1 head cabbage
90mL....6 Tbsp. pickling salt
2 1/2L ..10 cups boiling water
****

(1) Remove core and outer leaves from cabbage.
(2) Leave cabbage whole and place in a large non-metal container.

(3) Bring water and salt to a boil.
(4) Pour water over head of cabbage. Cabbage must be completely covered.
(5) Weigh down with heavy object. A plate with a clean rock placed on top works just fine.
(6) Let ferment for 2-3 weeks. Cabbage will ferment faster if kept warm.

* Can be frozen.
* Rinse cabbage leaves under cool water before using. Soak if too salty.
* Use sour head cabbage when making cabbage rolls.
* Chop 625mL (2 1/2 cups) sour cabbage, fry in 30mL (2 Tbsp.) butter. Peel and core 1 apple, slice over top of sour cabbage. Sprinkle with 15mL (1 Tbsp.) of brown sugar. Reduce heat, cover and simmer 10 minutes. Remove cover and saute until mixture begins to brown. Stir gently.
* Serve with pork.

Canned Tomatoes

1L ......1 quart peeled ripe tomatoes
1mL.....1/4 tsp. salt
2mL.....1/2 tsp. sugar
****

(1) Pour boiling water over tomatoes. Peel tomatoes and pack into 1L (1 Qt.) sterilized jars, leaving 2 1/2cm. (1-inch) space from top.

(2) Add salt and sugar. Seal and process for 20 minutes.

Frozen Cream Style Corn

15mL....1 Tbsp. fresh cream or
          evaporated milk
5mL.....1 tsp. sugar
1mL.....1/4 tsp. salt
........Dash pepper
****

(1) Select full kernel corn cobs. prepare corn the same day it is picked.
(2) Blanch corn in boiling water for 5 minutes. Drain.

(3) Using a sharp knife, cut kernels off cob. Using the back of the knife scrape the cob to remove small particles of corn.
(4) Measure into saucepan, for every cup of corn use the above amount of cream, salt, sugar, and pepper.
(5) Place over high heat. Stir constantly and bring to a full boil.
(6) Remove from heat; pour into mixing bowl. Place mixing bowl in a pan of ice to cool quickly.
(7) Pour into containers, label and freeze.

To Peel and Store Garlic/Ginger

To remove skin from garlic cloves, cut ends off cloves, lay on flat surface. Lay the flat side of knife on garlic clove. Press or smuck knife down hard with side of hand. The skins will be easy to remove. Mince garlic fine. Place in small jar, and cover with Scotch whiskey or salad oil.

5mL.....1 tsp. minced garlic   = 1 large clove.
2mL.....1/2 tsp. minced garlic   = 1 medium garlic clove.

*   Ginger can be prepared and stored, same as garlic cloves.

Sauces

Gravy

For meatballs, etc....

500mL...2 cups beef broth (cold)
75mL....1/3 cup flour
.........Salt & pepper to taste
****

(1) Mix beef broth and flour together, whip with wire wisk until all lumps are removed.

(2) Bring to a boil stirring constantly until thickened.
(3) Season to taste.
(4) Reduce heat, cook 5 minutes stirring occasionally.
(5) Serve immediately or cover and keep warm over low heat (do not boil).

Hot Mustard

Some like it hot...

50mL....1/4 cup flour
50mL....1/4 cup dry mustard
50mL....1/4 cup sugar
15mL....1 Tbsp. salt
.........Sprinkle of cayenne
         pepper **or**
.........Dash of tabasco sauce
50mL....1/4 cup vinegar (approx.)
****

(1) In a mixing bowl stir together dry ingredients.
(2) Add vinegar to desired thickness. This should thicken more when it sets.
(3) Add more vinegar, as desired.

Brown Sugar Syrup

375mL...1 1/2 cups brown sugar
175mL...3/4 cup water
2mL.....1/2 tsp. vanilla
1mL.....1/4 tsp. cinnamon
****

(1) Combine sugar and water.
(2) Stir until dissolved.
(3) Boil gently 3-4 minutes.
(4) Add flavouring, simmer 1 minute.

(5) Pour into sterilized jar, seal or cover and store in refrigerator.
(6) Serve hot over pancakes, waffles, or french toast.

* Makes 250mL (1 cup).

Cheez Whiz

Every bit as good...if not better than the purchased product...

500g.....1 lb. grated cheddar
        cheese
425mL...1 3/4 cups evaporated
        milk
45mL....3 Tbsp. sugar
15mL....1 Tbsp. flour
5mL.....1 tsp. dry mustard
15mL....1 Tbsp. vinegar
2mL.....1/2 tsp. garlic salt
2mL.....1/2 tsp. salt
1mL.....1/4 tsp. worcestershire
        sauce
1mL.....1/4 tsp. molasses
      ****

(1) In the top of double boiler, combine all ingredients.
(2) Cook, stir continually until cheese melts.
(3) Remove from heat, beat until smooth.
(4) Pour into sterilized jars.
(5) Cool, store in refrigerator.

*   Makes 875mL (3 1/2 cups).
*   Do not make cheez whiz in an aluminum saucepan as the cheese will discolour.

Chocolate Sauce

50mL....1/4 cup butter
5mL.....1 tsp. instant coffee
        powder
5mL.....1 tsp. vanilla
........Pinch salt
8........8 squares semi-sweet
        chocolate
125mL...1/2 cup chopped pecans
        or walnuts

(1) In a small saucepan melt butter until bubbling. Stir in coffee powder, vanilla and salt.
(2) Add chocolate squares, turn off heat. Stir until all chocolate is melted, and mixture is smooth. Stir in nuts.
(3) *Pour into glass jar. Cool and refrigerate. Serve warm over ice-cream.

Maple Syrup

You can adjust the water content for a thicker, or thinner consistency...

175mL...3/4 cup water
250g.....1/2 lb. maple sugar
      ****

(1) Bring slowly to a boil, until sugar is dissolved.

(2) Simmer slowly for 5 minutes.
(3) Stir occasionally. Pour into a sterilized jar.
(4) Seal while hot or store in refrigerator.

Mock Maple Syrup

250mL...1 cup brown sugar
45mL....3 Tbsp. cornstarch
750mL...3 cups water
15mL....1 Tbsp. butter
7mL.....1 1/2 tsp. maple flavour-
         ing
10mL....2 tsp. vanilla
****

(1) In a medium saucepan combine sugar and cornstarch.
(2) Add water and bring to a boil. Boil 5 minutes stirring until slightly thickened. Reduce heat and boil gently 10 minutes longer.

(3) Stir in butter, remove from heat. Add maple flavouring and vanilla.
(4) Pour into sterilized jar, cool and refrigerate.

* Warm before pouring over pancakes.
* Makes 750mL (3 cups).

Carmel Syrup

This will double as a browning sauce...

250mL...1 cup sugar
250mL...1 cup water
****

(1) In a heavy saucepan, over medium low heat, melt sugar to golden brown. *Do not stir.

(2) Cautiously add water, stir, and cook until all the carmelized sugar is dissolved, and a rich syrup is formed.

* This makes a basic syrup, bottle and refrigerate.

Caramel Cream Sauce

125mL...1/2 cup caramel syrup
125mL...1/2 cup cream
2mL.....1/2 tsp. vanilla
5mL.....1 tsp. rum (Opt.)
****

(1) Mix together very well.
(2) Pour into sterilized jar.
(3) Cover and refrigerate.
(4) Serve over ice-cream.

Fresh Fruit Dip

Prepare seasonal fruit of your choice...Cut into desired shapes...

125mL...1/2 cup evaporated milk
170g.....6 oz. semi-sweet chocolate
         chips
30mL....2 Tbsp. brandy
****

(1) In a small saucepan scald milk, remove from heat.
(2) Add chocolate chips, stir until chocolate melts and mixture is smooth.

(3) Stir in brandy.

* Makes 250mL (1 cup).

Mixed Herb Dip

125mL...1/2 cup sour cream
250mL...1 cup mayonnaise
5mL.....1 tsp. tarragon
5mL.....1 tsp. thyme
15mL....1 Tbsp. chopped chives
15mL....1 Tbsp. chopped parsley
1mL.....1/4 tsp. paprika
.........Salt & pepper to taste
60mL....4 Tbsp. bacon flavoured
        bits
        ****

(1) Combine all ingredients and re-frigerate.
(2) Serve with potato chips, crackers or fresh vegetable sticks.

* Makes 375mL (1 1/2 cups).

Raw Vegetable Dip

250mL...1 cup mayonnaise
5mL.....1 tsp. horseradish
5mL.....1 tsp. dry mustard
5mL.....1 tsp. curry powder
.........Dash lemon juice
30mL....2 Tbsp. sour cream
        ****

(1) In a mixing bowl combine all ingredients together.
(2) Mix well and chill.
(3) Serve with prepared raw vegetables.

Vegetable Dip

250mL...1 cup sour cream
125mL...1/2 cup miracle whip
15mL....1 Tbsp. green onion
10mL....2 tsp. dried parsley
5mL.....1 tsp. dill weed
2mL.....1/2 tsp. seasoning salt
        ****

(1) Blend sour cream and miracle whip together.
(2) Chop green onions very fine, add to sour cream mixture.
(3) Stir in dried parsley, dill weed and seasoning salt.
(4) Blend well. Serve chilled.

* Store in refrigerator.

Garlic Dip

250mL...1 cup blender mayonnaise
        p. 14
30mL....2 Tbsp. vinegar
2mL.....1/2 tsp. garlic powder
        ****

(1) Mix mayonnaise with vinegar and garlic powder.
(2) Serve with potato chips.
(3) Use as dressing for coleslaw.

46

Italian Dip

30g......1 oz. pkg. spaghetti sauce mix	(1) Combine all ingredients in a small bowl.
250mL...1/2 pint (1 cup) sour cream	(2) Chill 30 minutes.
5mL.....1 tsp. worcestershire sauce	(3) Serve with prepared vegetables.
2mL.....1/2 tsp. garlic salt	

****

*   Makes 250mL (1 cup).

Fresh Vegetable Dip

125mL...1/2 cup mayonnaise	(1) Combine ingredients together.
125mL...1/2 cup sour cream	(2) Mix well. Chill.
15mL....1 Tbsp. Dijon mustard	(3) Serve with prepared raw vege-
15mL....1 Tbsp. worcestershire sauce	tables.
30mL....2 Tbsp. tomato sauce	
2mL.....1/2 tsp. grated onion	
1/2mL...1/8 tsp. garlic powder **or** 1 clove grated garlic	

****

Guacamole Dip

Just right to start the party...

3........3 medium ripe avocados	(1) In a bowl mash avocados, add lemon juice, salt & pepper. Set aside.
30mL....2 Tbsp. lemon juice	
2mL.....1/2 tsp. salt	
1mL.....1/4 tsp. pepper	
250mL...1 cup sour cream	(2) In another bowl combine sour cream, salad dressing and taco seasoning. Set aside.
125mL...1/2 cup salad dressing	
35g......1 pkg. taco seasoning mix **or** 125mL (1/2 cup) taco sauce. *Recipe to follow	(3) In a 17x25cm. (7x10-inch) serv- ing dish, spread beans evenly over bottom. Top with avocado mixture, layer sour cream on top.
398mL...14 oz. refried beans *Recipe to follow	
.........Large bunch green onions (chopped)	(4) Sprinkle with onion and tomato.
2........2 medium tomatoes (chopped)	(5) Top with cheese.
500mL...2 cups grated cheese	
1........1 large pkg. taco chips	

****

*   Use taco chips as dippers.

Boiled Beans/Refried Beans

500g.....1 lb. pinto beans
1 3/4L ..7 cups water
2mL.....1/2 tsp. salt
125mL...1/2 cup lard
****

(1) Wash and sort beans, check carefully for small stones.
(2) Place in a large bowl, cover with water, let soak overnight.
(3) Transfer to saucepan.

(4) Add salt and lard. Cook slowly until tender.
(5) Add water as needed to keep beans covered.

Refried Beans

Use in Tacos, Nachos, or Guacamole Dip...

500mL...2 cups cooked pinto beans
          including juice to barely
          cover
30mL....1 Tbsp. bacon drippings
50mL....1/4 cup tomato paste
1mL.....1/4 tsp. onion powder
1mL.....1/4 tsp. garlic powder
114mL...4 oz. can green chilies
****

(1) Drain beans, reserve liquid. In a medium saucepan place 150mL (2/3 cup) of the measured beans.
(2) With a potato masher, mash beans, add reserved liquid, drippings, tomato paste, onion powder, garlic powder, and green chilies.

(3) Over medium low heat cook and stir 5 minutes. Reduce heat.
(4) Using a sharp knife cut remaining beans a bit to reduce their size. Do not cut too small. Fold them into the mashed ingredients, heat through. Gently stir occasionally.

Taco Sauce

75mL....1/3 cup tomato paste
105mL...1/3 cup water plus
          2 Tbsp. water
15mL....1 Tbsp. cornstarch
5mL.....1 tsp. chili powder
2mL.....1/2 tsp. oregano
1mL.....1/4 tsp. salt
1........1 clove minced garlic
15mL....1 Tbsp. minced onion
30mL....2 Tbsp. peeled minced
          green chilies
****

(1) In a saucepan combine tomato paste, water and cornstarch.
(2) Blend in the rest of the ingredients.
(3) Cook and stir over medium low heat for 5 minutes.
(4) Store in a sterilized jar.
(5) Cool and refrigerate.

* Makes 150mL (2/3 cup).
* Recipe can be doubled.

Dill Sauce

250mL...1 cup sour cream
2mL.....1/2 tsp. dill
5mL.....1 tsp. finely chopped
        onion
........Salt & pepper to taste
        ****

(1) Blend all ingredients together.
(2) Chill.
(3) Store in refrigerator.
(4) Use as vegetable or potato chip dip.

Russian Dressing

A tasty dip for raw vegetables...

125mL...1/2 cup mayonnaise or
        salad dressing
125mL...1/2 cup sour cream
15mL....1 Tbsp. Dijon mustard
15mL....1 Tbsp. worcestershire
        sauce
30mL....2 Tbsp. tomato sauce
2mL.....1/2 tsp. grated onion
1........1 clove grated garlic **or**
1/2mL...1/8 tsp. garlic powder
        ****

(1) In a mixing bowl combine ingredients together.
(2) Place in a sterilized jar and refrigerate.

Cranberry Sauce

250mL...1 cup water
250mL...1 cup sugar
750mL...3 cups cranberries
        ****

(1) In a saucepan mix water and sugar, stir to dissolve sugar. Bring to a boil.

(2) Add cranberries, return to a boil, reduce heat. Boil gently for 10 minutes, stirring occasionally.
(3) Pour into sterilized jars and seal, or cool completely at room temperature, then refrigerate.

* Makes 750mL (3 cups).

Sweet & Sour Sauce #1

500mL...2 cups brown sugar
30mL....2 Tbsp. flour
125mL...1/2 cup vinegar
50mL....1/4 cup water
30mL....2 Tbsp. soy sauce
15mL....1 Tbsp. ketchup
        ****

(1) In a saucepan stir together sugar and flour.
(2) Slowly add vinegar, water, ketchup and soy sauce.
(3) Bring to a boil, cook for 1 minute, stirring constantly.
(4) Pour over meatballs etc.

49

Sweet & Sour Sauce #2

You're sure to be pleased with this sauce...

15mL....1 Tbsp. butter
1........1 small chopped onion
75mL....1/3 cup vinegar
15mL....1 Tbsp. soy sauce
250mL...1 cup water
50mL....1/4 cup ketchup
175mL...3/4 cup white sugar
30mL....2 Tbsp. cornstarch
****

(1) In a small saucepan heat butter.
(2) Saute onion until limp.
(3) Transfer onion to separate bowl.
(4) In same saucepan combine rest of ingredients.
(5) Cook until thickened.
(6) Stir in onions.
(7) Serve with meat or rice.

Spaghetti Sauce #1

Kountry Koop Special, thick and flavourful...

500g.....1 lb. sliced fresh mush-
           rooms
45mL....3 Tbsp. butter or margar-
           ine
1........1 medium chopped onion
4........4 diced cloves garlic
15mL....1 Tbsp. olive oil
340mL...13 oz. can tomato paste
284mL...10 oz. can undiluted
           tomato soup
2mL.....1/2 tsp. salt
2mL.....1/2 tsp. pepper
5mL.....1 tsp. basil
5mL.....1 tsp. oregano
125mL...1/2 cup sliced ripe olives
****

(1) In a medium saucepan saute mushrooms in 30mL (2 Tbsp.) of butter, until juicy.
(2) Remove to bowl. In the same saucepan saute onion and garlic in remaining 15mL (1 Tbsp.) of butter until limp. Do not brown.
(3) Add 15mL (1 Tbsp.) olive oil, tomato paste and tomato soup; Mix well.
(4) Add salt, pepper, basil and oregano. Blend well.
(5) Cover and cook over very low heat for 10 minutes.

(6) Do not boil, sauce should be very thick.
(7) Add mushrooms and olives.
(8) Cook 10 minutes longer over very low heat.

* This sauce may be preserved or frozen.
* Spread over pizza, blend with cooked ground beef (drained of all fat) or serve hot over spaghetti.
* Makes 4 cups.

Tomato Spaghetti Sauce #2

30mL....2 Tbsp. salad oil
375g.....1 1/2 lbs. ground beef
1/4......1/4 medium chopped
        onion
284mL...10 oz. can mushroom
        pieces, including juice
42g......1 pkg. spaghetti sauce mix
370mL...13 oz. can tomato paste
218mL...7/8 cup water
........Salt & pepper to taste

(1) In medium saucepan, brown ground beef. Add onion.
(2) Stir in remaining ingredients.
(3) Simmer for 30 minutes.
(4) Stir occasionally.
(5) Serve hot over spaghetti.

****

White Sauce

The method used for thin, medium and thick white sauce is the same procedure; only the amounts of ingredients differ. Therefore it will be easy to remember when it comes to making the sauce that you prefer. The quantity in milk will remain the same in each sauce. The butter and flour will be in equal amounts. Bear in mind:

Thin sauce: Used for making soups.

15mL....1 Tbsp. butter
15mL....1 Tbsp. flour
250mL...1 cup milk

Medium sauce: Used for sauces with vegetables or fish

30mL....2 Tbsp. butter
30mL....2 Tbsp. flour
250mL...1 cup milk

Thick sauce: Used for souffles

45mL....3 Tbsp. butter
45mL....3 Tbsp. flour
250mL...1 cup milk

To make sauce:

In a saucepan melt butter until bubbling. Stir in the flour, cook 5 minutes after mixture bubbles. Gradually add the milk. While stirring constantly, cook until the mixture is thick and smooth. When making creamed vegetables, cook vegetables in a separate saucepan first; combine after both sauce and vegetables are cooked. Drain vegetables before adding sauce.

*   Salt & pepper to taste.
*   250mL (1 cup) white sauce covers 250mL (1 cup) vegetables.

Tartar Sauce (White)

125mL...1/2 cup salad dressing
2mL.....1/2 tsp. grated onion
15mL....1 Tbsp. finely chopped
        chives
15mL....1 Tbsp. finely chopped
        pickles
15mL....1 Tbsp. lemon juice
3........3 or more drops tabasco
        sauce
      ****

(1) Combine all ingredients.
(2) Stir together well.
(3) Serve with fish, or use as vegettable dip.

* Makes 175mL (3/4 cup).

Tartar Sauce (Red)

Serve with cold shellfish...
Excellent on crab or shrimp cocktail...

125mL...1/2 cup tomato paste
175mL...3/4 cup chili sauce
15mL....1 Tbsp. creamed horse-
        radish
15mL....1 Tbsp. vinegar
15mL....1 Tbsp. minced green
        onion
15mL....1 Tbsp. lemon juice
      ****

(1) In a small mixing bowl blend tomato paste and chili sauce together.
(2) Stir in remaining ingredients. Blend well, pour into sterilized jar. Chill thoroughly.

* Makes 250mL (1 cup).

Very Hot Mustard

50mL....1/4 cup dry mustard
10mL....2 tsp. sugar
1mL.....1/4 tsp. salt
30mL....2 Tbsp. water
1mL.....1/4 tsp. lemon juice
      ****

(1) Mix mustard, sugar and salt together, add water gradually, then lemon juice.
(2) Blend well.

* Makes 50mL (1/4 cup).

Sweet Mustard

This is an old recipe handed down through generations...
I'm pleased to have it in this collection...

250mL...1 cup sugar	(1) In a saucepan stir sugar, corn-
50mL....1/4 cup cornstarch	starch, celery seed, tumeric and
5mL.....1 tsp. celery seed	mustard powder together. Slow-
5mL.....1 tsp. tumeric	ly add the pickle juice.
15mL....1 Tbsp. mustard powder	(2) Add water, combine well.
250mL...1 cup sweet pickle juice	(3) Stir mixture constantly and
250mL...1 cup water	cook over medium heat until
*********	thickened. Lower heat and sim-
	mer 15-20 minutes.

*   This may be used as a spread on cold meat, lovely on scrambled eggs, or used in potato salad.

Shrimp Dip

113g.....1-4 oz. can small shrimp	(1) Drain shrimp well, wrap in
250g.....1-8 oz. pk. cream cheese	paper towel to dry.
125mL...1/2 cup whipped salad	(2) Soften cream cheese with a
dressing	fork, mix in ketchup, tabasco
30mL....2 Tbsp. ketchup	sauce and green onion.
1mL.....1/4 tsp. tabasco sauce	(3) Fold in shrimp. Keep in refrig-
10mL....2 tsp. chopped green	erator until ready to serve.
onion	(4) Serve with crackers or celery.
*********	

Cheese Sauce

45mL....3 Tbsp. butter	(1) In a medium saucepan, melt
45mL....3 Tbsp. flour	butter until bubbling.
375mL...1 1/2 cups milk	(2) Stir in the flour and cook 5
250mL...1 cup mild grated cheddar	min. after mixture bubbles.
cheese	Gradually add the milk while
2mL.....1/2 tsp. salt	stirring constantly. Cook until
1/2mL...1/8 tsp. paprika	the mixture is thick and
........Sprinkle of cayenne	smooth.
pepper	(3) Reduce heat, stir in grated
*********	cheese.

(4)   Add salt, paprika and cayenne pepper. Stir the mixture until the cheese is melted.

*   Keep cheese sauce hot but do not boil.

Veloute Sauce

A smooth, creamy, white sauce made from meat stock...
Use chicken, turkey, pork or veal stock...

To make meat stock, place cut up meat into saucepan. Add cold water to cover 3/4 of the meat. Simmer slowly for 1 1/2-2 hours. Stir occasionally. Strain and cool.

To make Veloute Sauce:

500mL...2 cups meat stock
75mL....1/2 cup flour
........Salt
........White pepper
****

(1) In a small saucepan, combine flour and cold meat stock. Use a wire wisk and wisk vigorously until no lumps of flour remain.

(2) Place over medium heat, bring to a boil stirring constantly until thickened. Cover and cook slowly for 5 minutes. Cool.

* Makes 500mL (2 cups).

Hollandaise Sauce

45mL....3 Tbsp. lemon juice
45mL....3 Tbsp. water
2mL.....1/2 tsp. salt
1........1 egg
2........2 egg yolks
125mL...1/2 cup butter
****

(1) In a small saucepan, bring lemon juice, water and salt to simmer. Warm butter in separate pan, set aside and keep warm.

(2) In a small saucepan beat egg and egg yolks. Beat vigorously with a wire whip until they are light coloured and thick. Set over low heat and wisk in the hot lemon juice very slowly. Keep beating until foamy. Remove from heat just as it starts to steam.

(3) Beat in warm butter very slowly, adding enough butter to make thick, creamy sauce.

* As bacteria works quickly in egg yolks, it is best to make Hollandise Sauce in small quantities. Make it, serve it, then discard any unused sauce.

Beef

Preparing Tough Cuts of Meat

When preparing tough cuts of meat, place 125mL (1/2 cup) flour, 5mL (1 tsp.) salt, 1mL (1/4 tsp.) pepper, in a plastic bag. Add steak and pound with edge of plate. Do not pound with china plate if there is a bone in the steak. Use a metal pie plate. Pound both sides of steak, shaking flour around it in the bag until steak is covered with flour as you pound it.

Heat fat in frying pan until very hot. Place steak in the pan. It will spatter somewhat. Do not camouflage with spices. Let the true flavour of the meat come through. Salt & pepper are all that is needed to bring the flavour out. Sear 5 minutes. Add some drippings, turn steak over and fry for another 5 min. If the steak is not too very tough, this should be sufficient cooking time. If steak is not tender add a small amount of water, lower heat, cover and cook until tender. Do not discard unused flour in bag. Use it to make gravy after the steak is finished cooking. 75mL (1/3 cup) flour will thicken 500mL (2 cups) of liquid.

This unused flour cannot be stored in the refrigerator as the meat juices will spoil.

To Marinate Tough Cuts of Meat

Mix equal parts vinegar and heated bouillon. Marinate 2 hours.
To tenderize steak rub in a mixture of oil and vinegar. Marinate 2 hours.

Basic Cooking Method for Roasting Meat

Preheat oven to 200°C (400°F).
For your more tender cuts of beef such as: standing rib, rolled rib or sirloin tip. Also for leg of lamb and pork roast.

Rub roast with oil, sprinkle with salt & pepper. *There is no need to rub a pork roast with oil. Place fat side up on a rack in a shallow baking pan. Do not cover. Do not baste. Do not add water.
Roast in oven at 200°C (400°F) for 30 minutes. Reduce heat to 160°C (325°F) until done.

Less tender cuts will take longer to cook.

Less tender beef roast should be started at a lower heat 160°C (325°F).

55

Cook in a covered roaster, add small amounts of water when needed.
Ask your butcher for fat strips to lay on top of beef roasts, especially for dry roasts. For additional flavour, lay thick slices of onion on top of roast under fat strips. The use of a meat thermometer is an accurate way to tell when a roast is as done as you like it. Make sure the tip of the thermometer is not in fat or touching any bones. Lay tinfoil loosely over roast if it is drying.
If roast is frozen, place thermometer in meat when partially cooked.

This timetable is only a guide as stoves differ in temperature.
Mark dcwn the temperatures that work best for you.

Cooking time: 20-30 minutes per 500g. (1 lb.)

Temperature	Meat	Weight	Roasting Time	Thermometer Reading
160°C (325°F)	Beef	2-3kg. (4-6 lbs.)	2-4 hrs.	140°Rare 160°Med 170°Well

Allow cooked roast to stand 15-20 minutes before carving.
Before placing ham in oven remove rind. Cut fat diagonally two ways.
Stick whole cloves into squares at random.
A mixture of honey, Dijon mustard and margarine may be used to glaze the ham as it cooks.

Beef Marinade

675mL...2 3/4 cups cider vinegar
575mL...2 1/3 cups water
3.......3 medium sliced onions
1.......1 sliced lemon
1.......1 clove pressed garlic
2.......2 bay leaves
8.......8 whole black peppers
8.......8 whole cloves
****

(1) In a mixing bowl combine all the ingredients.
(2) Place steaks or roast into marinade; cover. (Plastic wrap may be used if none other is available.)
(3) Refrigerate 12 hours for steaks, 24-30 hours for roasts. Turn occasionally.

(4) Drain, pat dry with paper towel before cooking.

Beef Stew

Especially good on those chilly winter days...

1kg .....2 1/2 lbs. stewing beef cut up	(1) In a 3L (3 Qt.) casserole mix beef with flour.
50mL....1/4 cup flour	(2) Dissolve bouillon cube in boil-
250mL...1 cup boiling water	ing water. Add soy sauce, salt
1........1 beef bouillon cube	& pepper and pour over meat.
50mL....1/4 cup soy sauce	(3) Chop onions, potatoes and car-
2mL.....1/2 tsp. salt	rots into 2.5cm. (1-inch) pieces.
2mL.....1/2 tsp. pepper	Chop celery into 1cm. (1/2-
500mL...2 cups each onions, pota- toes, and carrots	inch) pieces.
	(4) Stir into meat mixture. Cover.
250mL...1 cup celery	(5) Bake just below centre in 150°C
*********	(300°F) oven for 3 hrs. or until meat is tender.

*   Makes 8 servings.

Meat Loaf

250g.....1/2 lb. ground pork	(1) In a mixing bowl combine beef
750g.....1 1/2 lbs. ground beef	and pork. Mix well.
75mL....1/3 cup finely chopped onion	(2) Add onion, garlic, parsley, celery, bread crumbs, tomatoes,
1........1 small finely chopped garlic clove	egg, salt, pepper and seasoning.
	(3) Blend well. Place in a greased
30mL....2 Tbsp. chopped parsley	loaf pan.
45mL....3 Tbsp. finely chopped celery	(4) Cover with aluminum foil.
	(5) Bake just below centre in 180°C
175mL...3/4 cup soft bread crumbs	(350°F) oven for 1 1/2 hours.
175mL...3/4 cup canned tomatoes	
1........1 beaten egg	
7mL.....1 1/2 tsp. salt	
1/2mL...1/8 tsp. pepper	
2mL.....1/2 tsp. poultry seasoning	
*********	

*   Serves 8.

Basic Mix for Meatballs

You may add your choice of gravy or spices to suit your taste...

750g.....1 1/2 lbs. ground pork
750g.....1 1/2 lbs. ground lean beef
375mL...1 1/2 cups fresh white bread torn into fine pieces
375mL...1 1/2 cups finely chopped onions
2........2 eggs
15mL....3 tsp. salt
5mL.....1 tsp pepper
10mL....2 tsp. oregano
10mL....2 tsp. thyme
........Flour for dredging, drippings for browning
****

(1) In a mixing bowl combine ground pork and beef together very well.
(2) Mix in bread crumbs, onions, eggs and spices.
(3) Roll meat into balls 2cm. (3/4-inch) in diameter. Roll in flour.
(4) In a frying pan over medium heat, brown meatballs in drippings, turning once.
(5) Transfer to 2 1/2L (10 cup) casserole.
(6) Cover with sweet and sour sauce **or** gravy of your choice.

(7) Cover and bake just below centre in 180°C (350°F) oven for 30-40 min. or until cooked through.

Variations for Meatballs

* For quick oven browning after meatballs have been dredged in flour, place them in a single layer on a greased cookie sheet.
  Bake just above center in 190°C (375°F) for 8-10 minutes or until cooked through. Turning once or twice to brown uniformly.
* Serve on a tray as an appetizer. Have toothpicks handy.
* They also go very well over buttered parsleyed noodles.
* For Swedish meatballs, omit oregano and thyme and add:
  10mL...2 tsp. sugar
  10mL...2 tsp. salt
   5mL...1 tsp. nutmeg
   1mL...1/4 tsp. allspice

Hawaiian Sweet-N-Sour Meatballs

One of our families' favorites...it's sure to be yours too...

5mL.....1 tsp. salt
150mL...2/3 cup evaporated milk
750g.....1 1/2 lbs. ground beef
125mL...1/2 cup chopped onion
150mL...2/3 cup cracker crumbs
****

(1) Combine evaporated milk, beef, onions, cracker crumbs and salt.
(2) Form into 2cm. (3/4-in.) balls.
(3) In a frying pan brown meatballs and transfer to casserole.

Sauce

426g.....15 oz. can drained chunk pineapple, reserve juice
.........Water
30mL....2 Tbsp. cornstarch
50mL....1/4 cup vinegar
50mL....1/4 cup brown sugar
30mL....2 Tbsp. soy sauce
****

(4) Place drained pineapple into casserole with meatballs.
(5) Add water to pineapple juice to fill 250ml (1 cup).
(6) Mix juice, cornstarch, vinegar, brown sugar and soy sauce together. Cook stirring until thick and clear.

(7) Pour over meatballs and pineapple.
(8) Bake just below centre in 180°C (350°F) oven for 30 minutes.

Saucy Short Ribs

1kg......2 lbs. short ribs
625mL...2 1/2 cups canned tomatoes (drained)
30mL....2 Tbsp. shortening
250mL...1 cup tomato juice from tomatoes
1........1 onion
15mL....1 Tbsp. prepared horse-radish
5mL.....1 tsp. salt
2mL.....1/2 tsp. pepper
1........1 large bay leaf
****

(1) Cut beef into pieces and remove some of the excess fat.
(2) In a heavy frying pan heat shortening, add short ribs and fry until golden brown.
(3) Pour off fat.
(4) Transfer meat into casserole and cover with the remaining ingredients that have been mixed together.
(5) Cover. Bake just below centre in 180°C (350°F) oven for 1 1/2 hours or until tender. Remove bay leaf.

* Makes 4-6 servings.

Liver Teriyaki

45mL....3 Tbsp. olive oil or
       salad oil
500g.....1 lb. beef liver
45g......1 1/2 oz. soy sauce
45mL....3 Tbsp. brown sugar
       ****

(1) Heat oil in frying pan.
(2) Cut liver into small cubes.
(3) In hot oil quickly stir fry liver,
     add soy sauce.
(4) When liver is almost done, add
     brown sugar.

(5) Cook and stir, coating all pieces of meat.
(6) Cook 5 minutes or until cooked through.
(7) Liver should remain tender.

*   Serves 2.

Chili Con Carne

This deluxe recipe comes from the files of the Boy Scout Leaders...
a winner...

500g.....1 lb. ground beef
1........1 clove garlic minced
375mL...1 1/2 cups chopped onion
250mL...1 cup chopped celery
1........1 chopped green pepper
795mL...1-28 oz. can tomatoes
213mL...1-7 1/2 oz. can tomato
       sauce
5mL.....1 tsp. salt
1mL.....1/4 tsp. pepper
45mL....3 Tbsp. chili powder
7mL.....1 1/2 tsp. vinegar
10mL....2 tsp. worcestershire sauce
795mL...2-14 oz. cans kidney beans
       ****

(1) In a large saucepan combine all
     ingredients.
(2) Stir to combine.
(3) Cover and cook very slowly,
     for about 1 hour. Stir occasion-
     ally until tender.

*   Can be doubled or tripled when larger amounts are needed.
*   Can be processed or frozen.
*   Mash half the beans for thicker consistency.

Sloppy Joes

500g.....1 lb. ground beef
50mL....1/4 cup uncooked rice
50mL....1/4 cup chopped green
.............pepper
2mL.....1/2 tsp. sugar
1mL.....1/4 tsp. celery seed
250mL...1 cup sliced onions
1........1 clove garlic (minced)
1mL.....1/4 tsp. mustard
2mL.....1/2 tsp. salt
500mL...2 cups tomatoes **or**
375mL...1 1/2 cups tomato juice
.............*********

(1) In a heavy frying pan brown beef, turning over gently so meat stays chunky.
(2) Drain off excess fat.
(3) Add remaining ingredients.
(4) Bring to a boil.
(5) Reduce heat to low, cover and cook 25 minutes.
(6) Turn over gently, occasionally.
(7) Stir and serve hot on buns.

* Serves 4.

Canned Beef

Ready for unexpected guests or a busy day...
Not to mention the taste that's hard to beat...

Select fresh stewing beef. Cut into approx. 5cm. (2-inch) pieces.
Pack loosely into sterilized 1L (1 Qt.) jars. Do not fill jar completely.
Leave 2.5cm. (1-inch) at the top of the jar. Add 5mL (1 tsp.) salt, 2mL (1/2 tsp.) pepper to each 1L (1 Qt.) jar.

* Do not add water. Wipe edge of jar very well, rubbing hard with a sterilized cloth. Seal jars according to directions on canning lids.
* Process in pressure cooker according to manufacturers instructions.
* Store in a cool, dark room.

* For a quick meal:

In a saucepan combine 500mL (2 cups) of cold water, 175mL (1/3 cup) flour, 2 chopped green onions, **or** 15mL (1 Tbsp.) cooking onions. Bring to a boil, stirring constantly. Reduce heat and cook until thickened. Add canned beef, fold in gently as not to break up beef cubes. Salt & pepper to taste. Keep heat low and slowly simmer until heated through.

* Serve with mashed potatoes.

Beef Jerky

1kg .....2 lbs. very lean beef **or**
        venison
175mL...1/3 cup soy sauce
1........1 clove minced garlic
****

*   If meat is slightly frozen it will be very easy to slice into uniform strips.

(1) Slice the meat lengthwise with grain into 10cm. (4-inch) x 2.5cm. (1-inch) x .6cm. (1/4-inch) thick strips.
(2) Combine soy sauce and garlic in mixing bowl.
(3) Add meat. Marinate for 20 minutes, stirring occasionally.
(4) Drain and arrange in single layer on wire racks. Set in cookie sheet.
(5) Bake just above centre in 48°C (150°F) oven overnight or up to 12 hours until dry.
(6) Blot meat on paper towel to remove excess fat.
(7) Store in tightly covered container.

*   Does not require refrigeration.

Beef Steak

As you like it...

........Beef steak 2 1/2cm.
     (1-inch) thick
........Salt & pepper
........Garlic salt (Opt.)
****

(1) Turn oven to broil. Spray broiler pan with *Pam; place into oven until very hot.

(2) Place beef steaks onto hot broiler pan. Place on highest position in the oven. If broiler plan is too high place one position lower; leave oven door slightly open.
(3) Broil steaks 4-5 minutes for rare; 6 minutes for medium rare. Turn steaks over, sprinkle with salt, pepper and garlic salt. Broil 4,5 or 6 minutes. Serve immediately on warmed plates.

*   Pam contains a pure vegetable product in oil form.
*   The use of Pam eliminates excess smoking under high heat.
*   Choose tender cuts of meat for broiling (T-bone, Sirloin, Porterhouse, etc.)

Hamburgers

500g.....1 lb. medium ground beef	(1)	In a bowl combine beef,
1mL.....1/4 tsp. salt		seasoning salt, salt & pepper,
1mL.....1/4 tsp. pepper		then blend in egg.
2mL.....1/2 tsp. seasoning salt	(2)	Shape into 4 patties, place onto
1........1 egg		greased broiler pan.
4........4 slices cheese (Opt.)	(3)	Broil just above center for
*********		3 minutes.

(4) Turn patties over and cook 3 more minutes.
(5) Place cheese on top of patty. Broil only until slightly melted.
(6) Serve at once on buns.
(7) Serve with chopped or sliced onions, relish, hamburger sauce, ketchup and mustard.

Marinated Short Rib Steaks

Ask your butcher to cut you some short rib steaks...

150mL...2/3 cup brown sugar	(1)	Mix first 5 ingredients together
175mL...3/4 cup soy sauce		until sugar is dissolved.
2........2 crushed garlic cloves	(2)	Pour over steaks.
3........3 thin slices ginger root	(3)	Marinate steaks from 8-20
15mL....1 Tbsp. sesame oil		hours, in refrigerator.
4........4 short rib steaks 1.5cm.	(4)	Turn from time to time.
(1/2-inch) thick	(5)	Drain. Bar-B-Q, or broil steaks.
*********		

Hamburger (Large amount)

Chuckwagon Rodeo Style...

Makes 28 patties:
3kg .....6 lbs. ground beef
500mL...2 cups fine bread crumbs
22mL....1 1/2 Tbsp. salt
7mL.....1 1/2 tsp. pepper
22mL....1 1/2 Tbsp. worcestershire
          sauce
75mL....1/3 cup evaporated milk
       ****

Makes 14 patties:
1.5kg....3 lbs. ground beef
250mL...1 cup fine bread crumbs
15mL....1 Tbsp. salt
5mL.....1 tsp. pepper
15mL....1 Tbsp. worcestershire
          sauce
50mL....1/4 cup evaporated milk
       ****

(1) In a mixing bowl combine beef, bread crumbs, salt & pepper.
(2) Stir the worcestershire sauce into the milk, pour over beef mixture. Combine thoroughly.
(3) Form into patties using 125mL (1/2 cup) to each pattie. Place wax paper between each pattie. *(May be frozen at this stage.) Patties may be B.B.Q.ed or broiled. Broil just above centre of oven 3-4 minutes on each side or until cooked through.
(4) Serve with onions, lettuce, hamburger sauce, relish, mustard, etc.

* Reduce bread crumbs if very lean meat is used.

Hamburger Mix (Large)

Chuckwagon Rodeo Style...

6kg .....12 lbs. meat
1L ......1 quart fine bread crumbs
45mL....3 Tbsp. salt
15mL....1 Tbsp. pepper
45mL....3 Tbsp. worcestershire
          sauce
197mL...3/4 cup plus 2 Tbsp.
          evaporated milk
       ****

(1) In a large mixing bowl combine beef, bread crumbs, salt & pepper.
(2) Stir the worcestershire sauce into the milk, pour over meat mixture. Combine thoroughly.
(3) Form into patties using 125mL (1/2 cup) to each pattie. *(May be frozen at this stage).

Patties may be B.B.Q.ed or broiled. Broil just above centre of oven 3-4 minutes on each side, or until cooked through.
(4) Serve with onions, lettuce, hamburger sauce, relish, mustard, etc.

* Makes 56 patties.

Pork

Pork Chops with Rice

30mL....2 Tbsp. drippings
6........6 pork chops
1 1/4L ..5 cups water (divided)
1........1 pouch onion soup mix
500mL...2 cups brown rice
****

(1) In a frying pan melt drippings.
(2) Brown pork chops on both sides.
(3) Lift pork chops out of frying pan. Set aside.
(4) Discard fat from frying pan.

(5) Place 250mL (1 cup) of the water and onion soup mix in frying pan.
(6) Stir well, scraping up brown particles from the bottom.
(7) Place rice in 3L (3 Qt.) casserole.
(8) Add remaining three cups of cold water.
(9) Stir in onion soup mix from frying pan.
(10) Mix well. Set pork chops on top of rice, cover.
(11) Bake just below center in 180°C (350°F) oven for 45 minutes or until cooked through.

*   Serves 6.

Pork Chops

Quick?... Yes... Tasty?... Very... Serve with?... Mashed Potatoes...

30mL....2 Tbsp. drippings
6........6 pork chops
........Salt & pepper
540mL...19 oz. can mushroom
         soup (undiluted)
****

(1) In a large frying pan melt drippings.
(2) Brown pork chops on both sides. Salt & pepper both sides.
(3) Drain off fat, lower heat.

(4) Spoon mushroom soup over pork chops. Cover.
(5) Cook slowly until tender, turning pork chops once.
(6) If frying pan is kept on lower heat and if you do not stir mushroom soup, just move it around a bit, it will stay somewhat in a gravy form.

Bacon Curls

360mL...12 1/2 oz. can water
         chestnuts
15mL....1 Tbsp. worcestershire
         sauce
15mL....1 Tbsp. seasoned salt
30mL....2 Tbsp. lemon juice
6........6 slices bacon (cut in
         halves
      ****

(1) Drain water chestnuts, sprinkle with salt, worcestershire sauce and lemon juice.
(2) Wrap each in a half slice of bacon and secure with a toothpick.
(3) Place on broiler rack and broil for 2 minutes on each side or until bacon is crisp.

* Serves 4.

Pork and Beans

A scrumptious old fashioned baked in flavour...

1kg .....2 lbs. small white beans
1 1/2L ..6 cups water
2........2 large onions (chopped)
1.36L....48 oz. can tomato juice
540mL...19 oz. can tomato soup
        (undiluted)
250mL...1 cup bacon drippings
250g.....1/2 lb. bacon or leftover
        hambone
30mL....2 Tbsp. prepared mustard
150mL...2/3 cup brown sugar
50mL....1/4 cup molasses
      ****

(1) Wash and sort beans; check carefully for tiny stones.
(2) Place in large kettle, cover well with cold water.
(3) Bring water and beans to a boil.
(4) Add onions, tomato juice, bacon fat, bacon or hambone, mustard, brown sugar and molasses.
(5) Cover.
(6) Bake in 120°C-150°C (250°F-300°F) oven until beans are tender. Approx. 3 hrs.

(7) Add tomato soup 1 1/2 hours after started. Stir well.
(8) Stir beans occasionally and add more liquid, if needed.

* Soy beans may be used in place of small white beans, but must be cooked longer. Test for doneness. More water may be needed, depending on the dryness of beans.

Mountain Boy Pork and Beans (Large)

1 . . . . .1 large diced onion
500g. . . . .1 lb. diced bacon
4.5L. . . . .1 gallon cheap pork and
        beans
5mL. . . . .1 tsp. worcestershire
        sauce
2mL. . . . .1/2 cup molasses
        ****

(1) In a large dutch oven saute
     onions and bacon until onions
     are clear.
(2) Add pork and beans, worcester-
     shire sauce and molasses.
(3) Mix well and simmer for 2-3
     hours.

* Makes enough for a crowd.

Breakfast Sausage

750g. . . . .1 1/2 lb. ground pork **or**
        beef
7mL. . . . .1 1/2 tsp. sage
7mL. . . . .1 1/2 tsp. salt
1mL. . . . .1/4 tsp. pepper
3mL. . . . .3/4 tsp. thyme
. . . . .Small amount water
        ****

(1) In a mixing bowl combine meat
     and spices.
(2) Mix until thoroughly blended.
     Add water, if needed, to hold
     meat together.
(3) Shape into patties or stuff into
     sausage casings, tie off into
     10cm. (4-inch) links with string.

(4) Refrigerate in air tight container for 2 days to allow flavours to blend.
(5) In a frying pan, over medium heat, cook sausages until golden brown.

Ham Steaks

4 . . . . . . .4-2cm. (3/4-inch) ham
        steaks
15mL. . . .1 Tbsp. oil
        ****

(1) In a heavy frying pan heat oil.
     Add hams steaks and fry over
     medium low heat for 10 min.
     on each side.

* Do not have frying pan too hot.
* Serves 4.

Broiled Ham with Pineapple

4 . . . . .4-2cm. (3/4-inch) slices of
        fully cooked ham
4 . . . . . . .4 pineapple slices
        ****

(1) Preheat broiler, place ham slices
     on slightly greased broiler pan.
(2) Broil for 5 min. on each side.

(3) Place a slice of pineapple onto each slice of ham.
(4) Broil an additional 5 minutes.

* Serves 4.

Chinese Meat Balls

An attractive dish with a sweet and sour taste.

1kg .....2 lbs. ground pork	(1) Mix first 8 ingredients together.
125mL...1/2 cup chopped onion	(2) Shape into 2.5cm. (1-inch)
1mL.....1/4 tsp. pepper	balls.
5mL.....1 tsp. salt	(3) Bake on a broiler pan just
250mL...1 cup finely chopped	above centre in a 180°C (350°F)
mushrooms	oven until brown on both sides.
45mL....3 Tbsp. soy sauce	(May be frozen at this point
30mL....2 Tbsp. cornstarch	when cooled).
5mL.....1 tsp. sugar	

****

Sauce:

370mL...13 oz. tin pineapple	(1) Drain pineapple, reserve juice.
chunks	(2) In a frying pan combine juice,
30mL....2 Tbsp. light brown sugar	brown sugar, soy sauce, vine-
5mL.....1 tsp. soy sauce	gar, pepper, salt and salad oil.
30mL....2 Tbsp. vinegar	(3) Stir and bring to a boil.
1ml .....1/4 tsp. pepper	(4) Add carrots and green pepper.
1mL.....1/4 tsp. salt	(5) Simmer covered for 5 minutes.
30mL....2 Tbsp. salad oil	(6) Remove from heat.
250mL...1 cup thinly cut carrots	(7) Combine cornstarch with 50mL
1........1 medium green pepper,	(1/4 cup) water to smooth
cut in 2.5cm. (1-inch)	paste.
strips	(8) Stir into frying pan, bring to a
15mL....1 Tbsp. cornstarch	boil, stirring constantly. Mix-
50mL....1/4 cup water	ture will thicken and become
1........1 large tomato (cut in	transparent.
wedges)	(9) Add meat balls, pineapple and
	tomatoes.

****

(10)   Cover and simmer for 10 minutes.

* This can be kept on low heat until served.
* Add a little water if it thickens.
* Serve over rice.

Sweet and Sour Spare Ribs

This is a #1 favorite. Flavour improves when rewarmed...
If there are any left over...

2kg .....4 lbs. spare ribs (cut into serving pieces	(1) Brown spare ribs in a heavy pan and transfer to casserole.
250mL...1 cup chopped onions	(2) Drain off fat, add 50mL (1/4
50mL....1/4 cup brown sugar	cup) hot water to frying pan.
10mL....2 tsp. dry mustard	(3) Stir and scrape off browned
5mL.....1 tsp. paprika	particles; add to casserole.
5mL.....1 tsp. salt	(4) Add onions.
250mL...1 cup ketchup	(5) Stir together sugar, mustard,
10mL....2 tsp. worcestershire sauce	paprika, salt, ketchup, vinegar
250mL...1 cup water	worcestershire sauce and water.
50mL....1/4 cup vinegar	Pour over spare ribs. Cover.

****

(6) Bake in 180°C (350°F) oven for 1 hour.
(7) Remove cover 10 minutes before finished.

Oriental Spare Ribs

A good blend of ingredients...

1.5kg....3 lbs. pork spare ribs cut into small serving pieces	(1) In a large saucepan, mix together water, 50mL (1/4 cup) soy sauce, salt and garlic.
500mL...2 cups water	
125mL...1/2 cup soy sauce (divided)	(2) Place ribs in liquid, bring to a boil.
5mL.....1 tsp. salt	(3) Reduce heat, cover and cook
30mL....2 Tbsp. brown sugar	slowly for 1 hour.
1........1 clove garlic (minced)	(4) Remove cover, bring to a boil
15mL....1 Tbsp. cornstarch	and cook 20 minutes longer.
15mL....1 Tbsp. sesame seeds	(5) Drain, reserving 50mL (1/4
30mL....2 Tbsp. finely chopped green onions	cup) of cooking liquid.
1mL.....1/4 tsp. ginger	(6) Mix together with remaining 50mL (1/4 cup) soy sauce,

****

brown sugar, cornstarch, sesame seeds, green onions and ginger.
(7) Place spare ribs and reserved 50mL (1/4 cup) cooking liquid in frying pan.
(8) Pour seasoned soy sauce mixture over ribs and cook, turning ribs often and spooning sauce over to glaze ribs until glaze is thickened and sticks to ribs, about 10 minutes.

* Keep warm until served.
* Serves 6.

69

Spare Ribs and Sauerkraut

6........6 slices bacon chopped
1........1 medium sliced onion
796mL...2-14 oz. cans sauerkraut
2mL.....1/2 tsp. caraway seed
      (Opt.)
1.5kg....3 lbs. spare ribs, cut up
2........2 medium apples
****

(1)   In a frying pan cook bacon. Drain off fat, leaving enough to brown onion slightly.

(2)   Drain and rinse sauerkraut. Place in buttered casserole. Mix in bacon and onions. Sprinkle with caraway seed, if desired.

(3)   In same frying pan brown ribs and mix them with sauerkraut. Drain fat from frying pan, add 50mL (1/4 cup) water. Stir while scraping up browned particles. Pour over ribs. Peel apples, cut into quarters, mix into sauerkraut. Cover.

(4)   Bake just below center in 180°C (350°F) for 1 1/2 hours.

* For crispy spare ribs, transfer spare ribs only to cookie sheet. Place under broiler until crisp, turning once. Serve over sauerkraut on warmed platter.
* Or, remove cover 15-20 minutes before serving.
* Serves 6-8.

Variation:

* Spicy meat may be used in place of spare ribs. Kaulbasa, Debreziener (hot German wiener), and Bavarian sausages are excellent.
* Place spicy meat, just below center in 190°C (375°F) oven approx. 15 minutes to remove fat. Do this before adding to sauerkraut in casserole.

Pork in Apple Sauce Bake

750g.....1 1/2 lbs. pork cut up in-
      to bite size pieces **or** use
      4 pork chops
5mL.....1 tsp. garlic powder
30mL....2 Tbsp. flour
2mL.....1/2 tsp. salt
1/2 mL ..1/8 tsp. pepper
250mL...1 cup boiling water
398mL...1-14 oz. can apple sauce
22mL....1 1/2 tsp. lemon juice
****

(1)   In a frying pan brown pork pieces in small amount of fat. Transfer to a buttered casserole.

(2)   Drain off fat, leaving 30mL (2 Tbsp.) in pan. Have fat hot. Combine garlic salt, flour, salt & pepper together. Stir into hot fat, mix well.

(3)   Add water, stir constantly until mixture thickens. Add apple-sauce and lemon juice, mix well. Pour over pork. Cover.

(4)   Bake just below center in 180°C (350°F) oven for 1 hour.

* Serves 4.

Chicken

Canned Chicken

So handy for sandwiches...or meal time:

(1) Select mature chicken, dress, soak in cold water for 12 hours.
(2) Cut up chicken, remove large bones.
(3) Pack into sterilized jars. Leave 2.5cm. (1-inch) space at top.
(4) Add 5mL (1 tsp.) salt and 2mL (1/2 tsp.) white pepper to each 1L (1 Qt.) jar. Do not add water. Wipe top of jars hard using a sterilized cloth.
(5) Seal jars according to directions on canning lids.
(6) Process in pressure cooker according to manufacturers instructions.
(7) Store in a cool dark room.

* For chicken soup; dice chicken into smaller pieces, add water, noodles, cooked vegetables or rice. Adjust seasoning. Simmer until heated through.

Chicken Pickens

2kg .....4 lbs. wingetts or chicken breasts
500mL...2 cups fine dry bread crumbs
5mL.....1 tsp. garlic powder
125mL...1/2 cup buttermilk
1........1 egg
2mL.....1/2 tsp. salt
50mL....1/4 cup melted butter or margarine
.........Pepper
****

(1) If breasts are used, skin and debone. Pound to 1cm. (1/2-inch) thickness. Cut into 5cm. (2-inch) strips.
(2) Place wax paper on a pie plate and put bread crumbs and garlic powder on it. Set aside.
(3) Wisk buttermilk, egg and salt together. Set aside.
(4) Dip each piece of chicken into the buttermilk mixture, then into the bread crumbs.

(5) Place single layer on a greased cooked sheet. Drizzle with melted butter. Sprinkle with salt & pepper.
(6) Bake just above center in 200°C (400°F) oven for 15-20 minutes or until tender. Turn once, sprinkle with salt & pepper again after turning.

Catalina Chicken

45mL....3 Tbsp. margarine
3kg .....3 lbs. chicken cut into
    serving pieces
398mL...14 oz. can pineapple
    chunks (well drained)
500mL...16 oz. bottle catalina salad
    dressing
398mL...14 oz. can mandarin
    oranges (well drained)
15mL....1 Tbsp. cornstarch
.........Rice
****

(1) Heat margarine in frying pan.
(2) Brown chicken on both sides.
(3) Drain off all fat.
(4) Place in greased roaster.
(5) Add pineapple chunks, mandarin oranges, pour catalina salad dressing over all.
(6) Bake just below centre in 180°C (350°F) oven for 1 hour.
(7) Using a slotted spoon, lift out pineapple chunks, chicken and orange sections.

* Arrange on a platter of prepared rice.

(8) Thicken sauce with cornstarch. Mix cornstarch with small amount of water. Blend into sauce and stir until thick. Cook for 3 minutes.

* Serve sauce separately.

Chicken Souper Supper

2kg .....4 lbs. chicken breasts
15mL....1 Tbsp. butter or margar-
    ine
2mL.....1/2 tsp. salt
1mL.....1/4 tsp. pepper (lemon
    pepper, if available)
284mL...10 oz. can cream of mush-
    room soup
1........1 envelope dry onion soup
    mix
250mL...1 cup sour cream
2mL.....1/2 tsp. curry powder
5mL.....1 tsp. lemon juice
****

(1) Debone chicken breasts, cut into serving pieces, place in greased casserole. Sprinkle with melted butter, salt & pepper.
(2) Thoroughly blend all remaining ingredients in a bowl and pour mixture over the chicken.
(3) Bake just below center in 180°C (350°F) oven for 1 hour or until tender.

* Makes approx. 6 servings.

Pure D. Chicken

The D. stands for delicious. . . cook the gravy right along with the chicken to pick up deep rich flavour. . .

175mL. . .3/4 cup flour	(1) Place wax paper on a plate.
5mL. . . . .1 tsp. salt	(2) On it mix flour, salt & pepper.
1mL. . . . .1/4 tsp. pepper	(3) Debone chicken breasts.
50mL. . . .1/4 cup butter or margarine	(4) Place bones in saucepan.
	(5) Cover half way up with water.
1kg . . . . .2 lbs. chicken breasts	Cook until meat falls off the
50mL. . . .1/4 cup chopped onions	bones (turn bones over twice).
625mL. . .2 1/2 cups chicken broth	Drain and reserve broth.
1/2mL. . .1/8 tsp. thyme	(6) Cut breast fillets into serving
1/2mL. . .1/8 tsp. oregano	pieces.
15mL. . . .1 Tbsp. parsley	(7) In a heavy frying pan, heat butter hot but not smoking.

****

(8) Dredge chicken pieces in flour, covering both sides.
(9) Brown in hot butter on both sides, turning once.
(10) Sprinkle with thyme and oregano.
(11) Transfer chicken to greased casserole.
(12) In same frying pan, cook onions until tender.
(13) Transfer to casserole.
(14) Add flour (use flour that remains on plate adding more if needed to make up 75mL (1/3 cup).
(15) Slowly add 625mL (2 1/2 cups) chicken broth (use reserved broth from bones). Stir well.
(16) Bring to a boil, cook 5 minutes, stirring up all particles from the bottom of the frying pan.
(17) Pour over chicken pieces. Cover.
(18) Bake just below center in 180°C (350°F) oven for 30 minutes or until chicken is cooked through.
(19) Garnish with parsley.

Chicken Casserole

30mL. . . .2 Tbsp. margarine	(1) Heat margarine in frying pan.
750g. . . . .1 1/2 lbs. chicken pieces	(2) Brown chicken pieces on both
4. . . . . . .4 green onions (chopped)	sides. Drain off fat.
15mL. . . .1 Tbsp. soy sauce	(3) Place in greased casserole.
15mL. . . .1 Tbsp. brown sugar	(4) Add green onions.
2mL. . . . .1/2 tsp. salt	(5) Mix soy sauce, sugar, salt &
1/2mL. . .1/8 tsp. pepper	pepper and broth together.
250mL. . .1 cup chicken broth	Pour over chicken and cover.

****

(6) Bake just below centre in 180°C (350°F) oven for 1 hour or until the chicken is cooked through.

73

Chicken Marengo

125mL...1/2 cup flour
5mL.....1 tsp. salt
1mL.....1/4 tsp. pepper
45mL....3 Tbsp. butter or margarine
1.5kg....3 lbs. chicken parts
500g.....1 lb. (about 16) whole white onions (small)
1........1 clove garlic, minced (Opt.)
284mL...10 oz. can tomato soup
284mL...10 oz. can cream of mushroom soup
****

(1) Place wax paper on a pie plate.
(2) On it mix flour, salt & pepper.
(3) In a heavy frying pan heat butter until hot but not smoking.
(4) Dredge chicken pieces in flour mixture, covering both sides.
(5) Brown in hot butter on both sides, turning once.
(6) Transfer to casserole.
(7) Add onions and garlic.
(8) Drain fat from frying pan.
(9) Add tomato and mushroom soups.

(10) Stir with wooden spoon scraping up browned bits.
(11) Add flour that remains on plate. Cook 5 minutes.
(12) Pour over chicken. Cover.
(13) Bake just below center in a 180°C (350°F) oven for 45 minutes.
(14) Remove cover and cook 15 minutes longer or until chicken is cooked through.

Chicken Cordon Bleu

1........1 chicken breast
2........2 thin slices cooked ham
2........2 slices mozzarella cheese .6cm. (1/4-inch) thick and the same length as the ham
175mL...3/4 cup flour
5mL.....1 tsp. garlic powder
5mL.....1 tsp. onion powder
5mL.....1 tsp. salt
1mL.....1/4 tsp. pepper
284mL...10 oz. can mushroom soup
........Butter for frying
****

(1) Skin and debone chicken breast and split in half.
(2) Place breast meat one at a time in a plastic bag.
(3) Pound flat with mallet.
(4) On each portion place ham, then the cheese. Tuck ends of chicken towards the centre.
(5) Roll and secure with toothpicks.
(6) Mix flour, garlic powder, onion powder, salt & pepper together.
(7) Coat each roll in flour mixture. Let stand 30 minutes.
(8) Heat butter in frying pan.

(9) Recoat each roll in flour mixture. Fry in hot butter until brown on all sides.
(10) Pour undiluted mushroom soup over rolled chicken.
(11) Cover and steam 15-20 minutes before serving.

* An electric frying pan may be used.
* Serve over warm rice, if desired.
* Serves 2.

Chicken Strips

Just right for snacking...

4........4 chicken breasts
125mL...1/2 cup salad dressing
5mL.....1 tsp. dry mustard
5mL.....1 tsp. onion powder
125mL...1/2 cup sesame seeds
125mL...1/2 cup dried, crushed
            bread crumbs
125mL...1/2 cup thickened poultry
            veloute stock p. 54
            ****

(1) Skin and debone breasts, pound to 1cm. (1/2-inch) thickness. Cut into 5cm. (2-inch) wide strips.

(2) In a medium bowl, combine salad dressing, mustard and onion powder. Set aside.

(3) Place wax paper on a pie plate. On it mix sesame seeds, bread crumbs and thickened poultry stock.

(4) Coat chicken pieces with salad dressing mixture, then with bread crumb mixture.
(5) Place on an ungreased cookie sheet.
(6) Bake just above centre in 180°C (350°F) oven for 20-30 minutes or until cooked through.
(7) Serve hot with following Dip of your choice.

Marmalade Dip

50mL....1/4 cup salad dressing
20mL....4 tsp. citrus marmalade
10mL....2 tsp. minced onion or
            minced garlic
            ****

(1) In a small bowl mix together well.

Honey Dip

125mL...1/2 cup salad dressing
45mL....3 Tbsp. honey
            ****

(1) Melt honey slightly.
(2) Mix with salad dressing.

Chili Dip

50mL....1/4 cup chili sauce
10mL....2 tsp. lemon juice
            ****

(1) Mix chili sauce and lemon juice together.

Curried Chicken

1.5kg....3 lbs. chicken wings or
           wingetts
125mL...1/2 cup flour
5mL.....1 tsp. salt
2mL.....1/2 tsp. pepper
45mL....3 Tbsp. butter or margar-
           ine
1080mL..2-19 oz. cans mushroom
           soup
284mL...1-10 oz. can evaporated
           milk
2mL.....1/2 tsp. curry or to taste
        ****

(1) Melt butter in frying pan.
(2) Place a sheet of wax paper on a plate, on it stir flour, salt & pepper.
(3) Dredge chicken wings in flour mixture. Brown on both sides.
(4) Transfer to casserole.
(5) Combine soup and milk. Add curry and adjust seasoning. Pour over chicken parts.
(6) Bake just below centre in 180°C (350°F) oven for 1 hour or until chicken is cooked through.

*   Serve with rice.
*   Serves 4.

Turkey Nuggets

These tasty little morsels are so easy to prepare...

2........2 boneless turkey breasts
50mL....1/4 cup parmesan cheese
50mL....1/4 cup finely grated
           cheddar cheese
125mL...1/2 cup fine dry bread
           crumbs
125mL...1/2 cup butter or margar-
           ine
5mL.....1 tsp. thyme
5mL.....1 tsp. basil
2mL.....1/2 tsp. salt
1mL.....1/4 tsp. pepper
        ****

(1) Cut turkey into 4cm. (1 1/2-inches) cubes.
(2) In a bowl, mix parmesan cheese, cheddar cheese, bread crumbs, thyme, basil, salt & pepper.
(3) Melt butter, dip turkey pieces in butter, then roll in dry crumb mixture to coat completely.
(4) Arrange on a foil-lined baking sheet. Bake just above centre in 200°C (400°F) oven for 15-20 minutes.

(5) Serve hot or cold.

Honey Glazed Chicken Wings

If you like a somewhat sweet taste to your meat...you will enjoy these wings...

1.5kg....3 lbs. chicken wings
30mL....2 Tbsp. oil
5mL.....1 tsp. salt
2mL.....1/2 tsp. pepper
125mL...1/2 cup honey (melted)
50mL....1/4 cup soy sauce
1........1 clove garlic minced
30mL....2 Tbsp. ketchup
****

(1) Cut off tips from chicken wings.
(2) Cut remaining pieces in two.
(3) Arrange side by side in shallow baking pan.
(4) Sprinkle wings with oil, then salt & pepper.
(5) Combine honey, soy sauce, garlic and ketchup.

(6) Pour over wings.
(7) Bake just above centre in 190°C (375°F) oven until browned and cooked through. Approx. 1 hour.

Celestial Chicken

1.36kg...3 lbs. chicken wings
50mL....1/4 cup prepared mustard
125mL...1/2 cup honey
2mL.....1/2 tsp. curry powder
****

(1) Snip tips off wings. Cut wings in half. Place single layer in shallow baking pan.
(2) In a small bowl combine mustard, honey and curry powder. Pour over wings. Bake in 180°C (350°F) oven for 50 minutes turning once.

Kountry Koop Fried Chicken

Crisp and flavorful...our favorite...

125mL...1/2 cup flour
5mL.....1 tsp. salt
2mL.....1/2 tsp. pepper
2.72kg...2-3 lbs. fryers or 1-6 lb. roasting chicken cut up or parts
30mL....2 Tbsp. butter or margarine
****

(1) Place wax paper on pie plate. On it mix flour, salt & pepper.
(2) In a heavy frying pan heat butter, hot but not smoking.
(3) Dredge chicken pieces in flour on both sides.
(4) Brown pieces on both sides, turning once. Sprinkle both sides with salt & pepper.

(5) Transfer onto a greased cookie sheet, skin side up.
(6) Sprinkle again with salt.
(7) Bake just above center in 200°C (400°F) oven for 45 minutes for small pieces; 1 hour for large.

Oriental Chicken Wings

1.36kg...3 lbs. chicken wings
1........1 slightly beaten egg
250mL...1 cup flour
250mL...1 cup butter or margarine
****

(1) Cut off tips from chicken wings.
(2) Cut remaining piece in two. In a heavy frying pan heat butter, hot but not smoking.

Sauce

45mL....3 Tbsp. soya sauce
45mL....3 Tbsp. water
250mL...1 cup sugar
125mL...1/2 cup vinegar
5mL.....1 tsp. accent
2mL.....1/2 tsp. salt
****

(3) Dip chicken into egg, then into the flour. Brown on both sides turning once until crisp. Transfer into a greased shallow baking pan, 22x33cm. (9x13-inch).
(4) Pour sauce over chicken.
(5) Bake just below center in 150°C (300°F) oven for 2 hours. Do not cover.
(6) Baste sauce over wings while cooking.

Teriyaki Chicken

2kg......4 lbs. chicken parts
1........1 bottle teriyaki sauce
****

(1) Marinate chicken in teriyaki sauce for 1 hour. Transfer onto a well greased, shallow baking pan.

(2) Bake just below center in 180°C (350°F) oven until done, approx. 1 hour, depending on size of chicken parts. Brush chicken often with teriyaki sauce, turn chicken over two or three times.

Chicken and Dumplings

On my Mama's coal and wood stove, they were sooo good...

2 1/2 kg .5-6 lbs. stewing fowl
.........Water
125mL...1/2 cup diced celery
125mL...1/2 cup diced onions
2mL.....1/2 tsp. salt
1/2mL...1/8 tsp. pepper
****

(1)   Cut up stewing fowl and place in a large kettle.
(2)   Add cold water to almost cover.
(3)   Add celery, onion, salt & pepper.

(4)   Bring to a boil. Reduce heat and simmer for approx. 3 hours or until meat is well done.

*   Dumplings to follow.

(5)   Remove meat from kettle, (use slotted spoon).
(6)   If you prefer a somewhat drier dumpling, leave part of the meat in the kettle, you must have sufficient liquid to have juicy dumplings. Otherwise they will be dry and tough.

Dumplings

250mL...1 cup flour
2mL.....1/2 tsp. salt
7mL.....1 1/2 tsp. baking powder
.........Dash of pepper
3........3 eggs
****

(1)   Mix flour, salt, baking powder and pepper together.
(2)   In a separate bowl, beat eggs until foamy.
(3)   Stir dry ingredients into eggs quickly and thoroughly.

(4)   Have broth in kettle boiling gently.
(5)   Dip metal tablespoon into hot liquid, spoon egg mixture, one spoon at a time into the kettle right on top of chicken. Place dumplings side by side. Work quickly. Do not crowd them as they expand while cooking.
(6)   Dip spoon into hot liquid each time. This prevents egg mixture from sticking to the spoon.
(7)   Cover immediately, boil very gently for 15 minutes.

*   Do not lift cover until time is up.

Roasting Chicken or Turkey

* Wash chicken and dry with paper towel.
* Stuff fowl loosely with stuffing.
* Rub chicken breast and legs with margarine.
* Sprinkle with salt & pepper and poultry seasoning.
* Place breast side up on a rack in a roaster. Cover legs and breast with tin foil.
* Bake just below centre in preheated 200°C (400°F) oven for 30 minutes.
* Reduce heat to 160°C (325°F) until done. Remove lid and tin foil last 15 minutes of cooking.
* For easier carving allow fowl to stand 20-30 minutes.

Temperature	Meat	Weight	Roasting Time
200°C	Chicken	2-3kg.	3 hours
(400°F)		(5-6 1/2 lbs.)	
	Turkey	5-7kg.	5 hours
		(12-15 lbs.)	

Cooking times for poultry: 25-30 minutes per 500g (1 lb.).

* If roast chicken is to be used in sandwiches or salad, it is much easier to remove meat from bones when slightly cool, before refrigerating.

Pan Gravy

(1) Pour off all fat from frying pan except 45mL (3 Tbsp.).
(2) Add 500mL (2 cups) of chicken stock, or water if no stock is available.
(3) Add 75mL (1/3 cup) of flour to stock. Stir until smooth.
(4) Cook over low heat stirring continually until thickened. Cover.
(5) Turn heat to lowest setting, keeping gravy warm. *Do not boil after gravy has finished cooking. (If heat is too hot, place frying pan just partially off element.

* Use canned cream of mushroom soup as part of the liquid in making gravy for variation.
* Serves 8.

Dressing (Stuffing)

These spices blend well together, to give you a traditional bread stuffing...
Use to stuff fish, fowl, heart, etc....

125mL...1/2 cup melted butter or margarine
250mL...1 cup chopped onion
125mL...1/2 cup chopped celery
2L ......8 cups cubed, stale bread
125mL...1/2 cup boiling water
2mL.....1/2 tsp. salt
1mL.....1/4 tsp. pepper
5mL.....1 tsp. thyme
5mL.....1 tsp. sage
7mL.....1 1/2 tsp. poultry seasoning
****

(1) In a frying pan, heat 50mL (1/4 cup) butter.
(2) Saute onion and celery until limp. Set aside. Tear bread into .6cm. (1/2-inch) pieces.
(3) In a large bowl toss bread pieces with hot water and remaining butter.
(4) Cover and let steam 5 minutes.
(5) Add onions and celery to bread pieces and toss lightly.
(6) Mix salt, pepper, thyme, sage and poultry seasoning together in a separate bowl.

(7) Sprinkle half spice mixture over surface of bread mixture, toss lightly, then sprinkle remaining half; mix well.
(8) Stuff dressing into cavity of fish or fowl, stuff heart or flank steak.
(9) Dressing expands when it cooks. Do not stuff too tightly.
(10) Should there be extra dressing, enclose it loosely in tin foil, cook it separately in a baking dish. Do not overbake.
(11) When fowl is finished cooking, remove dressing from cavity and pat gently into square pan. Cut into slices to serve.
(12) Drippings from roast may be sprinkled on top of dressing to keep it moist.
(13) Cover and keep warm.

* Refrigerate leftovers.
* Makes enough to stuff one large turkey or 2 roasting chickens.

Chicken Oscar

1........1 large chicken breast
1........1 small bay leaf
6........6 peppercorns
2mL.....1/2 tsp. salt
1........1 small piece star anise
.........1/2 cup EACH sliced
          celery, carrot and onion
120mL...1-4 oz. can crab meat
     ****

(1) Place chicken, spices and vegetables in a medium saucepan. Add water to barely cover. Cover and simmer until cooked, approx. 25 minutes.

(2) Lift chicken out with slotted spoon. Remove bones, skin and gristle, discard. Save stock for other use.

(3) Divide chicken breast in half. Place each half on a warmed dinner plate. Top with 22mL (1 1/2 Tbsp.) crab meat. Spoon Bearnaise Sauce (recipe to follow) over crab meat.

Bearnaise Sauce

22mL....1 1/2 Tbsp. tarragon
          vinegar
22mL....1 1/2 Tbsp. water
3........3 thin onion slices
1mL.....1/4 tsp. salt
.........Dash paprika
30mL....2 Tbsp. warm butter
2........2 slightly beaten egg yolks
     ****

(1) In a small saucepan bring vinegar, water and onion to a boil, simmer 3 minutes. Discard onion.

(2) Place beaten egg yolks into top of double boiler. Gradually stir in the vinegar mixture, add salt and paprika. Cook, stirring constantly until mixture begins to thicken.

(3) Stir in butter 15mL (1 Tbsp.) at a time. Beat constantly until mixture is quite thick.

* Serve with 4 spears asparagus per serving.
* Serves 2.

Variation:

* This sauce is equally as good when served over crab meat and B.B.Qed, or broiled steak.
* As bacteria works quickly in egg yolks, it is best to make Bearnaise Sauce in small quantities. Make it, serve it, then discard any unused sauce.

Fish

Canned Salmon

Canned salmon is never as good, as when it is home canned...
** *Select fresh spring, sockeye or cohoe salmon.*

(1) Scale, dress and wash thoroughly. *Try to can salmon the same day it is caught. If not canned the same day, cover with plastic wrap and refrigerate. *Do not soak in water.
(2) Slice salmon, pack into sterilized 500g (pint) jars (include bones).
(3) Leave a 1cm. (1/2-inch) space at the top. Do not add water.
(4) Add 5mL (1 tsp.) salt and 5mL (1 tsp.) vinegar.
(5) Wipe top of jars hard, using a sterilized cloth.
(6) Seal jars according to directions on canning lids.
(7) Process in pressure cooker according to manufacturers directions.
(8) Store in cool, dark room.

* For super scrumptious sandwich filling, mix canned salmon with a small amount of whipped salad dressing, chopped green onions or cooking onions, salt and pepper to taste.
* For lunch serve canned salmon flaked; pass vinegar, onions, whipped salad dressing, lettuce and bread.

Freezing Fish

* To freeze fish pieces...

(1) To freeze fish pieces, place pieces in a milk carton.
(2) Fill with water, making sure fish is covered.

* To freeze whole fish...

(1) Place whole fish on a tray and put in freezer; add as much water as the tray will hold.
(2) When frozen, turn fish over and again add as much water as the tray will hold. Repeat until fish is completely covered with ice.
(3) Wrap in tin foil or heavy plastic bags.

* Alternate way to freeze fish...wrap tightly in tin foil and place in heavy plastic bags.

Easy Pickled Herring

(1) Make sure gills are removed before soaking.
(2) Fillet herring, if large.
(3) In a large crock, layer filleted herring with pickling salt.
(4) Place weight on top (eg. plate with 2 bricks that have been placed in a plastic bag).
(5) Put away in a cool spot for at least 2 weeks.
(6) Remove herring and soak in cold water overnight or longer if still salty.
(7) Drain, split skin and remove bones, cut into strips crosswise. Pack into sterilized jars.
(8) Cover herring completely with following pickling solution and store in a cool place.

* These will keep for 6 to 8 months.

Pickling Solution:

1........1 large onion
10mL....2 tsp. whole allspice
2........2 bay leaves
50mL....1/4 cup sugar
300mL...1 1/4 cups water
175mL...3/4 cup vinegar
****

(1) In a saucepan bring all ingredients to a boil.
(2) Boil 5 minutes. Cool.
(3) Pour over herring.
(4) Seal and let stand for 2 days.

Baked Salmon Loaf

500g.....1 large (1 lb.) can pink salmon
250mL...1 cup milk
250mL...1 cup bread crumbs (crusts removed)
1........1 slightly beaten egg
30mL....2 Tbsp. chopped parsley (Opt.)
30mL....2 Tbsp. finely chopped onion
10mL....2 tsp. lemon juice or vinegar
1mL.....1/4 tsp. salt
1mL.....1/4 tsp. pepper
****

(1) In a mixing bowl combine all ingredients, incl. liquid from can of salmon. Blend well.
(2) Spoon into a buttered loaf pan or casserole. *Do not cover.
(3) Bake just below center in 190°C (375°F) oven for 35-40 min. or until loaf is set in centre.
* Test—inserted knife comes out clean.
(4) Remove from oven.
(5) Cool for 5 minutes.
(6) Turn out onto a heated platter.

(7) Serve with slices of lemon, cream of mushroom or cream of celery soup that has been heated and flavoured to taste with curry powder.

* Serves 4-6.

Panfried Fish Fillets

500g.....1 lb. fish fillets, steak or
         small fish
2mL.....1/2 tsp. salt
50mL....1/4 cup buttermilk
125mL...1/2 cup fine bread crumbs
........Oil for frying
      ****

(1) Cut fish into serving portions.
(2) Combine salt and buttermilk.
(3) Heat .6cm. (1/4-inch) of oil in frying pan.
(4) Dip fish into buttermilk, then into bread crumbs.

(5) Fry in hot oil until browned.
(6) Sprinkle with salt & pepper.

* If there is not much oil in the frying pan, drizzle fish with oil.
* Gently turn and brown on other side.
* Fish is done when it is light coloured and it flakes easily.
* Do not overcook.
* Serve piping hot.
* Makes 2 servings.

Curried Shrimp

30mL....2 Tbsp. butter
1........1 medium chopped onion
125mL...1/2 cup evaporated milk
113g.....4 oz. can shrimp (drained
         and rinsed in cold
         water)
540mL...19 oz. can mushroom
         soup (undiluted)
142g.....5 oz. can button mush-
         rooms (drained)
2mL.....1/2 tsp. curry or to taste
      ****

(1) In a medium saucepan saute onions until limp. (Do not brown).
(2) Stir in milk, shrimp, mushroom soup and mushrooms.
(3) Add curry, blend well, stirring gently.
(4) Simmer slowly until heated through.
(5) Serve over warm rice.

Shrimp Cocktail

500g.....1 lb. small cooked shelled
         shrimp
1........1 minced green onion
         (Opt.)
175mL...3/4 cup red tartar sauce
         p. 52
1........1 lettuce
      ****

(1) Break lettuce into bite size pieces.
(2) Place 125mL (1/2 cup) into each stemmed glass (6).
(3) Add shrimp, sprinkle with green onion, if desired.
(4) Drizzle with red tartar sauce.

* Serve chilled.
* Serves 6.

Baked Salmon

The flavour and juices are sealed in aluminum foil and the fish steams in its own liquid...

1 . . . . 1 fresh or frozen dressed salmon or any other fish

. . . . Bread dressing

4 . . . . 4 slices bacon

. . . . Salt & pepper

****

(1) Wash fish, dry with paper towel.

(2) Measure thickness of fish or piece of fish. Record.

(3) Place aluminum foil on shallow baking pan. (Foil must be large enough to wrap fish making folds at top). Grease foil.

(4) Lay fish on foil, stuff generously with Bread Dressing, p. 81. Don't worry if cavity doesn't close.

(5) Sprinkle with salt & pepper.

(6) Place sliced bacon diagonally over fish.

(7) Bring sides of foil up and make double folds in it. Pinch folds, turn up ends to make steam tight.

(8) Bake just below centre in 230°C (450°F) oven. Allow 10 minutes cooking time per 2.5cm. (1-inch) thickness for fresh fish and 20 minutes cooking time per 2.5cm. (1-inch) for frozen fish. Plus an additional cooking time for heat to penetrate foil and fish. An extra 5 minutes for fresh fish and 10 minutes for frozen fish is recommended.

* To test if fish is cooked, open foil and with a fork spread fish apart at the thickest part down to the backbone. It should be opaque in colour and can be easily flaked.
* Serve fish immediately while it is still piping hot.
* To serve: Transfer fish to heated serving plate. Bring fish to table, cut and serve each guest individually. With a sharp knife in one hand and a turner in the other hand, cut a 5-6.5cm. (2-2 1/2-inch) slice down to the bone (not through). Try not to press too hard as to squash the bottom half of the fish.
* Run turner under slice and above backbone, lift and serve; serve the dressing at the same time.
* When top layer has been served lift backbone off and discard. Serve the bottom half of fish as you did the top.
* Fish may be baked with fins and tail on. This helps keep the juices inside the fish. They are easily removed when cooked and before serving.
* Allow 250g (1/2 lb.) per serving.

Barbecued Salmon

One dressed salmon...the choice of size is yours...and a flat bottom dish...to hold the fish...

250mL...1 cup salad oil
.........Juice of one lemon
45mL....3 Tbsp. wine vinegar
30mL....3 Tbsp. worcestershire
         sauce
15mL....1 Tbsp. minced parsley
5mL.....1 tsp. salt
5mL.....1 tsp oregano
2mL.....1/2 tsp. basil
1mL.....1/4 tsp. thyme
1........1 clove crushed garlic
2........2 medium sliced onions
         ****

(1) In a bowl combine all ingredients.
(2) Pour over fish, let marinate for 1/2 hour.
(3) Turn fish over and let marinate an additional 1/2 hour.
(4) Grease a sheet of heavy duty foil. Spread 1/2 of the onion slices onto the foil.
(5) Place whole salmon on top of the onions. Cover with the remaining onions and sprinkle with marinade.

(6) Fold foil over fish, make your best leak proof seal. Fold ends securely.
(7) Wrap again in another sheet of foil.
(8) Make seam of second sheet on opposite side of first seam.
(9) Place on grill 15-18cm. (6-8-inches) above coals. Cook 30 minutes then turn over and cook an additional 30 minutes.)

* Allow 250g (1/2 lb.) per serving.

Canned Fish

This recipe is prepared for naturally dry fish as Pike, Pickerel, etc....

15mL....1 Tbsp. vinegar
15mL....1 Tbsp. ketchup
5mL.....1 tsp. salt
15mL....1 Tbsp. mazola oil
.........Fresh fish
         ****

(1) Into each 500mL (pint) jar, mix vinegar, ketchup, salt, and oil.
(2) Pour fish in jar, pack tight, leave a 1cm. (1/2-inch) space at the top.

(3) Wipe top of jar hard, using a sterilized cloth.
(4) Seal jars according to directions on canning lids.
(5) Process in pressure cooker according to manufacturers directions.
(6) Store in cool, dark room.

Crab Cocktail

........Lettuce Leaves
250mL...1 cup shredded lettuce
625mL...2 1/2 cups crab meat
250mL...1 cup tartar sauce
2........2 sliced hard cooked eggs
15mL....1 Tbsp. chopped chives
****

(1) Using a clear glass salad bowl line bottom with lettuce leaves. Place shredded lettuce, then crab meat.
(2) Pour over red or white tartar sauce p. 52.

(3) Top with sliced eggs. Sprinkle with chopped chives.
(4) Chill thoroughly.

* Makes 4-5 servings.

Pickled Fish

First Brine

1.5L.....6 cups water
175mL...3/4 cup salt
........Fresh fish
****

(1) In a medium sauce pan bring water and salt to a boil. Set aside until cold.

Second Brine

1L ......4 cups vinegar
15mL....1 Tbsp. salt
30mL....2 Tbsp. sugar
125mL...1/2 cup water
1........1 medium sliced onion
30mL....2 Tbsp. pickling spice
1........1 clove chopped garlic
1........1 chopped red pepper
****

(2) Fillet fish, remove fins and fatty portions. Slice fish into 2.5cm. (1-inch) slices.
(3) Pour the cold salt brine over fish and let stand 4 hours. Drain.
(4) In a saucepan bring vinegar, salt, sugar, water, onion, spices, garlic and red pepper to a simmer. Simmer 10 minutes. Set aside until cold.
(5) Pack fish slices into sterilized 1L (1 Qt.) jars, alternately, with slices of onion from second brine.
(6) Pour second brine over raw fish, seal. Let stand at least 1 week before use.

Casseroles

Italian Delight

Some extra time is needed to prepare, but...you will enjoy the freedom at serving time...plus there is only one bowl to wash afterwards...
* *Served with rolls it's a meal in itself...*

500g.....1 lb. ground beef
50mL....1/4 cup salad oil
1........1 medium chopped onion
1........1 clove minced garlic
          (Opt.)
1........1 chopped green pepper
250g.....8 oz. can tomato paste
284mL...10 oz. can tomato soup
284mL...10 oz. can mushroom
          soup
2mL.....1/2 tsp. salt
1mL.....1/4 tsp. pepper
3mL.....3/4 tsp. oregano
3mL.....3/4 tsp. thyme
15mL....1 Tbsp. worcestershire
          sauce
398mL...14 oz. can whole kernel
          corn (drained)
284mL...10 oz. can mushrooms
          drained (reserve juice)
250g.....8 oz. pkg. medium
          noodles
250mL...1 cup grated mozzarella
          ****

(1) Brown meat in oil, transfer to a large mixing bowl. Set aside.
(2) Saute onions, garlic and green peppers until limp.
(3) Stir in tomato paste, tomato soup, mushroom soup, salt, pepper, oregano, thyme, worcestershire sauce and liquid from mushrooms. Simmer 10 minutes.
(4)   Add corn and mushrooms with browned meat.
(5) Cook noodles until just tender, drain (do not over cook).
(6) Add noodles to meat mixture; Stir.
(7) Pour sauce over all and stir together, mixing well.
(8) Put into a well greased casserole, cover.
(9) Bake in 180°C (350°F) oven for 1 hour.
(10) Remove cover, sprinkle with cheese, return to oven uncovered and cook until cheese is hot and bubbling.

* Mix noodles with meat mixture as soon as they are drained, to prevent them from sticking together in a mass. Try to have noodles ready just prior to mixing everything together. There will be no change to the sauce if it is ready before the noodle.
* This dish freezes well. If freezing do not add cheese until reheated. After casserole is rewarmed, uncover. Sprinkle with cheese, return to oven until cheese is hot and bubbling. Approx. 10 minutes.

Lasagne

170g.....6 oz. lasagne noodles
30mL....2 Tbsp. oil
750g.....1 1/2 lb. ground beef
500g.....1 lb. ground pork
284mL...1-10 oz. can mushroom
stems and pieces
(reserve liquid)
250mL...1 cup tomato paste
250mL...1 cup water
15mL....1 Tbsp. worcestershire
sauce
15mL....1 Tbsp. sweet basil
5mL.....1 tsp. oregano
5mL.....1 tsp. salt
2mL.....1/2 tsp. pepper
500g.....1 lb. sliced mozzarella
cheese
****

(1) Cook lasagne according to directions on package.
(2) Combine beef and pork together. Mix well.
(3) In a heavy frying pan brown
meat in oil. Drain off fat.
(4) In a saucepan combine mushrooms and liquid, tomato paste,
water, salt, sweet basil, worcestershire sauce and oregano.
(5) Blend well. Simmer over low
heat for 5 minutes. Stir occasionally.
(6) Pour over meat, stir until meat
is coated.
(7) Simmer over low heat for 15
minutes.

(8) Spread a few spoonfuls of sauce in a 22x33cm. (9x13-inch) baking pan.
(9) Arrange 3 cooked lasagne noodles in a single layer on top of the meat
sauce in the pan.
(10) Spread half of the remaining sauce over the noodles.
(11) Arrange 3 cooked lasagne noodles over sauce.
(12) Spread remaining sauce over noodles.
(13) Arrange mozzarella cheese slices on top.
(14) Cover with tin foil.
(15) Bake just below centre in 180°C (350°F) oven for 30 minutes. Remove
tin foil and bake until cheese is bubbling hot.

* This freezes well. If freezing do not add cheese until reheated. After
lasagne is rewarmed, uncover, and arrange cheese slices on top, return to
oven until cheese is hot and bubbly. Approx. 10 minutes.

Macaroni Casserole

250mL...1 cup macaroni
125mL...1/2 cup grated cheddar
cheese
284mL...1-10 oz. can cream of
mushroom soup
50mL....1/4 cup milk
125mL...1/2 cup canned sliced
mushrooms (drained)
250mL...1 cup hot cooked peas
****

(1) Cook macaroni in 1L (4 cups)
of salted water. Drain well.
(2) Stir in grated cheese.
(3) Add soup and milk, combine
thoroughly.
(4) Fold in mushrooms and peas.
(5) Bake just below centre in 180°C
(350°F) oven for 20 minutes.

Baked Macaroni and Cheese

We still haven't lost the taste for this old time favorite...

500mL...2 cups uncooked macaroni
15mL....1 Tbsp. salt
2L ......8 cups water
125mL...1/2 cup cream
175mL...3/4 cup grated cheese
1mL.....1/4 tsp. paprika
........Salt & pepper
........Sprinkle cayenne
****

(1) Boil macaroni in salted water 8-10 minutes. Drain well.
(2) In a mixing bowl combine macaroni, cream, cheese, paprika, sprinkle salt & pepper to taste.
(3) Place in a buttered 16x25cm. (6x10-inch) oven proof pan. Sprinkle with small amount of cayenne.

(4)   Bake just below center in 180°C (350°F) for 30 minutes (uncovered).

*   Makes 4-6 servings.

Turkey Stew

This is one way to use any left over turkey...

125mL...1/2 cup butter or margarine
1........1 large chopped onion
375mL...1 1/2 cups chopped celery
375mL...1 1/2 cups flour
2L ......2 Qts. turkey or chicken broth including *mushroom liquid (below)
5mL.....1 tsp. salt
2mL.....1/2 tsp. pepper
3........3 egg yolks slightly beaten
284mL...10 oz. pkg. frozen sweet peas
250mL...1 cup sliced cooked carrots
284mL...1-10 oz. can mushrooms (drained, *reserve liquid)
1 1/4L ..5 cups cooked turkey (chunked)
****

(1) In a 2 1/2L (6 Qt.) saucepan melt butter over medium heat.
(2) Add onion and celery; saute until tender.
(3) Stir the flour in well. Reduce heat to medium low. Gradually stir in milk until smooth.
(4) Stir broth in slowly.
(5) Add salt & pepper.
(6) Stir 125mL (1/2 cup) of hot mixture into egg yolks.
(7) Slowly stir egg yolks into the hot mixture.
(8) Raise heat to medium.
(9) Add peas and carrots. Continue cooking 5 minutes.
(10) Add mushrooms and turkey, heat through.
(11) Pass side dish of grated sharp cheddar cheese for those who prefer it.

*   Serve with hot biscuits.

91

Pizza Crust

300mL... 1 1/4 cups warm water
15mL....1 Tbsp. yeast
825mL-
   1L ....3 1/2-4 cups flour
2mL.....1/2 tsp. salt
2mL.....1/2 tsp. black pepper
****

(1) In a mixing bowl dissolve yeast in warm water.
(2) Add 500mL (2 cups) of flour, salt & pepper.
(3) Beat until smooth.

(4) Gradually add enough of remaining flour to form a moderately stiff dough.
(5) Turn out onto a floured work surface.
(6) Knead until smooth and satiny about 5 minutes.
(7) Place in a greased bowl, grease top, cover with plastic wrap and a tea towel.
(8) Let rise in a warm place until doubled about 40 minutes. Punch dough down. Divide in half, cover one half with plastic wrap to keep from drying out.
(9) On a lightly floured pastry sheet, roll out each half into 33cm. (13-inch) circle.
(10) Place onto two lightly greased 30cm. (12-inch) pizza pans.
(11) Build excess crust up so the edge of the dough is even with the rim of the pan. Flute edge of crust using thumbs and index fingers, building a rim.

Pizza Filling (Shrimp)

1........1-30cm. (12-inch) pizza
142mL...5 oz. can shrimp
15mL....1 Tbsp. butter or margar-
              ine
30mL....2 Tbsp. finely chopped
              onion
15mL....1 Tbsp. chopped garlic
              clove
175mL...3/4 cup pizza sauce
2mL.....1/2 tsp. oregano
375mL...1 1/2 cups grated mozzar-
              ella cheese
****

(1) Drain shrimp; rinse in cold water.
(2) In frying pan heat butter, saute garlic and onion until tender.
(3) Remove from heat, add pizza sauce and oregano.
(4) Spread sauce evenly over pizza crust.
(5) Distribute shrimp over sauce.
(6) Sprinkle cheese over all.
(7) Bake just below center in 230°C (450°F) oven for 20-25 minutes; until crust is browned and cheese melts.

* Makes 6-8 servings.

92

Pizza Filling (Pepperoni)

175mL...3/4 cup pizza sauce
200g.....7 oz. pepperoni on the
     spicy side, if preferred
540mL...19 oz. pineapple tidbits,
     drained
284mL...10 oz. sliced, drained
     mushrooms
500mL...2 cups grated mozzarella
     cheese
****

(1) Spread pizza sauce evenly over the top of pizza crust.
(2) Arrange pepperoni in single layer, add pineapple then mushrooms.
(3) Sprinkle cheese evenly over pizza.
(4) Bake just below centre in 230°C (450°F) oven for 20-25 minutes, or until cheese is melted and crust is browned.

* Makes 6-8 servings.

Tofu Manicotti

Different...a little fussy to make, but worth every minute it takes to prepare...

8........8 manicotti shells
125mL...1/2 cup chopped fresh
     mushrooms
50mL....1/4 cup chopped onion
15mL....1 Tbsp. snipped parsley
2mL.....1/2 tsp. dried basil
1mL.....1/4 tsp. salt
1/2mL...1/8 tsp. paprika
........Dash pepper
2........2 beaten eggs
284mL...10 oz. fresh tofu
50mL....1/4 cup grated parmesan
     cheese
30mL....2 Tbsp. flour
30mL....2 Tbsp. butter
375mL...1 1/2 cups milk
250mL...1 cup mozzarella cheese
........Ground nutmeg
****

(1) Cook pasta shells according to pkg. directions. Rinse in cold water,drain, set aside.
(2) In a saucepan saute mushrooms and onions until tender.
(3) Add parsley, basil, salt, paprika and dash pepper. Remove from heat, cool.
(4) Combine eggs, tofu, parmesan cheese.
(5) Stir in vegetable mixture.
(6) Stuff each manicotti shell with 50mL (1/4 cup) of tofu mixture. Arrange in buttered 30x19x5cm. (12x7 1/2x2-inch) baking dish.
(7) In a saucepan melt butter, add flour and dash of pepper. Add milk all at once.

(8) Cook and stir until thickened and bubbly.
(9) Remove from the heat, stir in mozzarella cheese until melted.
(10) Pour cheese sauce over pasta; sprinkle with nutmeg, if desired. Cover with foil.
(11) Bake just above centre in 180°C (350°F) oven for 20-25 minutes.

* Serves 6.

Seven Layer Dinner

Use a roasting pan large enough to suit your family's needs...

1.......1 layer sliced potatoes
1.......1 layer sliced onions
1.......1 layer sliced carrots
1.......1 layer rice
1.......1 layer peas
.........Salt & pepper
1.......1 can *tomato soup
50mL....1/4 cup ketchup (Opt.)
1.......1 layer cooked sausage
****

(1) In a roasting pan layer vegetables, sprinkle each layer slightly with salt & pepper.
(2) Dilute tomato soup with a small amount of water and pour over vegetables.
(3) Dot with ketchup.
(4) Add water enough to barely cover peas.

(5) Bake just below centre in 160°C (325°F) oven for 2 1/2 hours.
(6) In the meantime fry sausage slowly in frying pan until just about cooked.
(7) Drain off all the grease.
(8) Arrange sausage on top of vegetables half an hour before finished.

* If making large amount, use 540mL (19 oz.) tomato soup (small amount use 284mL (10 oz.) tomato soup).

Cabbage Rolls

1L ......4 cups water
250mL...1 cup vinegar
1.......1 large head cabbage
500g.....1 lb. finely diced ham
500g.....1 lb. ground beef
250mL...1 cup rice
1.......1 large chopped onion
10mL....2 tsp. onion soup mix
2mL.....1/2 tsp. salt
2mL.....1/2 tsp. pepper
796mL...28 oz. can tomatoes
540mL...19 oz. can tomato soup
2mL.....1/2 tsp. sugar
****

(1) In a large saucepan bring water and vinegar to a boil.
(2) Scald cabbage head in water let steam until leaves can be easily taken apart. Remove leaves as they become soft. Discard core and any heavy central ribs.
(3) Mix ham, beef, rice, onion, soup mix, salt & pepper.
(4) Spoon the meat mixture onto one end of the cabbage leaf; roll up and place in a small roaster. Layer when bottom is filled.

(5) Mix tomatoes, tomato soup and sugar together. Pour over cabbage rolls.
(6) Cover and bake just below centre in 160°C (325°F) oven for 3-4 hours.

* May add 15mL (1 Tbsp.) red pepper sauce or stuff one green pepper with meat; set on top of cabbage rolls to cook.

Egg Noodles

250mL...1 cup flour
2mL.....1/2 tsp. salt
2........2 beaten eggs
2 1/2L ..10 cups chicken stock
****

(1) In a mixing bowl stir flour and salt together.
(2) Make a well in the centre of the flour; add eggs.

(3) Gradually mix in the surrounding flour.
(4) Turn out onto a floured surface, knead vigorously.
(5) Add slight amount of flour or water to make a workable dough.
(6) Divide dough in half.
(7) Wrap dough in plastic wrap, chill 1/2 hour. Dough may be frozen at this point.
(8) On a well floured work surface roll dough out very thin. Sprinkle with flour if sticky.
(9) With a sharp knife cut dough into 6cm. (1/4-inch) strips.

*   You may add noodles directly to simmering chicken stock or hang to dry.
*   A broom handle placed on the back of two chairs is an ideal place to hang noodles to dry.
*   When thoroughly dry, place them in a closed jar.

2 1/2L ..10 cups of chicken stock is needed to cook 250g (8 oz.) of noodles.
1 1/4L ..5 cups chicken stock is needed for 125g (4 oz.) of noodles (half of the recipe).

(10) Bring chicken stock to a boil, add noodles.
(11) Reduce heat, cover and simmer for 30-40 minutes until tender.

*   They will be chewy if not cooked enough.

Macaroni and Tomatoes

Another old favorite by request...

500mL...2 cups uncooked macaroni
15mL....1 Tbsp. salt
2L ......8 cups water
15mL....1 Tbsp. margarine
375mL...1 1/2 cups canned tomatoes (drained)
.........Salt & pepper
****

(1) Boil macaroni in salted water 10-12 minutes. Drain well.
(2) Return to saucepan. Stir in margarine, tomatoes, salt & pepper to taste. Serve hot.

*   Makes 4-6 servings.

Tomato Sauced Zucchini

New and deliciously different...serve hot as a vegetable casserole, or on toast...

3.2kg....7 lbs. peeled ripe tomatoes
2........2 large onions
1/4......1/4 head celery
2........2 green peppers
1/2......1/2 bunch parsley
2........2 medium unpeeled
           zucchini
750mL...3 cups ketchup
15mL....1 Tbsp. garlic powder
15mL....1 Tbsp. sugar
5mL.....1 tsp. salt

(1) Cut all vegetables into cubes, keep zucchini separate.
(2) In a large kettle combine all ingredients except zucchini.
(3) Simmer to boiling. Remove from heat, stir in zucchini.
(4) Pour into sterilized jars.
(5) Seal and process 30 minutes.

****

*   Makes approx. 5 1/2L (7 Qts.).

Fettuccine

400g.....12 oz. uncooked fettuccine
           noodles
4........4 slices cooked, crumbled
           bacon
75r..L....1/3 cup butter or margar-
           ine
2........2 cloves minced garlic
250mL...1 cup chopped green
           onions (include tops)
175mL...3/4 cup chopped mush-
           rooms
250mL...1 cup whipping cream
1/2mL...1/8 tsp. nutmeg
30mL....2 Tbsp. chopped parsley
125mL...1/2 cup parmesan cheese
           (Opt.)
........Salt & pepper

(1) Cook noodles according to package directions. Drain well.
(2) Fry bacon nearly crisp, drain off grease. Crumble bacon and set aside.
(3) In same frying pan melt butter until bubbling. Add garlic, onions, and mushrooms. Cook and stir for 3 minutes. Add cream, nutmeg, parsley.
(4) Gently stir in cooked noodles, parmesan cheese, salt & pepper to taste. Serve hot.

****

*   Makes 6 servings.

Spaghetti in Tomato Sauce with Cheese

3L ......12 cups water
5mL.....1 tsp. salt
10mL....2 tsp. margarine
250g.....1/2 lb. spaghetti
15mL....1 Tbsp. margarine
540mL...1-19 oz. can tomato soup
       (undiluted)
125mL...1/2 cup grated medium
       cheddar cheese
****

(1) In a large saucepan bring water to a boil, add salt, margarine and spaghetti.
(2) Boil continuously for 8 minutes.
(3) Place colander in sink; drain spaghetti. Do not rinse.
(5) Place 15mL (1 Tbsp.) margarine into hot saucepan, melt.
(5) Return spaghetti to hot saucepan.

(6) Immediately stir in tomato soup.
(7) Add cheese and combine gently.
(8) Heat over very low heat until cheese melts.

Chicken and Broccoli Casserole

1........1 large chicken breast
1/2......1/2 small bay leaf
6........6 peppercorns
2mL.....1/2 tsp. salt
1........1 small piece star anise
125mL...1/2 cup EACH sliced
       celery, carrot and onion
500mL...2 cups broccoli
30mL....2 Tbsp. butter
1/2mL...1/8 tsp. curry powder
30mL....2 Tbsp. flour
1mL.....1/4 tsp. salt
375mL...1 1/2 cups milk
125mL...1/2 cup grated cheddar
       cheese
15mL....1 Tbsp. butter
15mL....1 Tbsp. grated parmesan
       cheese
125mL...1/2 cup bread crumbs
****

(1) Place chicken, spices and vegetables in a medium saucepan. Add water to barely cover. Cover and simmer until cooked, approx. 25 minutes.
(2) Lift chicken out with slotted spoon. Remove bones, skin and gristle, discard. Save stock for other use. Cut meat into bite size chunks. Set aside. Keep warm.
(3) While chicken is cooking, boil broccoli until just slightly tender. Do not overcook. Place broccoli in buttered 2L (2 Qt) casserole. Top with chicken. Keep warm.
(4) In a medium saucepan heat 30mL (2 Tbsp.) butter until bubbling. Stir in curry powder,

salt, then flour. Cook 3 minutes stirring constantly. Gradually stir in milk. Stir vigorously until smooth and thickened. Pour sauce over chicken.
(5) Grate cheddar cheese, sprinkle over sauce.
(6) Combine 15mL (1 Tbsp.) butter, parmesan cheese and bread crumbs until crumbly. Sprinkle over cheese. Do not cover.
(7) Bake just below center in 180°C (350°F) oven until bubbling and lightly browned, approx. 15 minutes.

* Serves 2.

Beef Stroganoff

750g.....1 1/2 lbs. beef steak
          partially frozen
45mL....3 Tbsp. oil
250mL...2 cups water
2........2 beef boullion cubes **or**
          10mL (2 tsp.) powdered
          beef base
50mL....1/4 cup ketchup
6........6 peppercorns
1........1 small bay leaf
5mL.....1 tsp. salt
1........1 medium sliced onion
284mL...1-10 oz. can sliced mush-
          rooms
30mL....2 Tbsp. butter or margar-
          ine
30mL....2 Tbsp. flour
250mL...1 cup sour cream
        ****

(1) In a medium saucepan combine water, beef boullion cubes (or powder), ketchup, peppercorns, bay leaf, and salt. Bring to a boil, reduce heat, stir until boullion cubes are dissolved. Cover and simmer while browning meat.

(2) Cut meat into slices approx. 7x2 1/2cm. (3x1-inch) x 1cm. (1/4-inch) across grain. In an ovenproof heavy pot, brown meat in hot oil (Do not over crowd or meat will steam instead of brown).
Transfer pieces to plate as they brown.

(3) In same pan saute onions and drained mushrooms until slightly browned. Add small amount of oil, if needed. Return meat to pan with onions and mushrooms.

(4) Strain simmering broth into measuring cup, add water to make 500mL (2 cups) liquid. Pour over meat. Stir to combine, scraping up browned bits from bottom of pan.

(5) Bake just below center in 180°C (350°F) oven for 45 minutes to 1 1/2 hours or until meat is tender.

(6) Remove from oven, place over medium heat on top of stove. Melt butter, add flour, mix well. Add to boiling broth in small amounts at a time, stirring constantly until smooth. When thickened remove from heat. Fold in sour cream (fold gently, do not break up meat). Return to 160°C (325°F) oven for approx. 10 minutes. Do not let mixture boil as cream will curdle.

* Serve over cooked medium or wide noodles.
* Serves 4-6.
* Less tender cuts of meat (stewing beef or flank steak) may be used, but longer cooking is required, reduce heat to 160°C (325°F).
* May be frozen at end of method #5. Heat and start at method #6 when taken from the freezer.

Breads

Highlights on Making Bread

If you are unfamiliar with making bread, a few tips will help you to relax while doing this rewarding project:

* There are two yeasts that are used throughout this book; active dry yeast and instant yeast.
* The active dry type you soak in warm water and sugar. Have water at 40°C (105°F) when soaking yeast.
* Instant yeast is the type of yeast you mix with some of the flour. I find that the instant yeast does best when the water used in the mixture (not yeast) is at 52°C (115°F). As you will notice in the recipes where I use yeast I always put some flour in before the yeast. This will assure you that the liquid used will not be too hot as to kill the action of the yeast.
* Lay a dampened dish cloth under mixing bowl when mixing bread. This will keep it from moving around.
* When bread has been mixed and oiled, cover with plastic wrap. Lay plastic wrap right on top of dough. This will help keep the warmth in. **Keeping this dough warm is your main concern now. The recommended temp. is between 22-28°C (75-80°F). Run a few inches of very warm water in kitchen sink, set bowl of dough in water, cover sink with a towel to keep heat in. Make sure doors and windows are shut keeping out any drafts.
* While dough is rising prepare loaf pans. Loaf pans must be greased with solid fat. Soften fat slightly and generously brush inside of loaf pan.
* Do not use oil to grease pans, as the dough absorbs the oil and your bread will stick to the pans.
* When dough has risen and it is time to put it into the pans, cut off a portion of the dough, weigh it on your kitchen scales (if you're wanting uniform size loaves). A good size loaf to make sandwiches from or for the slices to fit in the toaster is 800g (28 oz.) pan size 10x22x7.5cm. (4x7 1/2x3 1/2-inches).
* When you get acquainted with bread portions you will find you will not need to use scales. If you are selling bread you will want your weight accurate. Bread weighs the same after it is baked as the dough you put into the pans.
* Punch down each portion of dough, pushing out all air bubbles. Shape as close as possible to size of pan; by bringing ends and sides into centre. (Caution do not use too much oil or grease on hand at this stage or dough won't stick to itself). Pinch seam together with seam toward bottom. Lift dough up and smuck it down on the board. Do this several times until seam disappears. It will disappear quickly if dough doesn't

have too much flour in it, or if you haven't used too much oil on your hands while shaping loaf.

* Place seam side up in greased loaf pan. Punch down until dough is moved well into corners of loaf pan. Place right hand over loaf pan, with left hand tip dough out onto your right hand, replace dough back into loaf pan with seam side down. *****Did you follow that?***** This will give you a loaf of bread with no open cracks in it.
* Cover dough at this stage with a towel only and let rise to top of the bread pan. Remember the oven takes approximately 12 minutes to warm up.
* Do not let dough rise too high as bubbles will form under top layer of loaf. This is called overproofing.
* Any marks on the dough now will be there to haunt you after it is baked. If bubbles do form puncture them with a fine needle.
* Preheat oven to 190°C (375°F). Set bread pans just below centre and bake for 45 minutes. This temperature has worked for me every time.
* When bread is baked brush top with butter, remove from pans and place on racks to cool. Space loaves apart so vapour will not form between them.
* Bread must be completely cooled before wrapping.
* Bread freezes well.

Sourdough Starter #1

125mL...1/2 cup warm water	(1) In a bowl put 125mL (1/2 cup) warm water, stir in 5mL (1 tsp.) sugar until dissolved.
5mL.....1 tsp. sugar	
15mL....1 Tbsp. active dry yeast	
500mL...2 cups warm water	(2) Sprinkle yeast over top and let stand for 10 minutes.
15mL....1 Tbsp. sugar	
15mL....1 Tbsp. salt	(3) Stir well.
425mL...1 3/4 cup flour	(4) In a mixing bowl combine 500mL (2 cups) water, sugar and salt.
*********	

(5) Add flour and yeast mixture, beat vigorously until smooth.
(6) Pour into a large jug or crock (not metal). Allow ample space as mixture will expand to twice its size, then fall back on itself.
(7) Cover with a cloth. Let stand in a warm, draft-free place for 4 days.
(8) Stir down daily.
(9) After a portion of sourdough starter has been used for making bread replenish it by adding the following mixture to the unused portion:

375mL...1 1/2 cups warm water	(1) Stir together water, flour and sugar.
175mL...3/4 cup flour	
7mL.....1 1/2 tsp. sugar	(2) Pour it into the unused starter. Beat well for 1 minute. Cover.
*********	

(3) Let stand until ready to make bread again.

* Stir down occasionally.
* Store in the refrigerator until needed. It should be replenished once a week. Let come to room temperature before using.

Sourdough Bread #1

250mL...1 cup warm water
5mL.....1 tsp. sugar
30mL....2 Tbsp. active dry yeast
250mL...1 cup milk
30mL....2 Tbsp. margarine
30mL....2 Tbsp. sugar
5mL.....1 tsp. salt
375mL...1 1/2 cups sourdough
        starter #1
1 1/2-
1 3/4L ..6 1/2-7 cups flour
        ****

(1) In a bowl put 250mL (1 cup) warm water. Stir in 5mL (1 tsp.) sugar until dissolved.
(2) Sprinkle yeast over top and let stand for 10 minutes. Stir well before using.
(3) In a saucepan combine milk and margarine, heat until warmed and margarine has melted.
(4) Add sugar and salt, stir until dissolved.

(5) Pour milk mixture into mixing bowl.
(6) Stir in 500mL (2 cups) flour, then yeast mixture, and sourdough starter #1. Beat until smooth.
(7) Stir in remaining flour to make a soft dough.
(8) Turn out on floured surface, knead until smooth and elastic. Approx. 10 min.
(9) Place in a greased bowl. Oil top slightly and cover with plastic wrap.
(10) Let rise until doubled in bulk 1-1 1/2 hours. Punch down.
(11) Turn out onto floured surface, let rise 15 minutes.
(12) Divide dough in half. Shape each half into an oblong shape and place on a greased, cornmeal sprinkled cookie sheet.
(13) Cover with tea towel, place in a warm, draft-free place.
(14) Let rise until doubled in bulk.
(15) Brush with water and make diagonal slashes across tops with a sharp, single-edged razor blade (do not press down).
(16) Place melted butter in slashes.
(17) Bake just below centre in 190°C (375°F) oven for 45 minutes or until loaves sound hollow when tapped.
(18) Remove from pan. Place on racks to cool.

Sourdough Starter #2 Sponge Type

Maybe not exactly like the pioneers did it but it works out very well...

250mL...1 cup milk (not skimmed)
50mL....1/4 cup plain unflavoured
        yogurt
175mL...3/4 cup flour
        ****

(1) Warm milk and place into a warmed 500mL (2 cup) bowl (do not use a metal bowl).
(2) Stir yogurt into milk. Cover bowl with plastic wrap.

(3) Place oven rack just below the light in the oven.
(4) Turn oven on and heat just until warm. Approx. between 30-35°C (80-90°F). Turn oven off.

(5) Turn oven light on. Place bowl of starter near the light, but not touching it.
(6) Keep starter warm until mixture is the consistency of yogurt, takes about 18-20 hours.
(7) During this time if some clear liquid forms on the top, stir it back in.
(8) However, if mixture turns a light pink, discard it and start again.
(9) After a curd has formed, gradually stir 175mL (3/4 cup) of flour into the starter.
(10) Pour starter into a 2L (2 Qt.) sealer, cover and let stand in a warm place until starter is full of bubbles. About 2-4 days.

If clear liquid forms on top, stir it back into the mixture. If liquid turns pink save out 50mL (1/4 cup) of starter. Discard the rest. Then stir 250mL (1 cup) of flour into 250mL (1 cup) of warm milk and blend it into the 50mL (1/4 cup) of starter. Cover and let stand in a warm place until it is bubbly. Again stir 250mL (1 cup) of flour into 250mL (1 cup) warm milk, blend it into the starter. Let stand in a warm place until bubbly.

*   It is now ready to use.
*   To replenish sourdough supply after using, mix 250mL (1 cup) flour into 250mL (1 cup) warm milk. Stir into starter. Cover and let stand until bubbly. (An active starter will rise then fall back on itself). Store in the refrigerator until needed. Stir occasionally.
*   Starter must be at room temperature when used. Take it from the fridge, stir it, and leave it out overnight. To keep your starter at its best, if not using it every week, discard some of it if too much has accumulated and stir in equal amounts of flour and warm milk.

Sourdough Bread #2

Like the traditional sourdough bread, there is no yeast added...

375mL...1 1/2 cups sourdough starter #2
500mL...2 cups warm water
1 1/2L ..6 1/2 cups flour (divided)
15mL....3 tsp. sugar
10mL....2 tsp. salt
30mL....2 Tbsp. cornmeal
****

(1) In a 4L (4 Qt.) mixing bowl, (do not use metal) stir sourdough starter and warm water together.
(2) Stir in 1L (4 cups) of the flour.
(3) Cover bowl with lid or plastic wrap set in a warm place and let stand until mixture is full of bubbles. Approx. 8 hours.

*   I start my mixture the night before, cover it with a big bath sheet to keep it warm. In the morning, it is ready to finish.

(4) Mix sugar and salt into 500mL (2 cups) of the measured flour and gradually stir it into the sponge. Turn dough out onto a floured surface and knead dough until smooth, 5-10 minutes. Adding sprinklings of flour to prevent sticking.

(5) Place into buttered bowl, butter top, cover with plastic wrap and a tea towel.
(6) Let stand in a warm place until doubled in bulk, about 1 1/2-2 hours. In the meantime grease a large cookie sheet and sprinkle with cornmeal.
(7) Divide dough into 2 equal parts for long loaves or 3 equal parts for round loaves. Shape loaves and place onto a prepared cookie sheet. Cover with a tea towel, let stand in a warm place until doubled. About 1-1 1/2 hours.
(8) With a very sharp knife make three diagonal slashes in top of each oblong loaf, two slashes in criss-cross pattern in top of round loaves. Melted butter may be drizzled into slashes.
(9) Bake just below centre in 200°C (400°F) oven for 20 minutes. Reduce heat to 190°C (375°F) and bake for 15 minutes more or until loaves are browned and sound hollow when tapped.

* Cool on wire rack.

White Bread

125mL...1/2 cup warm water
5mL.....1 tsp. sugar
15mL....1 Tbsp. active dry yeast
45mL....3 Tbsp. margarine
125mL...1/2 cup milk
375mL...1 1/2 cups water
10mL....2 tsp. salt
45mL....3 Tbsp. sugar
1 1/2L ..6 1/2 cups flour
****

(1) In a bowl put 125mL (1/2 cup) of warm water, stir in 5mL (1 tsp.) sugar until dissolved.
(2) Sprinkle yeast over top and let stand 10 minutes, then stir well before using.
(3) In a medium saucepan, combine margarine, milk and water, heat until warmed and margarine has melted.

(4) Add salt and sugar stir until dissolved.
(5) Pour milk mixture into mixing bowl.
(6) Stir in 500mL (2 cups) flour and the yeast mixture.
(7) Beat until smooth. Stir in additional flour to make a soft dough.
(8) Turn out onto floured work surface and knead until smooth and elastic.
(9) Place in a greased bowl. Cover with plastic wrap and a tea towel. Place in a warm approx. 27°C (80°F) draft-free place.
(10) Let rise until double in bulk, about 1 hour.
(11) Punch down, butter top slighty.
(12) Cover with plastic wrap and a tea towel.
(13) Let rest for 15 minutes.
(14) Divide dough in half. Place into greased loaf pans. Oil top lightly, cover with a tea towel.
(15) Place in a warm 27°C (80°F) draft-free place. Let rise until doubled in bulk, about 1 hour.
(16) Bake just below centre in 190°C (375°F) oven for 45 minutes.
(17) For a soft crust brush top with butter. Remove from pans. Place on racks to cool.

Brown Bread

The busy homemaker will treasure this recipe...

500mL...2 cups warm water
30mL....2 Tbsp. sugar
30mL....2 Tbsp. active dry yeast
125mL...1/2 cup oil (use oil only)
2........2 eggs
30mL....2 Tbsp. sugar
15mL....1 Tbsp. salt
500mL...2 cups warm water
1 1/4L ..5 cups whole wheat flour
2 1/4L ..9 cups white flour
            ****

(1) In a medium bowl put 500mL (2 cups) warm water, stir in 30mL (2 Tbsp.) sugar until dissolved.
(2) Sprinkle yeast over top and let stand for 10 minutes. Stir well.
(3) In a 500mL (2 cups) measure put oil, eggs, sugar and salt.
(4) Beat thoroughly then add water to fill. Place in mixing bowl, add 500mL (2 cups) water. This should total 1 1/2L (6 cups) liquid.

(5) Beat in 1L (4 cups) flour, then yeast mixture.
(6) Gradually add remaining flour to make a soft dough. Add more oil as you finish kneading.
(7) Slightly oil top, cover with plastic wrap and a towel. Place in a warm 27°C (80°F) draft-free place.

*   Note the times:

(1) Let set 15 minutes, punch down and slightly oil.
(2) Let set 15 minutes, punch down again.
(3) Let set 15 minutes, (total of 45 minutes).
(4) Place in 4 well greased loaf pans.
(5) Cover with towel.
(6) Let rise until doubled in size.
(7) Bake just below centre in 190°C (375°) oven for 45 minutes.

*   For a soft crust brush top with butter.

(8) Remove from pans. Place on racks to cool.
(9) You may replace brown flour with cracked wheat flour, rye flour, stone ground flour, or use all white flour. This recipe may be doubled if more bread is needed.

100% Whole Wheat Bread

This recipe was designed by the manufacturers of a bread mixer...
A few shortcuts here, bread is ready to eat in 2 hours...

75mL....1/3 cup sugar
45mL....3 Tbsp. instant dry yeast
30mL....2 Tbsp. salt
150mL...2/3 cup oil (use oil only)
1 1/4L ..5 cups hot water 45°C
        (115°F)
3L ......12 cups whole wheat flour
        (approx. 4 lbs.)
       ****

(1) In a small bowl combine sugar, salt, yeast and 250mL (1 cup) of the measured flour. Set aside.
(2) In a large bowl of mixer place oil, hot water and 1 3/4L (7 cups) of the measured flour.
(3) Turn mixer on, blend well.
(4) Add sugar and yeast mixture. Blend well.

(5) While mixer is running, use a plastic scoop and gradually add additional flour until dough pulls away from the side of the bowl.
(6) Mix 10 minutes on medium speed.
(7) Oil hands and remove dough from mixer bowl. Cover and let stand 15 minutes.
(8) Place into 4 well greased loaf pans.
(9) Place pans just below center in a warmed 27°C (80°F) oven until dough is even with top of bread tins. **Do not have heat on in oven at this time.
(10) Turn heat to 190°C (375°F) and bake for 45 minutes.
(11) For a soft crust brush top with butter.
(12) Remove from pans. Place on racks to cool.

* For 60% whole wheat bread, mix 1 1/2L (6 cups) whole wheat flour with 1L (4 cups) white flour. **Use 3 1/4L (13 cups) flour in recipe when making 60% whole wheat bread.
* Makes 4 loaves.
* A plastic scoop is recommended just in case it comes in contact with beaters when adding the flour.

Raisin Bread

I created this recipe for use in a machine...
It is equally as good mixed by hand...

45mL....3 Tbsp. instant dry yeast
15mL....1 Tbsp. salt
2........2 beaten eggs
125mL...1/2 cup melted honey
500mL...2 cups warmed milk
125mL...1/2 cup melted butter or
        margarine
725mL...3 1/2 cups warm water
1L ......4 cups raisins or more
1 3/4L ..7 cups whole wheat flour
1 3/4L ..7 cups white flour
       *Stir the whole wheat
       flour and the white
       flour together
      ****

(1) In a small bowl combine yeast, salt and 250mL (1 cup) of the measured flour. Set aside.
(2) In large bowl of mixer, place egg, honey, milk, butter, water and 1 3/4L (7 cups) of the measured flour. Mix well.
(3) Add yeast mixture. Mix well.
(4) Dredge raisins with 125mL (1/2 cup) of the measured flour, and add to mixer.
(5) With mixer running use a plastic scoop and gradually add additional flour until dough pulls away from the side of the bowl.

(6) Mix for 10 minutes on medium speed.
(7) Oil hands and remove dough from mixer bowl.
(8) Place in greased bowl, oil top slightly.
(9) Cover with plastic wrap. Let rise in a warm draft-free place until doubled.
(10) Place into 5 well greased loaf tins.
(11) Cover with towel, let rise until doubled.
(12) Bake just below centre in 180°C (350°F) oven for 45 minutes.
(13) Brush top with butter, remove from pans and place on racks to cool.

* A plastic scoop is recommended just in case it comes in contact with the beaters when adding the flour.

French Bread

125mL...1/2 cup warm water
5mL.....1 tsp. sugar
30mL....2 Tbsp. active dry yeast
17mL....1 1/2 Tbsp. salt
30mL....2 Tbsp. sugar
30mL....2 Tbsp. margarine **or** oil
625mL...2 1/2 cups hot water
2L ......8 cups flour (approx.)
      ****

(1) In a bowl put 125mL (1/2 cup) warm water. Stir in 5mL (1 tsp.) sugar until dissolved.
(2) Sprinkle yeast over top and let stand for 10 minutes. Stir well before using.
(3) In a mixing bowl combine salt, sugar, margarine or oil and hot water. Stir until sugar is dissolved and margarine is melted; cool to lukewarm.

(4) Stir in 500mL (2 cups) flour, then the yeast mixture, beat until smooth. Stir in remaining flour to make a slightly stiff dough.
(5) Knead 10 minutes, or until smooth and elastic. Place in buttered bowl, butter top slightly and cover with plastic wrap and a tea towel. Let rise until doubled, 1-1 1/2 hours.
(6) Punch down and let rise 30 minutes.
(7) Divide dough in half. Shape each half into an oblong shape, and place on a buttered cookie sheet. Let rise until doubled. Make 3 slashes diagonally across top.
(8) Bake just below centre in 190°C (375°F) oven for 25-30 minutes or until done.

Bran Bread

20mL....4 tsp. sugar
37mL....2 1/2 Tbsp. instant dry yeast
20mL....4 tsp. salt
50mL....1/4 cup melt butter
250mL...1 cup molasses
1 1/4L ..5 cups warm water
1 1/4L ..5 cups natural bran
750mL...3 cups whole wheat flour
625mL...2 1/2 cups white flour
        *Stir the bran, whole wheat and white flour flour together.
        ****

(1) In a small bowl combine sugar, yeast, salt and 250mL (1 cup) of the measured flour. Set aside.
(2) In a large bowl of mixer place butter, molasses, water and 1 1/4L (5 cups) of the measured flour.
(3) Turn mixer on, blend well.
(4) Add yeast mixture. Blend well.
(5) While mixer is running use a plastic scoop and gradually add additional flour until dough pulls away from side of the bowl.

(6) Mix 10 minutes on medium speed.
(7) Oil hands and remove dough from mixer.
(8) Place in greased bowl, oil top slightly.
(9) Cover with plastic wrap.
(10) Let rise in a warm draft-free place until doubled.
(11) Punch down and let rise for 15 minutes.
(12) Place in 2 loaf pans, let rise until doubled.
(13) Bake just below centre in 190°C (375°F) oven for 35-40 minutes.
(14) Brush tops with butter, remove from pans.
(15) Place on rack to cool.

* Makes 2 loaves.
* A plastic scoop is recommended just in case it comes in contact with the beaters when adding the flour.

Cheese Bread

Wonderful flavour, try it toasted...

250mL...1 cup warm water
5mL.....1 tsp. sugar
15mL....1 Tbsp. active dry yeast
250mL...1 cup warm milk
50mL....1/4 cup butter or margarine
1........1 beaten egg
1L ......4 cups flour
500mL...2 cups shredded sharp cheddar cheese
15mL....1 Tbsp. salt
****

(1) In a bowl put warm water and stir in sugar until dissolved.
(2) Sprinkle yeast over top and let stand for 10 minutes, then stir well before using.
(3) In a mixing bowl, combine milk, butter, egg and yeast mixture.
(4) Combine 500mL (2 cups) of the flour, cheese and salt. Stir well to blend.

(5) Add flour cheese mixture to the milk mixture and beat together very well.
(6) Gradually add remaining flour beating well with wooden spoon.
(7) Cover with plastic wrap and a tea towel.
(8) Let rise in a warm draft-free place until doubled (about 45 min.).
(9) Stir down and place into two well greased loaf tins.
(10) Let rise until doubled (about 35 min.).
(11) Bake just below centre in 190°C (375°F) oven for 30-40 min.
(12) Remove from tins immediately.
(13) Place on racks to cool.

Whole Wheat Zucchini Bread

You will find this loaf very delicious...a good combination of ingredients...

750mL...3 cups whole wheat flour
5mL.....1 tsp. baking soda
2mL.....1/2 tsp. baking powder
15mL....1 Tbsp. cinnamon
125mL...1/2 cup chopped walnuts
500mL...2 cups grated zucchini (undrained)
500mL...2 cups brown sugar
250mL...1 cup oil
10mL....2 tsp. vanilla
5mL.....1 tsp. salt
3........3 beaten eggs
****

(1) Stir together flour, soda, baking powder, cinnamon, and walnuts. Set aside.
(2) Combine in a separate bowl, brown sugar, zucchini, oil, vanilla, salt and eggs.
(3) Add zucchini mixture to flour mixture. Mix well.
(4) Pour into two 10x20cm. (4x8-inch) well buttered loaf pans.
(5) Sprinkle top of loafs with finely chopped walnuts and cinnamon.

(6) Bake just below centre in 190°C (375°F) oven for 1 hour or until centre tests done.
(7) Let stand in pans for 5 minutes.
(8) Remove from pans. Place on racks to cool.

French Toast

2........2 slightly beaten eggs		(1)	Combine beaten eggs, milk,
175mL...3/4 cup milk			sugar and salt in a pie plate.
1mL.....1/4 tsp. salt		(2)	Stir thoroughly.
15mL....1 Tbsp. sugar		(3)	Melt butter in a skillet until
6........6 slices day old bread			bubbly, but not brown.
50mL....1/4 cup butter			
*********			

(4) Dip each slice into egg mixture, turning it to coat both sides. Allow bread to remain in mixture only long enough to absorb batter. If left too long, bread will become soft and hard to handle.

* Use a spatula when turning and removing slices from batter. Drain well.

(5) Place each slice in hot butter in skillet. Saute until golden brown. Turn and saute the other side.

* Add more butter as needed. Top with maple syrup, sugar, jam or honey.

Crepes

No one makes these as good as my mama...but we can try...

3........3 eggs, separated	(1)	Beat egg yolks well. Add salt,
1mL.....1/4 tsp. salt		sugar and 175mL (3/4 cup)
15mL....1 Tbsp. sugar		milk.
250mL...1 cup milk	(2)	Mix in flour, remaining milk
175mL...3/4 cup flour		and butter. Fold in stiffly whip-
15mL....1 Tbsp. melted butter		ped egg whites.
........Melted butter for frying	(3)	Have skillet very hot, add
*********		butter.

(4) Pour approx. 125mL (1/2 cup) crepe mixture onto hot, generously buttered skillet.
(5) Holding skillet by the handle tilt the skillet in a rotating motion to distribute mixture evenly, until very thin (try to keep crepe round).
(6) When crepe begins to dry around the edge, add 2mL (1/2 tsp.) butter.
(7) Flip crepe and fry the other side until browned.
(8) Reduce heat if pan becomes too hot during cooking. Remembering to keep it hot enough.
(9) Add more butter for each crepe when frying.
(10) Fold crepe in half and transfer to a warmed plate.
(11) Spread with jelly and roll up. Sprinkle with icing sugar.

* May be served for dessert, with sausages or bacon for breakfast, lunch or late supper.
* Serve immediately or roll in towel to keep warm.

Pancakes

375mL...1 1/2 cups flour
15mL....3 tsp. baking powder
2mL.....1/2 tsp. salt
30mL....2 Tbsp. sugar
300mL...1 1/4 cups milk
1........1 beaten egg
45mL....3 Tbsp. melted butter or
       margarine
1/2mL...1/8 tsp. vanilla
****

(1) In a medium mixing bowl stir together flour, baking powder, salt and sugar.
(2) In another bowl mix egg, milk, butter and vanilla together.
(3) Combine milk mixture with flour mixture.
(4) Mix only enough to moisten; leave slightly lumpy.

(5) Fry on hot, lightly buttered skillet.
(6) Pour approx. 50mL (1/4 cup) pancake mixture (to each pancake) onto hot, lightly buttered skillet.
(7) When bubbles form across pancake surface, flip them over and fry the other side until browned.

* Do not flip pancakes more than once.
* Do not butter skillet too heavily.
* If too much oil or butter is used in recipe or on skillet, pancakes will not brown evenly.
* Serve immediately.

Whole Wheat Buttermilk Pancakes

125mL...1/2 cup whole wheat flour
50mL....1/4 cup white flour
50mL....1/4 cup wheat germ
5mL.....1 tsp. baking powder
2mL.....1/2 tsp. baking soda
2mL.....1/2 tsp. salt
15mL....1 Tbsp. sugar (Opt.)
30mL....2 Tbsp. vegetable oil
1........1 slightly beaten egg
300mL...1 1/4 cup buttermilk
****

(1) Stir the flours together.
(2) Add baking powder, soda, salt and sugar. Set aside.
(3) In another bowl blend together oil, egg and buttermilk.
(4) Combine buttermilk mixture with flour mixture.
(5) Mix only enough to moisten, leave slightly lumpy.
(6) Fry on hot, lightly buttered skillet.

(7) Pour approx. 50mL (1/4 cup) of batter (for each pancake) onto hot, lightly buttered skillet.
(8) When bubbles form across pancake surface flip them over and fry the other side until browned.

* Do not flip pancakes more than once.
* Do not butter skillet too heavily.
* If too much oil or butter is used in recipe or on skillet, pancakes will not brown evenly.
* Serve immediately.
* Wheat germ adds vitamins and protein to pancakes without making them heavy.

110

Pancake Mix

1 1/2L ..6 cups flour
500mL...2 cups powdered milk
45mL....3 Tbsp. white sugar
45mL....3 Tbsp. brown sugar
15mL....1 Tbsp. salt
90mL....6 Tbsp. baking powder
****

(1) In a large bowl combine flour, powdered milk, white sugar, brown sugar, salt and baking powder.

(2) Mix well. Place in an air tight container. Store on cupboard shelf. *Makes 1kg. (2 lbs.)

To Make Pancakes:

1........1 slightly beaten egg
250mL...1 cup water
30mL....2 Tbsp. oil or margarine
375mL...1 1/2 cups pancake mix
45mL....3 Tbsp. wheat germ (Opt.)
****

(1) In a mixing bowl beat egg with a fork, add water, oil and 375mL (1 1/2 cups) pancake mix.

(2) Stir in wheat germ.

(3) Stir only enough to mix, leave slightly lumpy.
(4) Fry on hot, lightly buttered skillet.

Variations:

* You may replace one third of the flour with whole wheat flour, or other flour to your liking. Try oatmeal, soy flour, cornmeal, etc.
* Add wheat germ only when making pancakes. Wheat germ has to be stored in refrigerator. Wheat germ will go rancid if kept around too long.

Pancake Mix (Large)

3L ......12 cups flour
1L ......4 cups powdered milk
175mL...3/4 cup sugar (half white
        sugar, half brown sugar
30mL....2 Tbsp. salt
175mL...3/4 cup baking powder
****

(1) In a large bowl combine flour, powdered milk, sugar, salt and baking powder.

(2) Mix well. Place in air tight container. Store on cupboard shelf. Makes 2kg (4 lbs.)

To Make Pancakes:

1........1 slightly beaten egg
250mL...1 cup water
30mL....2 Tbsp. oil or margarine
375mL...1 1/2 cups pancake mix
45mL....4 Tbsp. wheat germ (Opt.)
****

(1) In a mixing bowl beat egg with a fork, add water, oil and 375mL (1 1/2 cups) pancake mix.

(2) Stir in wheat germ.

(3) Stir only enough to mix.
(4) Leave slightly lumpy. Fry on hot, lightly buttered skillet.

* You may replace one third of the flour with whole wheat flour, or other flour of your liking. Try soy flour, cornmeal, rye, or oatmeal.
* Add wheat germ only when making pancakes. Wheat germ has to be stored in refrigerator. Wheat germ will go rancid if kept around too long, or if not stored properly.

Waffles

500mL...2 cups flour
15mL....3 tsp. baking powder
2mL.....1/2 tsp. salt
5mL.....1 tsp. sugar
30mL....2 Tbsp. sugar
2........2 eggs (separated)
500mL...2 cups milk
90mL....6 Tbsp. melted butter
****

(1) In a medium mixing bowl combine flour, baking powder, salt and sugar.
(2) In another bowl beat egg yolks thoroughly; add milk. Add liquid to the dry ingredients.
(3) Mix only enough to make smooth. Stir in the melted butter. Fold in the stiffly whipped whites.

* Bake in preheated waffle baker until golden brown.
* Serve immediately or may be frozen.
* To freeze: Wrap each waffle in wax paper. Freeze individually before stacking into freezer container.
* To reheat: Pop waffle in toaster until heated through.

Sour Cream Waffles

250mL...1 cup flour
2mL.....1/2 tsp. salt
3mL.....3/4 tsp. baking soda
15mL....1 Tbsp. sugar
2........2 beaten eggs
250mL...1 cup thick sour cream
30mL....2 Tbsp. melted butter or
        margarine
****

(1) In a medium bowl stir together flour, salt, soda and sugar. Set aside.
(2) In another bowl mix eggs, sour cream and butter together.
(3) Combine sour cream mixture with flour mixture. Mix well.
(4) Bake in preheated waffle baker until golden brown.

(5) Serve immediately or may be frozen.

* To freeze: Cool on rack. Wrap each waffle in wax paper. Freeze individually before stacking into freezer container.
* To reheat: Pop waffle in toaster until heated through.

Sandwiches

Seafood Sandwich Loaf

Just right to serve at party time...

1kg . . . . . 32 oz. sandwich loaf	(1) Remove crusts from bread, cut in 4 slices lengthwise.
125mL. . . 1/2 cup butter	
126g. . . . . 8 oz. canned salmon (2-4 oz. cans)	(2) Cream butter and spread the two middle slices of bread on both sides.
126g. . . . . 8 oz. canned crab meat (2-4 oz. cans)	(3) Spread bottom and top layer on one side only.
126g. . . . . 8 oz. canned shrimp (2-4 oz. cans)	(4) Drain seafood well, rinse shrimp in cold water to remove salt, drain.
680g. . . . . 3-8 oz. pkg. cream cheese	
250mL. . . 1 cup salad dressing (Miracle Whip)	(5) Pat out moisture from seafood with paper towel.
. . . . Salt & pepper	

****

(6) Keeping seafood separately, mix into each a small amount of salad dressing, to make them spread easily; white tartar sauce could be used to mix with the shrimp.

(7) Place bottom slice of bread buttered side up onto a serving platter.

(8) Spread with salmon mixture.

(9) Sprinkle with salt & pepper.

(10) Cover with slice buttered on both sides.

(11) Spread with crab mixture.

(12) Sprinkle with salt & pepper.

(13) Cover with slices buttered on both sides.

(14) Spread with shrimp mixture.

(15) Cover with top slice buttered side down.

(16) Press under light weight. Place in fridge for 1 hour.

(17) Whip cream cheese, add salad dressing and mix together well.

(18) Spread dressing over prepared sandwich loaf, covering entire top and sides.

(19) Make swirling design with knife.

(20) Garnish with carrot curls, cherry tomatoes and parsley.

(21) Keep chilled until ready to serve.

(22) Cut in 2.5cm. (1-inch) slices for serving.

Toasted Cheese Sandwich

2........2 slices white or brown
       bread
125mL...1/2 cup grated cheddar
       cheese **or** cheese slices
       ****

(1) Butter one slice of bread, place it buttered side down on a plate.
(2) Put cheese on bread slice.

(3) Top with second slice of bread. Butter top of bread.
(4) Heat skillet over medium low heat.
(5) Place sandwich on skillet. When browned turn and brown other side.

Breakfast Sandwich

This makes a complete breakfast, saves precious time on those busy mornings...

8........8 slices bread
8........8 slices bacon or ham
8........8 slices sharp cheddar
       cheese
4........4 eggs
1mL.....1/4 tsp. salt
1mL.....1/4 tsp. pepper
1mL.....1/4 tsp. dry mustard
30mL....2 Tbsp. minced onion
30mL....2 Tbsp. chopped green
       pepper (Opt.)
5mL.....1 tsp. worcestershire sauce
375mL...1 1/2 cups whole milk
........Dash tabasco
........Special K or crushed
       Cornflakes
30mL....2 Tbsp. butter
       ****

(1) In a buttered 25x25cm. (10x10-inch) baking dish, put 4 slices of bread. Add pieces to cover bottom completely.
(2) Lay slices of bacon or ham on each slice of bread, lay slice of cheese on top of meat. Cover with the remaining bread in sandwich fashion.
(3) In a medium bowl beat eggs, salt & pepper. Add mustard, onion, green pepper, worcestershire sauce. Beat in milk and tabasco sauce.
(4) Pour over sandwiches, cover and place in refrigerator overnight.

(5) In the morning melt 30mL (2 Tbsp.) butter. Sprinkle Special K or crushed Cornflakes over sandwiches. Drizzle melted butter all over.
(6) Bake just above center in 180°C (350°F) oven for 1 hour. Let stand 10 minutes before serving.

*   Makes 4 sandwiches.

Beef Steak Sandwich

One way to a man's heart...

500g.....1 lb. thinly sliced hot roast beef	(1) In a frying pan melt butter, saute onions and mushrooms until onions are crisp tender.
15mL....1 Tbsp. butter	
2........2 large thinly sliced cooking onions	(2) Heat rolls in oven.
250g.....1 cup grated cheddar cheese	(3) Slice rolls and spread with mustard or mayonnaise.
4........4 submarine rolls	(4) Put 1/4 of the beef on each roll, top with onions, and mushrooms, then cheese.
.........Mustard and/or mayonnaise	
*********	(5) Put the top of the bun in place.

* Serve hot.
* Makes 4 servings.

Baked Ham Sandwich

3........3 slices raisin bread	(1) Butter one slice of bread; cover it with ham.
.........Butter	
.........Shaved black forest ham	(2) Butter both sides of next slice of bread, place it on top of ham. Cover with ham and a slice of cheese.
.........Swiss cheese	
*********	

(3) Butter next slice of bread on one side; and place it butter side down on top of cheese.
(4) Wrap sandwich in tin foil.
(5) Bake just above center in 120°C (250°F) oven for 1 hour.
(6) Open tin foil and broil until cheese melts.

* Makes 1 sandwich.
* This sandwich may be frozen. If frozen, thaw in the refrigerator before baking.

Turkey or Chicken Sandwich Filling

* Using a fork break cooked turkey or chicken into small pieces. Add salad dressing to make spreading consistency. Diced onions may be added, if desired.

Egg Salad Sandwich

2........2 hard boiled eggs
30mL....2 Tbsp. whipped salad
          dressing
30mL....2 Tbsp. chopped lettuce
15mL....1 Tbsp. chopped green
          onions
.........Salt & pepper
8........8 slices bread
.........Butter or margarine
          ****

(1) Grate eggs, stir in salad dress-
     ing, chopped lettuce and onions.
(2) Sprinkle salt & pepper to taste.
     Spread onto buttered bread.
     Cover with top slice.

* Makes 4 sandwiches.
* Finely chopped cucumbers or celery can be added, if desired.

Devilled Ham Sandwich

2........2 green onions chopped
          fine
30mL....2 Tbsp. butter
4........4 eggs
.........1/2 cup chopped cooked
          ham
.........Sprinkle salt & pepper
          ****

(1) In a frying pan fry onions in
     butter for 2 minutes.
(2) Add eggs and ham. Cook and
     stir until eggs are cooked but
     still moist.
(3) Season with salt & pepper.
     Spread between slices of butter-
     ed toast.

* Serve very hot.
* Makes 4 sandwiches.

Buns

Hot Cross Buns

10mL....2 tsp. cinnamon
2mL.....1/2 tsp. allspice
2mL.....1/2 tsp. cloves
1 3/4-2L .7-7 1/2 cups flour
30mL....2 Tbsp. sugar
125mL...1/2 cup water
30mL....2 Tbsp. active dry yeast
250mL...1 cup milk
125mL...1/2 cup sugar
50mL....1/4 cup butter or margarine
10mL....2 tsp. salt
175mL...3/4 cup water
2........2 well beaten eggs
250mL...1 cup mixed peel
250mL...1 cup currants
****

(1) Stir cinnamon, allspice, cloves, and 1 1/4L (5 cups) of the flour together. Set aside.
(2) Dissolve 30mL (2 Tbsp.) sugar in 125mL (1/2 cup) warm water; sprinkle with yeast, let stand for 10 minutes. Stir well.
(3) Scald milk, add sugar, butter and salt; stir until dissolved.
(4) Add 175mL (3/4 cup) of cool to lukewarm water. Pour into large mixing bowl.
(5) Add 500mL (2 cups) of the flour and spice mixture and the yeast; mix well.

(6) Add beaten eggs and 625mL (2 1/2 cups) of the flour and spice mixture. Beat until smooth.
(7) Dredge fruit with 125mL (1/2 cup) of the flour and spice mixture. Add to mixture.
(8) Add flour to make a soft dough.
(9) Turn out on a floured surface, cover with plastic wrap and a tea towel. Let rest 10 minutes. Knead until smooth and elastic, approx. 5 minutes.
(10) Place in a buttered bowl, butter top slightly, cover with plastic wrap and a tea towel. Set in a warm place 26-28°C (75-85°F).
(11) Let rise until doubled. About 1 1/2 hours.
(12) Shape into balls, place just touching in two buttered 22x33cm. (9x13-inch) pans. Cover with tea towel. Let stand until doubled.
(13) Bake just above centre in 180°C (350°F) oven for 20 minutes.
(14) Remove from oven after 15 minutes, brush with glaze (45mL (3 Tbsp.) sugar dissolved in 45mL (3 Tbsp.) water). Quickly return to oven and finish baking.
(15) When baked, brush again with glaze and place on rack to cool.
(16) When cool make crosses on top with following icing.

Icing for Hot Cross Buns:

1........1 egg white
325mL...1 1/3 cup icing sugar
1mL.....1/4 tsp. vanilla

(1) Gradually beat sugar into unbeaten egg white, add vanilla, beat well.

Cinnamon Buns

What can I say...try them you'll just love them...

375mL...1 1/2 cups warm water
10mL....2 tsp. sugar
30mL....2 Tbsp. active dry yeast
250mL...1 cup milk
125mL...1/2 cup sugar
6mL.....1 1/4 tsp. salt
90mL....6 Tbsp. butter or margarine
2........2 beaten eggs
1 3/4L ..7 cups flour
****

(1) In a bowl stir sugar into water until dissolved, sprinkle yeast over top. Let stand 10 minutes. Stir well.

(2) Scald milk. In a medium mixing bowl place sugar, salt and butter. Add hot milk, stir until butter is melted and sugar is dissolved.

(3) Cool to lukewarm.

(4) Add 250mL (1 cup) flour and yeast, mix well.
(5) Add 375mL (1 1/2 cups) flour, beat smooth. Beat in eggs.
(6) Add enough flour to make a soft dough.
(7) Turn out on floured surface, cover with plastic wrap and a tea towel. Let rest 10 minutes.
(8) Knead until smooth and elastic, 5 minutes.
(9) Place in a buttered bowl, butter top, cover with plastic wrap and a tea towel.
(10) Set in warm place 26-28°C (75-85°F).
(11) Let rise until doubled.
(12) Divide into two equal parts.
(13) Roll each piece into an oblong 6cm. (1/4-inch) thick 35x45cm. (14x18-inch). Spread with filling.

Filling:

125mL...1/2 cup butter or margarine
15mL....1 Tbsp. cinnamon
375mL...1 1/2 cups brown sugar
250mL...1 cup raisins
****

(1) Spread each half with 50mL (1/4 cup) butter, sprinkle with 7mL (1/2 Tbsp.) cinnamon, 175mL (3/4 cup) brown sugar, then 125mL (1/2 cup) raisins.

(2) Beginning at long edge roll up into thick roll.
(3) Cut into twelve 3cm. (1 1/4-inch) slices.
(4) Place just touching, cut side up in a well buttered 22x33x5cm. (9x13x2-inch) pan. Roll and prepare second half of dough.
(5) Let stand until doubled.
(6) Bake just above centre in 180°C (350°F) oven for 20-25 minutes.
(7) Cool on wire rack.

*   Makes 2 dozen buns.

118

More About Cinnamon Buns...

This is one place where parchment paper comes in very useful. Just line the bottom and partially line upsides and ends of pan. Just press sheet of parchment paper into pan letting edges cover sides. **Do not cut corners of parchment paper. The bottom corners will be useful to catch juices, especially if topping is used. Cinnamon buns can be left in pans if parchment paper is used.

Cinnamon Bun Toppings:

50mL....1/4 cup butter or margarine
150mL...2/3 cup brown sugar
50mL....1/4 cup chopped raisins
30mL....2 Tbsp. evaporated milk
30mL....2 Tbsp. kahlua
****

(1) In a saucepan melt butter, add sugar, raisins and milk.
(2) Simmer very slowly for 5 minutes.
(3) Remove from heat.
(4) Stir in kahlua, pour into glass jar. Cover.

(5) This topping may be drizzled over warm buns, or stored in a glass jar (in a glass jar for rewarming in the microwave) rewarmed and served over individual servings.

* Makes 3/4 cup.

Dinner Buns

You will be proud to serve these buns...superior taste...

15mL....1 Tbsp. active dry yeast
50mL....1/4 cup warm water
250mL...1 cup milk
125mL...1/2 cup butter or margarine
75mL....1/3 cup sugar
2mL.....1/2 tsp. salt
1L ......4-4 1/2 cups flour
2........2 eggs, well beaten
****

(1) Dissolve yeast in warm water, let stand 5 minutes, stir well.
(2) Heat milk. In a medium mixing bowl place butter, sugar and salt.
(3) Add hot milk. Cool to lukewarm.
(4) Add 250mL (1 cup) flour and yeast. Mix well.
(5) Add 325mL (1 1/2 cups) flour, beat smooth.

(6) Beat in eggs.
(7) Add enough remaining flour to make a soft dough. Turn out on a floured surface, cover with plastic wrap, let rest 10 minutes.
(8) Knead until smooth and elastic, approx. 5 minutes.
(9) Place in buttered bowl. Cover with plastic wrap and a tea towel. Set in a warm place 24-28°C (75-85°F). Let rise until doubled.
(10) Punch down and let rise until doubled.
(11) Shape in balls, place in buttered pans. Two 22x33cm. (9x13-inch). Let rise until doubled.
(12) Bake in 200°C (400°F) oven for 20-25 minutes. Cool on wire rack.

Dinner Rolls

Before you know it these buns will be ready to serve...super at any time...

1 3/4L ..7-8 cups flour (divided)
30mL....2 Tbsp. instant yeast
2........2 eggs
15mL....1 Tbsp. sugar
75mL....1/3 cup oil
7mL.....1 1/2 tsp. salt
750mL...3 cups very warm water
****

(1) In a medium bowl mix yeast with 1L (4 cups) flour. Set aside.
(2) In another bowl whip eggs, add sugar, oil, salt and water.
(3) Add yeast and flour mixture.
(4) Blend well, add remaining flour.

(5) Let rise 15 minutes. Punch down. Let rise 15 minutes.
(6) Shape into rolls, place just touching each other in a well buttered pan.
(7) Cover with towel, set in warm place 26-28°C (75-85°F). Let rise for 1 hour.
(8) Bake just above centre in a 180°C (350°F) oven for 15-18 minutes.

* If more crust is desired place rolls so they do not touch each other.

Baking Powder Biscuits

Serve these biscuits hot from the oven...pass the syrup please...

500mL...2 cups flour
25mL....5 tsp. baking powder
5mL.....1 tsp. salt
45mL....3 Tbsp. sugar
5mL.....1 tsp. cream of tartar
50mL....1/4 cup cold shortening
250mL...1 cup milk
****

(1) Combine flour, baking powder, salt, sugar and cream of tartar.
(2) Cut in shortening.
(3) Add milk all at once. Stir quickly but gently. Dough should be soft.
(4) Turn out onto floured surface.

(5) Knead gently just until dough masses together.
(6) Roll or pat out to 2cm. (3/4-inch) thickness.
(7) Cut with 6cm. (2 1/2-inch) cookie cutter.
(8) Place on ungreased cookie sheet.
(9) Bake just above center in 230°C (450°F) oven for 10-12 minutes.

* Makes 12 biscuits.

Baking Powder Biscuit Mix

So handy to have on hand...ready in minutes...

2L ......8 cups flour
60mL....1/4 cup plus 2 tsp. baking
　　　　　powder
15mL....1 Tbsp. salt
10mL....2 tsp. cream of tartar
5mL.....1 tsp. soda
375mL...1 1/2 cups milk powder
625mL...2 1/2 cups shortening
　　　　　(not lard)
　　　　　*********

(1) Combine these seven ingredients together.
(2) Store at room temperature.
(3) Use as needed in biscuits, dumplings, or pancakes below.

Biscuits

750mL...3 cups biscuit mix
150mL...2/3 cup milk or water
　　　　　*********

(1) Place mix into a medium bowl.
(2) Add milk all at once. Stir only enough to form a mass.

(3) Turn out onto a floured work surface. Gently form into a ball, knead 4 times. Sprinkle with flour just enough to handle.
(4) Pat into 15x15cm. (6x6-inch) square, 2cm. (3/4-inch) thick.
(5) Using a sharp knife cut into 9 or 12 squares. Place onto unbuttered cookie sheet.
(6) Bake just above centre in 230°C (450°F) oven for 10-12 minutes.
(7) Biscuits should be slightly browned. Serve hot from oven.

Drop Biscuits or Dumplings

* Mix as biscuits adding extra milk for drop batter.

Pancakes

550mL...2 1/4 cup biscuit mix
15mL....1 Tbsp. sugar
1........1 slightly beaten egg
250mL...1-1 1/2 cups milk
　　　　　*********

(1) Place mix into medium mixing bowl, add sugar. Stir egg into 250mL (1 cup) of the milk.
(2) Add liquid to dry ingredients.

　　Add enough remaining milk to make pancake batter consistency.
(3) Fry on hot, lightly buttered skillet, turning once.

Classic Biscuits

For that added touch...try these delicate biscuits...

500mL...2 cups flour
7mL.....1 1/2 tsp. baking powder
7mL.....1 1/2 tsp. cream of tartar
15mL....1 Tbsp. sugar
3mL.....3/4 tsp. baking soda
1mL.....1/4 tsp. salt
125mL...1/2 cup margarine
300mL...1 1/4 cup buttermilk
****

(1) In a medium bowl combine flour, baking powder, cream of tartar, sugar, soda and salt.
(2) Cut in margarine until mixture is crumbly, as in pie crust.
(3) Add buttermilk, mix together, turn out onto floured surface.
(4) Adding flour to keep from sticking, knead 4 times until smooth.

(5) Pat or roll gently into 2cm. (3/4-inch) thickness.
(6) With a sharp knife cut into 9 pieces, or cut into 7cm. (3-inch) circles.
(7) Place on unbuttered cookie sheet.
(8) Bake just above centre in 220-230°C (425-450°F) oven for 15-20 minutes, until slightly browned.

* For best results, buttermilk must be used.
* Serve hot.

Pull Aparts

This is similar to cinnamon buns...differing in shape with fruit added...

250mL...1 cup warm water
10mL....2 tsp. sugar
30mL....2 Tbsp. active dry yeast
250mL...1 cup milk
125mL...1/2 cup sugar
6mL.....1 1/4 tsp. salt
90mL....6 Tbsp. butter or margarine
2........2 beaten eggs
1 1/2L ..6 cups flour
****

(1) In a bowl stir sugar into water until dissolved. Sprinkle yeast over top. Let stand 10 minutes. Stir well.
(2) Scald milk. In a medium mixing bowl place sugar, salt and butter. Add hot milk until butter is melted and sugar dissolved.
(3) Cool to lukewarm.
(4) Add 250mL (1 cup) flour and yeast. Mix well.

(5) Add 375mL (1 1/2 cups) flour, beat smooth. Beat in eggs.
(6) Add enough flour to make a soft dough.
(7) Turn out on floured surface, cover with plastic wrap and a tea towel. Let rest for 10 minutes.
(8) Knead until smooth and elastic, approx. 5 minutes.
(9) Place in a buttered bowl, butter tops lightly, cover with plastic wrap and a tea towel. Set in a warm place 26-28°C (75-85°F).
(10) Let rise until doubled.
(11) Butter 25cm. (10-inch) tube pan well.

122

Fruit Mixture:

125mL...1/2 cup melted butter or margarine
15mL....1 Tbsp. cinnamon
375mL...1 1/2 cups brown sugar
125mL...1/2 cup chopped walnuts
125mL...1/2 cup raisins
125mL...1/2 cup maraschino cherries, drained and halved
****

(1) Place some of the raisins, nuts and cherries in bottom of tube pan.
(2) Having melted butter in one bowl, combine sugar and cinnamon in a separate bowl.
(3) Roll dough into 2 1/2cm. (1-inch) balls. Dip balls in melted butter then in sugar mixture.

(4) Place layer of balls on top of fruit in tube pan.
(5) Sprinkle with nuts, raisins and cherries.
(6) Repeat for second layer. **Place dough balls slightly apart.
(7) Sprinkle remaining sugar mixture and butter over the balls.
(8) Cover with tea towel, set in warm place 26-28°C (75-85°F) until doubled.
(9) Bake just above centre in 190°C (375°F) for 35-40 minutes.
(10) Invert pan on serving plate.

* Do not remove pan for a few minutes. Brown sugar mixture will run down over buns instead of clinging to pan.

Cheese Rolls

625mL...2 1/2 cups flour
250mL...1 cup butter
250mL...1 cup sour cream
.........Seasoned salt
.........White pepper
500mL...2 cups grated cheddar cheese
.........Paprika
****

(1) Mix flour and butter together.
(2) Add sour cream, mix well.
(3) Divide into four equal parts, wrap in plastic wrap, chill 4 hours.
(4) Roll out one at a time on a well floured surface to 30x15cm. (12x6-inch) rectangle.

(5) Sprinkle each lightly with seasoned salt and pepper, then with 45mL (3 Tbsp.) cheese.
(6) Starting with 30cm. (12-inch) side, roll up like a jelly roll. Moisten edges and ends with water. Seal.
(7) Place on buttered cookie sheet.
(8) Cut halfway through at 2.5cm. (1-inch) intervals using a sharp knife.
(9) Sprinkle with paprika.
(10) Bake just above centre in 180°C (350°F) oven for 30 minutes until golden brown.

* Makes 4 dozen.

Hamburger Buns

125mL...1/2 cup warm water
10mL....2 tsp. sugar
30mL....2 Tbsp. active dry yeast
50mL....1/4 cup butter or margarine
125mL...1/2 cup sugar
10mL....2 tsp. salt
250mL...1 cup milk
2........2 well beaten eggs
1 3/4L ..7-7 1/2 cups flour
****

(1) In a small bowl dissolve 10mL (2 tsp.) sugar in 125mL (1/2 cup) water, sprinkle with yeast. Let stand 10 minutes. Stir well.
(2) Scald milk, add sugar, butter and salt. Stir until dissolved.
(3) Add 175mL (3/4 cup) water, cool to lukewarm.
(4) Add 500mL (2 cups) flour and yeast. Mix well.

(5) Add beaten eggs and 625mL (2 1/2 cups) flour, beat until smooth.
(6) Add flour to make a soft dough.
(7) Turn out on a floured surface, cover with plastic wrap and a tea towel. Let rest for 10 minutes.
(8) Knead until smooth and elastic, approx. 5 minutes.
(9) Place in a buttered bowl. Butter top, cover with plastic wrap and a tea towel. Set in a warm place 26-28°C (75-85°F). Let rise until doubled.
(10) Punch down, cover and let rise until doubled.
(11) Divide dough in half. Roll dough 2cm. (3/4-inch) thick. Cut in 10cm. (3 1/2-4-inch) circles. **Use peanut butter lid or .45kg (1 lb.) coffee can.

*   If dough shrinks after cutting, divide into four portions, punch down, cover and let rest 10 minutes. Then reroll and recut.

(12) Place 2.5cm. (1-inch) apart on buttered cookie sheet.
(13) Bake just above centre in 190°C (375°F) oven for 20 minutes.

Croissants

300mL...1 2/3 cups warm water
125mL...1/2 cup skim milk
10mL....2 tsp. sugar
15mL....1 Tbsp. active dry yeast
900mL...3 2/3 cups flour
10mL....2 tsp. salt
45mL....3 Tbsp. sugar
75mL....1/3 cup shortening
500g.....1 lb. butter (no substitute) chilled
1........1 egg yolk
30mL....2 Tbsp. milk
****

(1) In a bowl put water and milk powder. Add 2 tsp. sugar. Stir until sugar is dissolved. Sprinkle yeast over top and let stand 10 minutes; stir well.
(2) In a large bowl, combine flour, salt and 45mL (3 Tbsp.) sugar.
(3) Mix the shortening into the flour mixture by rolling it lightly through your hands until the size of peas.
(4) Stir in the yeast mixture stirring only until dough forms a mass.

(5) Turn dough out onto a floured work surface (a pastry sheet is preferred). Using a pastry scraper, cut through dough in several places. Push pastry scraper under edge of dough and fold it in half, in the direction of the cuts. Repeat cutting and folding several more times, cutting in the opposite direction of previous cuts until dough is smooth. Place dough in buttered bowl; cover with plastic wrap and a towel. Set in a warm draft-free place until doubled in bulk. Approximately 2 hours.

(6) Punch down, cover with plastic wrap. Refrigerate for 2-4 hours.

(7) On a floured work surface, roll dough into a 46x25.4cm. (18x10-inch) rectangle. With a sharp knife cut butter lengthwise and place in centre third of dough, placing butter 2.54cm. (1-inch) in from two outside edges.

(8) To fold dough, pick up the right edge of the dough, fold it over the buttered third. With your left hand, pick up left edge of dough and fold it over both layers. Press two outside edges together securely.

(9) Give dough a 1/4 turn so that what was the top edge of dough is now at your right. Lightly flour work surface, roll dough into 30x60cm. (12x24-inch) rectangle. Fold dough into thirds as before. Give dough a 1/4 turn as before. This is your first turn.

(10) Repeat rolling out, folding and rotating dough to complete second turn. Cover and refrigerate for 45 minutes.

(11) Repeat rolling out, folding and rotating dough to complete third turn. Cover and refrigerate for 15 minutes.

(12) Repeat one more turn to complete fourth turn. Wrap and refrigerate 8-24 hours. *To help remember which turn I am on, I mark them down on a piece of paper:
   (1st turn and 2nd turn refrigerate for 45 minutes; 3rd turn refrigerate for 15 minutes; 4th turn refrigerate 8-24 hours).

(13) Divide dough in half. Wrap second half, and place in refrigerator. On lightly floured work surface, roll out dough into 5mm. (1/4-inch) thick, 40x52cm. (16x20-inch) rectangle.

(14) Cut dough in half lengthwise, cut out twelve 20x20x15cm. (8x8x6-inch) triangles.

(15) Beat egg yolk and milk together. Roll up each triangle from short base to tip. Brush tip with a small amount of egg wash (this helps to secure tip in place). Form croissant into crescent shape, place tip side down on lightly greased baking sheet. Don't use butter to grease pan as it burns quickly. Cover with tea towel. Repeat with remaining dough. Set in warm, draft-free place until almost double in bulk. Approximately 1 hour. Brush croissant with remaining egg wash. Bake just below centre in 230°C (450°F) oven for 10 minutes. Reduce heat to 190°C (375°F) and bake 6 minutes longer or until golden brown. Cool on racks.

*   Makes 24 large croissants.

Batter Rolls

Quick to make...quick to disappear...

125mL...1/2 cup warm water 50°C (115°F)
5mL.....1 tsp. sugar
5mL.....1 Tbsp. active dry yeast
375mL...1 1/2 cups warm milk
50mL....1/4 cup sugar
50mL....1/4 cup margarine
5mL.....1 tsp. salt
2........2 beaten eggs
925mL...3 3/4 cups flour
****

(1)   In a bowl, put warm water, stir in 5mL (1 tsp.) sugar until dissolved. Sprinkle yeast over top. Let stand 10 minutes.
(2)   Stir well before using.
(3)   In a medium saucepan combine milk, sugar, margarine and salt. Heat until warmed and margarine is melted.
      Add beaten eggs, mix well.

(5) Stir in 500mL (2 cups) flour and the yeast mixture.
(6) Beat vigorously with wooden spoon or electric mixer until smooth. About 3 minutes.
(7) Gradually stir in remaining flour. Batter will be soft.
(8) Cover with tea towel. Let rise in a warm draft-free place 28°C (80°F) until doubled (about 1 hour).
(9) Stir down dough and let stand 10 minutes. Fill buttered muffin tins 1/2 full.
(10) Let rise in a warm draft-free place until doubled (30-45 minutes).
(11) Bake just above centre in 190°C (375°F) oven for 20-25 minutes or until golden brown.
(12) Turn out of pans immediately.

*   Place on rack to cool.

Toasted Garlic Bread

250mL...1 cup butter or margarine
10mL....2 tsp. garlic powder
125mL...1/2 cup grated parmesan cheese (Opt.)
****

(1)   Select loaf bread of your choice (french, sourdough) *white bread.
(2)   Cut bread into thick slices or 17x4cm. (6x1 1/2-inch) strips.

(3)   Cover cookie sheet with tin foil. Place bread on tin foil.
(4)   In a small frying pan heat butter and garlic, stirring so butter gets a good garlic flavour.
(5)   Drizzle butter over bread, sprinkle with parmesan cheese.
(6)   Turn the oven to broil. Set cookie sheet just above center of oven. Broil until bread is toasted. Bread does not take long to toast. Watch closely.

*   The white bread recipe in this collection is excellent for toasted garlic bread.

126

Whole Wheat Rolls

125mL...1/2 cup warm water
5mL.....1 tsp. sugar
30mL....2 Tbsp. active dry yeast
250mL...1 cup milk
125mL...1/2 cup margarine
2mL.....1/2 tsp. salt
75mL....1/3 cup sugar
2........2 beaten eggs
875mL...3 1/2 cups whole wheat
         flour
500mL...2 cups white flour
         (Mix the two flours to-
         gether)
         ****

(1) In a bowl put 125mL (1/2 cup) warm water. Stir in 5mL (1 tsp.) sugar until dissolved.
(2) Sprinkle yeast over top and let stand 10 minutes. Stir well before using.
(3) In a saucepan combine milk and margarine; heat until warmed and margarine is melted.
(4) Add sugar and salt; stir until dissolved. Cool to lukewarm. Pour into a mixing bowl.

(5) Stir in 500mL (2 cups) flour, then the yeast mixture; beat until smooth. Stir in remaining flour to make a soft dough. Place on a floured surface; cover with plastic wrap; let rest 10 minutes.
(6) Knead until smooth and elastic (approx. 5 minutes). Place in buttered bowl, butter top, cover with plastic wrap and a tea towel. Let rise until doubled.
(7) Shape into balls. Place in two buttered pans 22x33cm. (9x13-inch). Let rise until doubled.
(8) Bake just above centre in 190°C (375°F) oven for 20-25 minutes.

* Place balls close together for soft sides; place apart for crusty sides.

Doughnuts

875mL-
   1L ....3 1/2-4 cups flour
2mL.....1/2 tsp. salt
2mL.....1/2 tsp. cinnamon
2mL.....1/2 tsp. nutmeg
5mL.....1 tsp. baking soda
5mL.....1 tsp. baking powder
250mL...1 cup sugar
2........2 beaten eggs
30mL....2 Tbsp. melted lard
5mL.....1 tsp. vanilla
250mL...1 cup sour milk or
         buttermilk
10-15cm .4-6-inches melted lard or
         oil for deep frying.
         ****

(1) Stir together flour, salt, soda, cinnamon, nutmeg and baking powder. Set aside.
(2) In a mixing bowl combine sugar, eggs, lard, vanilla and milk. Mix in the flour mixture. Blend well.
(3) Refrigerate 30 minutes.
(4) Roll out dough 1.5cm. (1/2-inch) thick, cut out with floured doughnut cutter.
(5) Place doughnuts on a lightly floured cookie sheet. Allow dough to dry 10 minutes.
(6) Heat lard to 190°C (375°F).

(7) Gently slip doughnuts into hot fat. **Do not crowd.**
(8) When lightly browned turn and cook other side.
(9) Drain on paper towel or brown paper.

Cinnamon-Sugar Doughnuts

(1) Place 50mL (1/4 cup) granulated sugar and 1mL (1/4 tsp.) cinnamon into a paper bag.
(2) Take doughnuts out of hot fat, lay them on a paper towel, then immediately place doughnuts into the paper bag and shake.
(3) Remove gently to tray, standing on edge to cool.

Glazed Doughnuts

(1) Stir together 125mL (1/2 cup) icing sugar, 1mL (1/4 tsp.) vanilla, 10mL (2 tsp.) hot milk.
(2) Add food colour, blend until smooth.
(3) Dip one side of doughnut into icing, then into crushed nuts, if desired.
(4) Place in single layer on tray until icing is dry.
(5) Stand on edge to store.

Raised Doughnuts

125mL...1/2 cup warm water
5mL.....1 tsp. sugar
15mL....1 Tbsp. active dry yeast
3........3 beaten egg yolks
175mL...3/4 cup sugar
1mL.....1/4 tsp. vanilla
175mL...3/4 cup oil
1mL.....1/4 tsp. salt
500mL...2 cups warm water
1 3/4L ..7 cups flour (approx.)
****

(1) In a small bowl put 125mL (1/2 cup) warm water. Stir in 5mL (1 tsp.) sugar until dissolved.
(2) Sprinkle yeast over top. Let stand 10 minutes. Stir well.
(3) In a medium bowl stir together egg yolks, sugar, vanilla, oil, salt and warm water. Add yeast mixture.

(4) Add flour to make a slightly sticky dough.
(5) Turn out onto a floured surface. Cover with plastic wrap and a tea towel. Let rest 10 minutes.
(6) Knead until smooth. Place in buttered bowl, butter top, cover with plastic wrap and a tea towel. Set in a warm place 26-28°C (75-85°F). Let rise until doubled (1 1/4 hours).
(7) Turn out onto a floured surface, knead dough slightly, let rest 10 minutes.
(8) Roll dough out to 1.5cm. (1/2-inch) thickness. Cut out with floured doughnut cutter. Cover with tea towel. Let rise 1 hour.
(9) Heat lard to 190°C (375°F) and gently slip doughnuts into hot fat. **Do not crowd.**
(10) When lightly browned, turn and cook other side. Drain on paper towel or brown paper.

Glaze for Doughnuts:

125mL...1/2 cup butter or margar-
        ine
250mL...1 cup sugar
125mL...1/2 cup milk
375mL...1 1/2 cups icing sugar
2mL.....1/2 tsp. vanilla
       ****

(1) In a saucpan place butter, sugar and milk.
(2) Stir and boil for 1 minute.
(3) Cool, add icing sugar, vanilla and salt.
(4) Dip doughnuts into glaze. Drain on wire rack.

*   Keep the glaze warm while dipping doughnuts.

Harvest Nuggets

875mL-
  1L ....3 1/2-4 cups 60% whole
        wheat flour
5mL.....1 tsp. baking powder
5mL.....1 tsp. nutmeg
5mL.....1 tsp. cinnamon
5mL.....1 tsp. baking soda
2mL.....1/2 tsp. salt
250mL...1 cup sugar
2........2 beaten eggs
30mL....2 Tbsp. melted lard
5mL.....1 tsp. vanilla
250mL...1 cup sour milk **or**
        buttermilk
10-15cm..4-6-inches melted lard **or**
        oil for frying
       ****

(1) In a mixing bowl stir together flour, baking powder, nutmeg, soda, cinnamon, salt and sugar.
(2) In another bowl mix eggs, 30mL (2 Tbsp.) melted lard, vanilla and sour milk. Add to dry ingredients. **Do not over mix.** Chill 30 minutes.
(3) Roll out 1.5cm. (1/2-inch) thick.
(4) Cut into circles 4cm. (1 1/2-inches) in diameter. Make a hole in centre with plastic straw .6cm. (1/4-inch) in diameter.
(5) Slip nuggets into hot fat 190°C (375°F) a few at a time. **Do not over crowd.**

(6) Cook until lightly browned, turn to cook other side.
(7) Remove from hot fat with slotted spoon.
(8) Drain on paper towel or brown paper.

*   To make sour milk add 30mL (2 Tbsp.) of vinegar to 250mL (1 cup) of sweet milk.

Sugar Nuggets

*   How to sugar doughnuts...place 125mL (1/2 cup) granulated sugar and 2mL (1/2 tsp.) cinnamon in a bag. Take nuggets out of hot fat, lay on paper towel, immediately place them into the sugar mixture and shake. Remove gently to tray, standing on edge to cool.

Butterhorns

For that extra special treat... try these... you won't be disappointed...

50mL.... 1/4 cup warm water
45mL.... 3 Tbsp. active dry yeast
50mL.... 1/4 cup shortening
125mL... 1/2 cup sugar
2mL..... 1/2 tsp. lemon juice
3 .... 3 eggs
1mL..... 1/4 tsp. vanilla
325mL... 1 1/2 cups milk
1 1/2L .. 6 cups flour
375mL... 3/4 lb. butter
          (no substitute)
1 .... 1 beaten egg
          ****

(1) Beat water and yeast together until dissolved. Set aside.
* This seems like alot of yeast, but it is needed in this recipe.
(2) Combine shortening, sugar, lemon juice, 3 eggs, milk, vanilla and yeast mixture.
(3) Beat with mixer on medium speed until combined, leave slightly lumpy.
(4) Work flour into above mixture by hand until thoroughly mixed.

(5) Dust with flour if too sticky, do not over work.
(6) Soften butter slightly and set aside.
(7) Place dough on a floured work surface, roll into an oblong shape 6cm. (1/4-inch) thick.
(8) Place softened butter in center third of dough.
(9) To fold dough, pick up the right edge of the dough; fold it over the buttered third. With your left hand pick up the left edge of the dough and fold it over both layers. Press two outside edges together securely. Let stand for 10 minutes.
(10) Roll again 6cm. (1/4-inch) thick dusting surface with flour if sticky and fold dough into three sections. Leave for 10 minutes. **Repeat this procedure once again and after the last fold refrigerate for 30 minutes.
(11) Roll dough into an oblong shape .6cm. (1/4-inch) thick, brush with beaten egg.
(12) Cut into 1.2cm. (1/2-inch) pieces and place in lightly greased cake pans. You will need two 22x33cm. (9x13-inch) pans.
     These rolls will lose their shape without help, so set them just touching.
(13) Cover with damp cloth and let rise until double in bulk.
(14) Bake just above centre in 200°C (400°F) oven for 10 minutes.
(15) Cool thoroughly. Ice with the following glaze.

Glaze:

250mL... 1 cup icing sugar
7mL..... 1 1/2 tsp. melted butter
.... Small amount of milk to
         make a smooth glaze
375mL... 1 1/2 cups crushed
         walnuts
         ****

(1) Mix icing sugar and melted butter together.
(2) Add enough milk to make a smooth glaze.
(3) Spread over butterhorns, sprinkle crushed walnuts over all before glaze sets.

Scones or Welsh Cakes

250mL...1 cup currants
750mL...3 cups flour
175mL...3/4 cup sugar
2mL.....1/2 tsp. salt
15mL....1 Tbsp. baking powder
5mL.....1 tsp. nutmeg
175mL...3/4 cup margarine
1........1 egg
175mL...3/4 cup milk
****

(1) In a small bowl cover currants with hot water. Let stand 5 minutes. Drain well. Set aside.
(2) In a large mixing bowl combine flour, sugar, salt, baking powder and nutmeg.
(3) Cut in margarine until mixture is crumbly.
(4) Stir in currants.

Topping:

1........1 egg white
5mL.....1 tsp. sugar
1/2mL...1/8 tsp. cinnamon
****

(5) Beat egg and milk together. Add to dry ingredients.
(6) On a lightly floured surface knead dough gently for 10-12 strokes.
(7) On a lightly floured surface roll dough to 1cm. (1/2-inch) thickness.
(8) Cut into 8.5cm. (3 1/2-inch) circles, place on an unbuttered cookie sheet.
(9) With a sharp knife score scone into thirds. Do not cut completely through.
(10) Whip egg white with fork until foamy, and brush on scone.
(11) Combine 5mL (1 tsp.) sugar and cinnamon, sprinkle over top.
(12) Bake just above centre in 190°C (375°F) oven 18 minutes or until light brown. Cool on wire rack.

* To make welsh cakes, roll dough out to 1cm. (1/2-inch) thickness. Cut into 7cm. (3-inch) circles. *Do not score.*
* Fry on a lightly buttered skillet over medium heat, browning both sides. Amount will depend on size of cookie cutter used.

Apple Fritters

550mL...2 1/4 cups flour
2mL.....1/2 tsp. nutmeg
250mL...1 cup sugar
2mL.....1/2 tsp. salt
10mL....2 tsp. baking powder
15mL....1 Tbsp. melted shortening
2........2 beaten eggs
5mL.....1 tsp. vanilla
175mL...3/4 cup milk
25mL....1 cup diced peeled apples
10-15cm .4-6-inches melted lard **or**
           oil for frying
        ****

(1) In a mixing bowl combine flour, nutmeg, sugar, salt and baking powder. Mix well.
(2) Add shortening, eggs, vanilla, milk and apples. Stir 1/2 minute.
(3) Heat oil to 190°C (375°F).
(4) Drop by heaping tablespoonfuls into hot lard.
(5) When lightly browned, turn and cook other side.
(6) Drain on paper towel or brown paper.

Glaze for Fritters:

500mL...2 cups sugar
500mL...2 cups water
5mL.....1 tsp. vanilla
        ****

(1) Bring sugar and water to a boil and boil 4 minutes or to the thread stage.

(2) Remove from heat. Stir in vanilla.
(3) Dip fritters into the syrup and drain on waxed paper.

Pastry

Graham Wafer Pie Shell

400mL...1 2/3 cups graham wafer
crumbs
50mL....1/4 cup sugar
50mL....1/4 cup butter or margarine
****

(1) Thoroughly blend wafer crumbs, sugar and butter together.
(2) Press firmly against bottom and sides of a 22cm. (9-inch) pie plate.

(3) Bake just above center in 190°C (375°F) oven for 8 minutes.

* Cool.
* If wafer crumbs are too fine, your crust will be too firm and difficult to cut.

Perfect Pie Crust #1

Perfect pie crust of excellent quality...

30mL....2 Tbsp. orange drink
crystals
.........Cold water
1........1 beaten egg
1 1/4L ..5½cups flour
15mL....1 Tbsp. sugar
5mL.....1 tsp. salt
500mL...1 lb. lard (not shortening)
****

(1) Mix orange crystals into 250mL (1 cup) cold water. Set aside.
(2) Beat egg with a fork until foamy.
(3) Pour beaten egg into 250mL (1 cup) measuring cup; add orange juice to make 250mL (1 cup). Set aside.

(4) In a large mixing bowl combine flour, salt and sugar.
(5) Mix the lard into the flour by rolling it through your hands. Particles should be the size of medium peas, with some pieces slightly larger.
(6) Gradually stir egg mixture into flour mixture. Toss ingredients together, quickly but gently until you can gather it into a ball. (Do not press too hard.)
(7) Divide mixture into eight 200g (7 oz.) balls, round up each ball slightly.

* Any unused portions should be wrapped individually in clear plastic wrap; then placed in a plastic freezer bag. Tie securely, refrigerate or freeze.

Perfect Pie Crust #2

Another perfect pie crust of excellent quality...

1........1 beaten egg	(1)	Beat egg with a fork until
........Cold water		foamy.
1 1/2L ..6 cups flour	(2)	Pour beaten egg into 250mL (1
15mL....1 Tbsp. sugar		cup) measuring cup. Add water
5mL.....1 tsp. salt		to make the 250mL (1 cup).
500g.....1 lb. lard (not shortening)		Set aside.

****

(3) In a large mixing bowl combine flour, salt and sugar.
(4) Mix the lard into the flour by rolling it through your hands. Particles should be the size of peas, with some pieces slightly larger.
(5) Gradually stir egg mixture into flour mixture. Toss ingredients together, quickly but gently until you can gather it into a ball. (Do not press together too hard.)
(6) Divide mixture into nine 170g (6 oz). portions. Round up each portion slightly. Each ball is sufficient for one 22cm. (9-inch) pie crust. (If you are making a double crust pie, you will need two 170g (6 oz.) balls.)

* You will need slightly more than one 170g (6 oz.) ball to make 12 tart shells.
* Any unused portions should be wrapped individually in clear plastic wrap, then placed in a freezer bag. Tie securely; refrigerate or freeze.
* When needed, set desired amount of dough out of freezer. Let thaw at room temperature for four hours or overnight.
* Pie crust should be kept cool. Do not hurry the defrosting.
* A plastic pastry sheet is ideal for rolling pie crust out. It helps immensely in lifting and turning dough. Wet the surface under the plastic pastry sheet to keep it from moving about as you roll the pie crust. (Some pastry sheets have the circles marked on them to help you to determine the size). It is very helpful when folding the pastry in half, you just lift the sheet and fold it over. If dough is stuck to pastry sheet, gently loosen it from the sheet unfolding the pastry sheet as the dough is loosened from it.
* Flatten dough slightly with hands. Roll out one portion of dough on a lightly floured surface into a circle 3cm. (1/8-inch) thick. Starting in the middle each time roll dough out in all directions (with gentle pressure of the rolling pin) into desired size. Sprinkle slightly with flour. Turning dough over every so often makes it easier to handle and not so likely to stick. **Use only enough flour to keep from sticking.
* No need to grease pie plate.
* Place in 22cm. (9-inch) pie plate. Gently press crust down to cover the bottom and sides. Do not trap any air between pie crust and plate. Top and bottom crust must extend 2mL (3/4-inch) over pie plate edge. Do not stretch. If pie crust is stretched at this stage, it will shrink while baking. If crust has to be patched, moisten edges with water and press securely together. Fill pastry-lined pie plate with filling. Moisten edge of bottom

crust with water. Roll out top crust, fold in half or quarters, cut slits or fancy designs near centre folds (not too close to outer edge) to let steam escape.

* Moisten edge of bottom crust again with water. Fit top crust over filling and press outer edges securely together. Trim off excess dough with a sharp knife, use a slashing motion against the pie plate. Pinch edges together, using thumbs and index fingers; forming a rim. Brush rim straight up with fingers. For a crispy-sugary top, brush with milk (using fingers or pastry brush). Sprinkle lightly with sugar, approx. 5mL (1 tsp.).

* Bake in 220°C (425°F) preheated oven for 15 minutes. Reduce heat and bake for 30 minutes longer. Bake pies on lowest rack in the oven when instructed.

* ## To make single pie crust:
Place centre of pie crust in centre of pie plate. (Here again the plastic pastry sheet is so helpful.) Unfold pie crust and using finger tips gently ease crust into place making sure there are no spaces between the pie crust and pie plate. The pie crust must extend 2cm. (3/4-inch) over outer edge of pie plate. Trim off excess dough with a sharp knife. Flute edge of crust using thumbs and index fingers build up a rim. Brush rim straight up with fingers. Set aside and allow dough to crust over and moisture to evaporate. This will help prevent crust from becoming soggy when making custard type pies (pumpkin, rhubarb, etc.).

* ## If crust is to be precooked before filling:
Prick holes in bottom and sides of pie crust using a fork. These holes prevent the pie crust from shrinking so make plenty. Perfect pie #2 recipe should be used when making precooked pie shells. It contains more flour, therefore, less shrinkage in baked pie shells.

* Bake just above centre in 230°C (450°F) oven for 10-12 minutes or until lightly browned.

* ## To make lattice for top of pies:
(First line bottom of a 22cm. (9-inch) pie plate. Set aside. Roll pastry to .3cm. (1/8-inch) thickness and 26.5cm. (10 1/2-inch) oblong from lattice work. With sharp knife, or fancy edge cutter; cut strips 1.5cm. (1/2-inch) wide 26.5cm. (10 1/2-inches) long for a 22cm. (9-inch) pie. You will need 14 strips for each pie.

* Pour filling into lined pie plate. Moisten edge of bottom crust with water. Place pastry stips over filling in basket weave effect. Lay seven pastry strips evenly spaced across top of filling. *Fold back every other strip. Lay one strip across pie plate approx. 2.5cm. (1-inch) from edge of pie plate; unfold previously folded strips back in place. Fold back the opposite strips that were not folded at first. Lay another strip of pastry across pie plate spacing approx. 2cm. (3/4-inch) from first pastry strip. Unfold strips. *Repeat until all pastry strips are in place. Press dough together at outer edge. Trim off excess evenly. Flute edge of pie crust by pinching dough together with thumbs and index fingers, building up a rim. Brush rim straight up with fingers. Bake as directed.

* To line tart shells:
* Roll one portion of pastry into .3cm. (1/8-inch) thickness.
* The size of the circles will differ according to tart tins.
* For tart tins measuring 6.5cm. (2 1/2-inches) across and .2cm. (3/4-inch) deep, you will need your circles cut 9cm. (3 1/2-inches) across.
* Wide mouth sealer screw lids work well. Place pastry circles in tart tins. With slight pressure arrange pastry evenly in each tart mould.
* Spoon filling into pastry fill 3/4 full. If shells are to be precooked prick generously before baking. Bake just above centre in 240°C (475°F) oven until delicately browned. Approx. 8-10 minutes.
** If a top is needed for tarts such as mincemeat, roll pastry .3cm. (1/8-inch) thick, cut into 5cm. (2-inch) circles. Lay pastry circles on top of the filling with tip of a knife gently press edges of circles, so they are laying flat.

Pastry Tips

* Pastry must be handled gently and as little as possible. Mixing the lard into the flour mixture should be done as quickly as possible to prevent the mixture from becoming too warm from the heat of your hands. (I find it so much faster to mix the lard into the flour by hand.) The lard should not be mixed to any smaller than the size of medium peas. It is these small particles of lard that expand when put into a preheated oven at a high temperature 220°C (425°F) for 15 minutes. Reduce heat to 190°C (375°F) and bake for an additional 30 minutes longer. Bake pies on the lowest rick of the oven unless otherwise stated. This is how you achieve a tender and flaky pie crust (custard pies must go on rack just above centre).
* For a crispy-sugary top, brush top of pastry with a little milk and sprinkle lightly with granulated sugar, approx. 5mL (1 tsp.).

To Measure Flour:

* It is important to measure flour accurately. Dip 250mL (1 cup) measure into flour, fill to overflowing. Scrape off straight across top with back edge of a table knife. *Do not pack or shake.

Puff Pastry

These simplified instructions make it easy for the beginner to try...

Remember to keep dough as cool as possible, wrap dough in plastic wrap, set in refrigerator to cool if butter gets too soft. The baking of puff pastry is very important. Preheat oven and follow temperature given.

800mL...3 1/4 cups flour	(1) In a large mixing bowl, stir to-
5mL.....1 tsp. salt	gether flour and salt.
500g.....1 lb. chilled butter	(2) Take butter from fridge, cut in-
(no substitute)	to 2.5cm. (1-inch) strips, then
300mL...1 1/4 cup ice water	into 1.5cm. (1/2-inch) and dice;
50mL....1/4 cup finely ground	add to the flour.
almonds	

****

* Use a metal spoon or fingertips and turn over and over quickly until butter is covered with the flour. Set bowl in fridge to cool if butter has softened.
* Blend in the water, mixing just enough to form a mass.
* Turn dough out onto a slightly floured work surface. A pastry sheet is preferred. Form dough into a ball by quickly pushing it together and rolling it over several times. Roll it out into a triangle 30x38cm. (12x15-inches). Flour top slightly.
* To fold dough, pick up the right edge of dough with your right hand, fold it over middle 1/3 of dough. Now with your left hand pick up left edge of dough and fold it over both layers. Pick up dough, scrape up any dough left on work surface.
* Flour slightly, then giving dough a 1/4 turn set it down so that what was the top edge is now at your right. Roll out again into a triangle, fold into three as before, give it a 1/4 turn so that what was the top edge is now at your right.
* Each roll, fold, turn is called a "turn". Repeat turns 2 more times.
* Wrap the dough in plastic wrap, place in fridge for 45 minutes or longer, to firm the butter.
* Give the dough 2 more turns, working it some first and letting it rest if it seems too hard.
* Roll dough into a triangle slightly thicker than .6cm. (1/4-inch). Brush with egg wash (beat 1 egg yolk, dilute with 10mL (2 Tbsp.) water).
* Sprinkle with very finely ground nuts, or leave plain.
* Using a very sharp knife cut into strips 5x7.5cm. (2x3-inches). Place on ungreased cookie sheet.
* Bake on lowest rack in preheated oven 260°C (500°F) for 10 minutes. Reduce heat to 190°C (375°F) and bake 10 minutes longer. Place on rack to cool.
* Makes 48 pieces.

Lemon Pie

Every bit as good as it looks...

One precooked, cooled 22cm. (9-inch) pie shell.

175mL...3/4 cup sugar	(1) In a double boiler combine sugar, cornstarch, salt and grated peel.
75mL....1/3 cup cornstarch	
1mL.....1/4 tsp. salt	
5mL.....1 tsp. grated lemon peel	(2) Gradually add water. Stir continually and cook until mixture is thick (about 12 min.).
375mL...1 1/2 cups water	
2........2 beaten egg yolks	
15mL....1 Tbsp. butter or margarine	(3) Cover and cook 10 minutes more. Stir occasionally.
90mL....6 Tbsp. lemon juice	(4) Remove mixture from the heat.

****

(5) Pour some of the mixture over beaten eggs, beat and return to mixture in double boiler. A few drops of yellow food coloring may be added.
(6) Cook and stir gently 5 minutes more.
(7) Remove from heat. Stir in butter and lemon juice. Cool 5 minutes. Stir gently twice to let steam escape.
(8) Pour mixture into pie shell.

Top with Meringue

2........2 egg whites	(1) Beat egg whites with cream of tartar until foamy.
1mL.....1/4 tsp. cream of tartar	
75mL....1/3 cup sugar	(2) Gradually add sugar and vanilla.
1mL.....1/4 tsp. vanilla	

****

(3) Whip until stiff enough to form peaks that curl over.
(4) Pile meringue on top of cooked pie.
(5) Bake just above center in 180°C (350°F) oven for 8-10 minutes, or until meringue is delicately browned.

Pumpkin Pie Filling

Served with a dollop of whipped cream...it's no surprise when they ask for seconds...

One deep 25cm. (10-inch) single, unbaked pie shell.

3........3 eggs	(1) Beat eggs slightly, set aside.
150mL...2/3 cup sugar	(2) In a mixing bowl combine
10mL....2 tsp. cinnamon	sugar, spices and salt.
5mL.....1 tsp. ginger	(3) Stir in pumpkin, butter, eggs,
2mL.....1/2 tsp. nutmeg	then milk. Stir well.
2mL.....1/2 tsp. salt	(4) Pour into unbaked pie shell.
375mL...1 1/2 cups cooked	(5) Bake just above centre in 200°C
pumpkin	(400°F) oven for 1 hour.
15mL....1 Tbsp. melted butter or	(6) Pie is done if silver knife insert-
margarine	ed in centre of pie comes out
375mL...1 1/2 cups milk	clean.

* Do not use more than 1 Tbsp. of butter in above recipe.
* If you double this recipe you will need three 22cm. (9-inch) single, unbaked pie shells.
* To help keep the bottom crust from becoming soggy, first brush it lightly with the white of an egg or melted butter. Allowing pie crust to sit several hours to dry out helps also.

Apple Pie

Straight to the heart goes this pie...no detours...
Serve with ice-cream or a piece of cheese, it's a taste treat that's hard to beat...

One 22cm. (9-inch) double, unbaked pie crust.

1L ......4 cups thinly sliced apples	(1) Peel and core apples, slice thin.
175-	(2) Spread apples in unbaked pie
250mL...3/4-1 cup sugar	shell.
1mL.....1/4 tsp. nutmeg	(3) Cover apples with sugar, sprin-
15mL....1 Tbsp. butter or margar-	kle with nutmeg. Dot with but-
ine	ter.
........Milk for brushing crust	(4) Brush outer edge with water.
5mL.....1 tsp. sugar	(5) Fit top crust over filling, press
*********	outer edge securely together.

(6) Brush top with milk, sprinkle with sugar.
(7) Bake on lowest rack in 220°C (425°F) oven for 15 minutes. Reduce heat to 190°C (375°F) and bake 30 minutes longer.

* Fresh apples from new crop require more sugar than mature apples.
* Different types of apples require more sugar, other types require less.
* Individual tastes are different. Choose what your family prefers.

Rhubarb Pie

One 22cm. (9-inch) single, unbaked pie shell.

4........4 egg yolks	(1) Beat egg yolks, set aside.
425mL...1 3/4 cups sugar	(2) Mix sugar, salt, cinnamon and
2mL.....1/2 tsp. salt	flour with evaporated milk.
5mL.....1 tsp. cinnamon	(3) Add to egg yolks.
3mL.....3/4 tsp. flour	(4) Stir in rhubarb. Let stand 15
175mL...3/4 cup evaporated milk	minutes. Stir.
625mL...2 1/2 cups cut up rhubarb	(5) Pour into pie shell.

****

(6) Bake just above center in 190°C (375°F) oven until set (approx. 1 hour).

Top with Meringue

2........2 egg whites	(1) Beat egg whites with cream of
1mL.....1/4 tsp. cream of tartar	tartar until foamy.
175mL...1/3 cup sugar	(2) Gradually add sugar and van-
1mL.....1/4 tsp. vanilla	illa.

****

(3) Whip until stiff enough to form peaks that curl over.
(4) Pile meringue on top of cooked pie.
(5) Bake just above center in 180°C (350°F) oven for 8-10 minutes or until meringue is delicately browned.

Blueberry Pie

One 22cm. (9-inch) double unbaked pie crust.

750mL...3 cups blueberries	(1) Prepare pastry and line 22cm.
175mL...3/4 cup sugar	(9-inch) unbaked pie shell.
45mL....3 Tbsp. flour	(2) Mix sugar and flour together,
15mL....1 Tbsp. lemon juice	add to blueberries and stir well.
15mL....1 Tbsp. butter	(3) Spread in unbaked pie shell.

****

(4) Sprinkle lemon juice over blue-berries.
(5) Dot with butter.
(6) Moisten edge of bottom crust with cold water.
(7) Roll out top crust, fold in half or quarters, cut slits or fancy designs near centre fold, to let steam escape.
(8) Moisten edge of bottom crust again with water, fit top crust over filling and press outer edges securely together.
(9) Trim edge evenly with sharp knife, leave .6cm (1/4-inch) of dough over edge if possible, flute edge with thumbs.
(10) Brush top crust with milk using fingers or pastry bursh.
(11) Sprinkle evenly with 5mL (1 tsp.) sugar.
(12) Bake on lowest rack in 220°C (425°F) oven for 15 minutes, reduce heat to 190°C (375°F) and bake 30 minutes longer.

Flapper Pie

One 20cm. (8-inch) baked, cooled, graham wafer pie shell...

Filling:

125mL...1/2 cup sugar
1mL.....1/4 tsp. salt
30mL....2 Tbsp. cornstarch
15mL....1 Tbsp. flour
500mL...2 cups milk
2........2 slightly beaten egg yolks
15mL....1 Tbsp. butter or margarine
5mL.....1 tsp. vanilla
****

(1) In a saucepan blend together sugar, salt, cornstarch, flour and gradually stir in the milk.
(2) Cook over medium heat, stirring constantly until mixture thickens and boils. Boil for 2 minutes.
(3) Remove from heat, stir a little hot mixture into egg yolks.

(4) Add egg yolks to hot mixture slowly. Stirring to blend.
(5) Boil 1 minute, stirring constantly.
(6) Remove from heat; blend in butter and vanilla.
(7) Cool 10 minutes. Pour into crumb crust.

Meringue:

2........2 egg whites
50mL....1/4 cup sugar
****

(1) Beat egg whites until soft peaks form.

(2) Gradually beat in sugar a little at a time, until meringue is stiff and glossy.
(3) Spread over filling to meet edge of crust.
(4) Sprinkle with fine graham crumbs.
(5) Bake just above centre in 220°C (425°F) oven for 5 minutes.
(6) Cool at room temperature for 3 hours before serving.

Peach Pie

One 22cm. (9-inch) double, unbaked pie crust.

1L ......4 cups sliced peaches
15mL....1 Tbsp. lemon juice
175mL...3/4 cup sugar
45mL....3 Tbsp. cornstarch
1mL.....1/4 tsp. salt
2mL.....1/2 tsp. nutmeg
15mL....1 Tbsp. butter
.........Milk
15mL....1 tsp. sugar
****

(1) In a bowl place sliced peaches, sprinkle with lemon juice.
(2) Mix sugar, cornstarch, salt and nutmeg together.
(3) Combine sugar mixture with peaches. Place into pie shell. Dot with butter.
(4) Cover with top crust.
(5) Flute edges. Brush with milk and sprinkle with sugar.

(6) Bake on lowest rack in 220°C (425°F) oven for 20 minutes. Reduce heat to 190°C (375°F) and bake 35 minutes longer.

Walnut Pie/Pecan Pie

This luscious pie has a jelly-like base, while crunchy walnuts rise to the top...
Top with whipped cream or vanilla ice-cream MMMMMMM...

One 22cm. (9-inch) single, unbaked pie shell.

150mL...2/3 cup sugar	(1) Stir together dry ingredients.
2mL.....1/2 tsp. salt	Set aside.
2mL.....1/2 tsp. cinnamon	(2) In a bowl combine egg, butter
2mL.....1/2 tsp. nutmeg	and corn syrup.
2mL.....1/2 tsp. cloves	(3) Add dry ingredients, beat all to-
3........3 eggs	gether with a rotary beater.
75mL....1/3 cup melted butter	(4) Mix in chopped walnuts.
250mL...1 cup dark corn syrup	(5) Pour into pie crust.
250mL...1 cup chopped walnuts **or**	(6) Bake on lowest rack in 190°C
pecans	(375°F) oven for 40-50 minutes.

****

Topping:

250mL...1 cup whipping cream	(1) Beat together whipping cream,
10mL....2 tsp. instant coffee	instant coffee and sugar until
15mL....1 Tbsp. sugar	stiff.
*********	(2) Spread on pie or pass in side
	dish.

Raisin Pie

One 22cm. (9-inch) double, unbaked pie crust...

500mL...2 cups raisins	(1) In a medium saucepan combine
500mL...2 cups water	raisins, water and lemon rind.
5mL.....1 tsp. grated lemon rind	(2) Cover, cook 5 minutes until
125mL...1/2 cup sugar	tender.
30mL....2 Tbsp. flour	(3) In a bowl combine sugar, flour
.........Pinch of salt	and salt. Stir into raisin mix-
15mL....1 Tbsp. butter	ture.
45mL....3 Tbsp. lemon juice	(4) Cook slowly, stirring constantly
*********	until mixture begins to boil.

(5) Boil 1 minute. Remove from heat.
(6) Stir in butter then lemon juice, mix well.
(7) Pour hot mixture into prepared pie shell.
(8) Cover with top crust.
(9) Bake on lowest rack in 220°C (425°F) oven for 15 minutes, reduce heat to 190°C (375°F) and bake 30 minutes longer.

Boston Cream Pie

One 22cm. (9-inch) round sponge cake.

Cream Filling:

125mL...1/2 cup sugar
75mL....1/3 cup cornstarch
1mL.....1/4 tsp. salt
500mL...2 cups milk
4........4 slightly beaten egg yolks
15mL....1 Tbsp. butter
2mL.....1/2 tsp. vanilla
****

(1) In a medium saucepan, combine sugar, cornstarch and salt. Gradually add milk.
(2) Over medium heat, bring mixture to a boil and boil for 2 minutes, stirring constantly to ensure even thickening, remove from heat.

(3) In a mixing bowl, gradually stir half of hot mixture into the egg yolks, return to hot mixture.
(4) Over medium heat, bring mixture to a boil and boil for 2 minutes, stirring constantly.
(5) Remove from heat. Add vanilla. Chill thoroughly at room temperature.

Chocolate Glaze:

30mL....2 Tbsp. butter
1........1 square unsweetened
        chocolate
250mL...1 cup icing sugar
30mL....2 Tbsp. boiling water
****

(1) In a small saucepan, melt butter and chocolate over low heat. Let cool.
(2) Add sugar and boiling water, beat just until smooth and well combined.

To Assemble Pie:

(1) Cut sponge cake into 2 even layers.
(2) Place bottom layer cut side up, on a serving plate.
(3) Spread with cooled cream filling.
(4) Top with remaining layer cut side down.
(5) Spread chocolate glaze over top of sponge cake.

* Refrigerate if not serving immediately.

Apple Strudel

The easy way... without sacrificing flavour...

Pastry for double crust 25x36x2cm. (10x14x5/8-inch) cookie sheet.

1 1/4L ..5 cups thinly sliced apples	(1) In a bowl combine apple slices, sugar and spices.
150mL...2/3 cup sugar	
2mL.....1/2 tsp. cinnamon	(2) Stir until combined.
2mL.....1/2 tsp. nutmeg	(3) Place in pastry lined cookie sheet.
1mL.....1/4 tsp. cloves	
30mL....2 Tbsp. butter	(4) Dot with butter. Moisten edge of bottom crust with water.
........Milk	
10mL....2 tsp. sugar	(5) Cover with pastry, seal trim and flute edges (see Pastry Tips p. 136).
*********	

(6) With a sharp knife cut through top crust at intervals to let steam escape.

* Make gashes in pattern for easier cutting into 16 pieces later, as shown below.

(7) Brush with milk (using pastry brush or fingers).
(8) Sprinkle with 10mL (2 tsp.) sugar.
(9) Bake just above centre in 190°C (375°F) oven for 45 minutes or until browned.

* Makes 16 pieces.

DIAGRAM: showing gashes in pattern for easier cutting

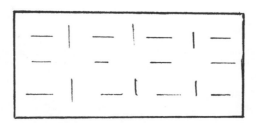

144

Chocolate Pie

Everyone's favorite chocolate pie...truly a taste sensation...

One precooked, cooled 22cm. (9-inch) graham wafer pie shell.

625mL...2 1/2 cups milk	(1) In a double boiler heat milk, add chocolate.
2........2 squares unsweetened chocolate	(2) In a separate bowl stir flour and milk together until smooth.
75mL....1/3 cup flour	Add salt, sugar and cinnamon.
50mL....1/4 cup milk	(3) Stir into double boiler with the chocolate mixture. Cook 15 minutes.
1mL.....1/4 tsp. salt	
250mL...1 cup sugar	
4........4 beaten egg yolks	(4) Pour 125mL (1/2 cup) of hot mixture over beaten egg yolks; beat and add to mixture in double boiler.
30mL....2 Tbsp. butter	
5mL.....1 tsp. vanilla	
*********	

(5) Stir and cook for 3 minutes. Add butter.
(6) Remove from heat, beat gently until very smooth.
(7) Add vanilla. Cool. Stir twice to let steam escape.
(8) Pour into prepared pie shell.

* Cover with whipped cream when completely cooled.

Cherry Pie

One 22cm. (9-inch) double, unbaked pie crust.

625mL...2 1/2 cups pitted cherries fresh or canned	(1) If cherries are canned, drain and reserve 175mL (3/4 cup) liquid.
175mL...3/4 cup fruit juice	
50mL....1/4 cup cornstarch	* If cherries are fresh bring to a boil with 175mL (3/4 cup) water; simmer 5 minutes, drain, reserve juice. Cool 50mL (1/4 cup) of the reserved juice, mix in cornstarch.
175mL...3/4 cup sugar	
5mL.....1 tsp. lemon juice	
15mL....1 Tbsp. butter	
1mL.....1/4 tsp. almond extract	
........Dash of salt	
*********	

(2) In a saucepan combine fruit juice, sugar and cornstarch mixture. Cook and stir over low heat until clear (about 3 minutes).
(3) Remove from heat, add lemon juice, butter, almond extract and salt.
(4) Place cherries in the pie shell, pour the hot juice over them. Cover with top crust.
(5) Bake on lowest rack in 220°C (425°F) oven for 15 minutes, reduce heat to 190°C (375°F) and bake 30 minutes longer.

* Lattice topped pie crust may be used.

Sour Cream Raisin Pie

The sour cream blends in to make a most delicious company fair pie...

One 22cm. (9-inch) double, unbaked pie crust.

500mL...2 cups chopped dark raisins
500mL...2 cups water
45mL....3 Tbsp. golden syrup
125mL...1/2 cup brown sugar
45mL....3 Tbsp. cornstarch
........Pinch of salt
30mL....2 Tbsp. butter or margarine
5mL.....1 tsp. vanilla
5mL.....1 tsp. grated lemon rind
45mL....3 Tbsp. lemon juice
75mL....1/3 cup sour cream
****

(1) In a saucepan combine raisins and water, cover; cook 5 minutes.
(2) Add syrup.
(3) Combine sugar, cornstarch and salt.
(4) Stir into raisins. Cook slowly, stirring constantly, until mixture begins to boil.
(5) Boil 1 minute. Remove from heat.
(6) Stir in butter, vanilla, lemon rind, lemon juice and sour cream.

(7) Pour hot filling into unbaked pie shell.
(8) Moisten outer edge with water.
(9) Fit top crust over filling and press outer edge securely together.

* **Important:** Read about Perfect Pie Crust p. 133; also Pastry Tips p. 136.
* Brush top with milk, using pastry brush or fingers.
* Sprinkle with 5mL (1 tsp.) sugar.
* Bake on lowest rack in 220°C (425°F) oven for 15 minutes, reduce heat to 190°C (375°F) and bake 30 minutes longer.

Banana Cream Pie

(1) Make cream filling as in Coconut Cream Pie p. 147. Omit coconut, add 1 large sliced banana.
(2) Banana may be mixed into filling or pour half the filling into precooked pie shell, add sliced banana, cover with remaining half of filling.
(3) Top with meringue or whipped cream.

* Slices of banana may be placed on top of pie. To keep them from discolouring sprinkle slices with "Ever Fresh" before placing on pie. They give a nice appearance stuck edgewise periodically through the whipped cream. Do this just prior to serving.

146

Coconut Cream Pie

One precooked, cooled 22cm. (9-inch) pie shell.

75mL....1/3 cup cornstarch
125mL...1/2 cup sugar
1mL.....1/4 tsp. salt
500mL...2 cups milk
4........4 well beaten egg yolks
15mL....1 Tbsp. butter
2mL.....1/2 tsp. vanilla
125mL...1/2 cup medium sweetened coconut
  ****

(1) In a medium saucepan combine sugar, cornstarch and salt. Gradually add milk, stir well.

(2) Over medium heat, bring mixture to a boil, boil 2 minutes, stirring constantly to ensure even thickening. Cook slowly for 10 minutes, stirring gently occasionally. Remove from heat.

(3) In a mixing bowl, stir half of the hot mixture into the egg yolks; return to hot mixture.

(4) Over medium heat, bring mixture to a boil and boil for 2 minutes; stirring constantly but gently. Remove from heat, stir in butter, vanilla and then the coconut. Blend well.

(5) Pour into pie shell. Top with meringue or whipped cream. Sprinkle with flaked coconut. Chill thoroughly at room temperature.

* For best results, serve cream pie the same day it's prepared.
* To ward off bacterial activity, refrigerate cream pie if not used the same day.
* Pie may become watery when refrigerated.

Blueberry Pie Filling

1L ......4 quarts blueberries
375mL...1 1/2 cup water, divided
250mL...1 cup cornstarch
750mL...3 cups sugar
50mL....1/4 cup lemon juice
50mL....1/4 cup butter or margarine
  ****

(1) In a large kettle place berries and 125mL (1/2 cup) of the water. Cook slowly 5 minutes until juice has formed.

(2) Dissolve cornstarch in remaining water. Stir cornstarch and sugar into the berries, stir constantly until mixture thickens.

(Stir gently so berries do not become mushy.)
(3) Add lemon juice and butter. Simmer 15 minutes, stir often.
(4) Pour into sterilized jars and seal.

* May be frozen.
* Makes 3 1/2L (3 1/2 Qts.).
* Serve over ice-cream, cake, fruit cobbler, pancakes.
* Use as filling for pie, in unbaked, double crust or lattice topped pie shell. Bake on lowest rack in 220°C (425°F) for 15 minutes, lower heat to 190°C (375°F) for 25 minutes or until pie crust is browned.

Saskatoon Pie

The filling is precooked...not so likely to run over in the oven...

One 22cm. (9-inch) double, unbaked pie crust.

750mL...3 cups saskatoons
125mL...1/2 cup water
175mL...3/4 cup sugar
45mL....3 Tbsp. Jello lemon pie filling
15mL....1 Tbsp. butter
****

(1) In a saucepan bring berries and water to a boil, reduce heat, cover and cook 5 minutes.
(2) Stir sugar and pie filling together and stir into berries.
(3) Stir berries constantly and cook 5 minutes.

(4) Pour into prepared pie shell, dot with butter. Cover with top crust, or make lattice topped pie crust.
(5) Bake on lowest rack in 220°C (425°F) oven for 15 minutes. Reduce heat to 190°C (375°F) oven for 30 minutes longer or until crust is browned.
(6) Serve warm with ice-cream or whipping cream.

Saskatoon Pię Filling

4L ......4 quarts saskatoons
250mL...1 cup water
750mL...3 cups sugar
113g.....1 envelope (3/4 cup) Jello lemon pie filling
****

(1) In a large kettle bring saskatoons and water to a boil, reduce heat. Cover and cook 5 minutes.

(2) Mix sugar and pie filling together and stir into berries. Stir berries constantly and cook 7 minutes.
(3) Pour into sterilized jars and seal. May be frozen.

* Makes 4L (4 Qts.)
* To make Saskatoon Pie, fill uncooked pie shell. Dot with butter, cover with top crust or make lattice topped pie crust. Bake as in Saskatoon Pie.

Lemon or Cream Tarts

* Use Lemon Pie filling, p. 138, or cream filling as in Coconut Cream Pie, p. 147.
* Omit coconut, if desired.
* 1 batch makes 2 1/2 dozen.

Butter Tarts

The golden stamp of approval...our favorite...

Sixteen unbaked tart shells.

75mL....1/3 cup butter or margar-   (1)   Cream butter and sugar to-
         ine   gether. Blend in milk.
250mL...1 cup brown sugar   (2)   Add egg, vanilla and currants.
30mL....2 Tbsp. evaporated milk (3)   Fill unbaked tart shells 3/4 full.
1........1 beaten egg   (4)   Bake just above centre in 180°C
5mL.....1 tsp. vanilla   (350°F) oven for 30 minutes.
125mL...1/2 cup currants
          ****

*   Makes 16 tarts.

Mincemeat Tarts

Twelve unbaked tart shells.

250mL...1 cup mincemeat   (1)   Combine mincemeat and rye
30mL....2 Tbsp. rye whiskey (Opt.)   whiskey.
          ****

(2) Fill tart shells 3/4 full.
(3) Cover with Pastry Circles p. 136.**
(4) Bake just below centre in 190°C (375°F) oven for 30 minutes or until
     pastry is browned.

Mincemeat Pie

One 22cm. (9-inch) double, unbaked pie crust.

750mL...3 cups mincemeat   (1)   Combine mincemeat and rye
50mL....1/4 cup rye whiskey (Opt.)   whiskey.
          ****

(2) Spread into unbaked pie shell.
(3) Moisten edge of bottom crust with cold water.
(5) Cover with top crust. Brush with milk, sprinkle with sugar.
(6) Bake on lowest rack in 220°C (425°F) oven for 15 minutes. Reduce heat
     to 190°C (375°F) and bake 30 minutes longer.

Choice Fruit Slice

Pastry for single crust 25x36x2cm. (10x14x5/8-inch) cookie sheet.

1L ......4 cups finely chopped
　　　　　prune plums
10mL....2 tsp. minute tapioca
500mL...2 cups sugar (divided)
375mL...1 1/2 cups flour
175mL...3/4 cup oatmeal
175mL...3/4 cup butter
****

(1)　In a mixing bowl stir plums, tapioca and 50mL (1/4 cup) sugar together.
(2)　Line cookie sheet with pastry, bringing dough up to edge to form a rim. Pour in fruit, spread evenly.

(3)　Combine flour, sugar, oatmeal and butter until crumbly. Spread evenly over top. Pat gently.
(4)　Bake just below center in 180°C (350°F) oven for 45 minutes to 1 hour.

* 　Cut into 5x7cm. (2x2 3/4-inch) slices, approx. 25.
* 　Variation: Use sliced apples, add 5mL (1 tsp.) cinnamon; cherry pie filling, add 2mL (1/2 tsp.) almond extract; rhubarb is delicious also.

Puddings

Rice Pudding

50mL....1/4 cup uncooked rice
500mL...2 cups milk
2........2 egg yolks
50mL....1/4 cup sugar
1mL.....1/4 tsp. salt
5mL.....1 tsp. vanilla
30mL....2 Tbsp. sugar
50mL....1/4 cup raisins
****

(1) In top of double boiler combine rice and milk. Cook uncovered for 15 minutes.
(2) Add raisins and cook 10 minutes longer or until rice is tender.
(3) Beat together egg yolks, sugar and salt.

(4) Stir some of the rice mixture into the beaten egg mixture.
(5) Add egg mixture to the hot rice mixture.
(6) Cook 3-4 minutes longer, stirring constantly.
(7) Remove from heat, add vanilla.
(8) Pour into individual serving dishes.

Creamy Rice Pudding

The delicious flavour comes from the long, slow cooking...

1L ......4 cups milk
75mL....1/3 cup uncooked rice
75mL....1/3 cup sugar
1mL.....1/4 tsp. salt
1mL.....1/4 tsp. nutmeg **or**
        cinnamon
75mL....1/3 cup raisins
****

(1) Combine all ingredients except the raisins.
(2) Place in a well buttered baking dish 1.5L (1 1/2 Qts.).
(3) Bake just below centre in 140°C (275°F) oven for 2-3 hours or until rice is tender and creamy.

(4) Stir occasionally during first hour of cooking, to prevent rice from settling on the bottom.
(5) After 1 1/2 hours cooking, stir in raisins.

* Pudding will thicken as it cools
* Serve warm or cold.
* Do not over cook rice or have oven too hot as the rice will turn to an undesirable brown colour.

Apple Crisp Pudding

Delicious! Easy to prepare dessert...

1 1/2L ..6 cups thinly sliced apples
15mL....1 Tbsp. lemon juice
250mL...1 cup brown sugar
175mL...3/4 cup flour
3mL.....3/4 tsp. cinnamon
3mL.....3/4 tsp. nutmeg
125mL...1/2 cup butter or margarine
****

(1) Arrange apples in the bottom of a greased 15x25cm. (6x10-inch) baking dish.
(2) Sprinkle with lemon juice.
(3) In a bowl combine, sugar, flour, spices and butter.
(4) Rub through fingers until consistency of peas.

(5) Spread over apple slices.
(6) Bake just above centre in 180°C (350°F) oven for 30 minutes.
(7) Serve warm with milk, cream or ice-cream.

* Serves 6-8.
* For a slightly different crust; replace flour with 250mL (1 cup) graham wafer crumbs and reduce sugar to 125mL (1/2 cup).

Rice-Cream Mould

750mL...3 cups water
500mL...2 cups milk
175mL...3/4 cup rice (uncooked)
3mL.....3/4 tsp. salt
........Dash cinnamon
3........3 envelopes unflavoured gelatine
175mL...3/4 cup sugar
10mL....2 tsp. vanilla
250mL...1 cup whipping cream whipped
****

(1) Combine water, milk, rice, salt and cinnamon in top of double boiler.
(2) Cover and cook over simmering water 40 minutes or until rice is tender. Stir occasionally.
(3) Mix gelatine with sugar; stir into rice until gelatine dissolves.
(4) Pour into large bowl and cool.
(5) Add vanilla. Chill until slightly thickened.
(6) Fold in whipped cream.

(7) Rub mould with a slight amount of salad dressing (makes it easier to remove rice mould from ring before serving).
(8) Pour into a 2L (8 cup) ring mould.
(9) Chill until firm. Unmould and serve with strawberries or kiwi fruit.

* Makes 8-10 servings.

Custard

Good at any time...but especially when soft diet is needed...

4........4 eggs or 8 egg yolks	(1)	Beat eggs slightly, add sugar and salt.
75mL....1/3 cup sugar		
1mL.....1/4 tsp. salt	(2)	Stir in milk and vanilla until well blended.
750mL...3 cups milk		
2mL.....1/2 tsp. vanilla	(3)	Pour into 6 buttered individual custard moulds, or into baking dish 22x22cm. (9x9-inches).

****

(4) Set moulds or baking pan in a pan of warm water.
(5) Bake just below centre in 160°C (325°F) oven for 30-40 minutes, or until knife inserted near the edge of the cup comes out clean.

* Set moulds on wire rack to cool.

Rich Plum Pudding

750g.....1 1/2 lbs. raisins	(1)	Wash raisins and currants. Drain.
500g.....1 lb. currants		
250g.....1/2 lbs. dates cut up	(2)	Leave on cloth over night to dry.
500g.....1 lb. mixed peel		
125mL...1/2 cup thick jam	(3)	Cut dates. Combine all fruit; add jam and mix well.
500g.....1 lb. suet		
500mL...2 cups flour	(4)	Add ground suet to fruit mix and blend.
5mL.....1 tsp. salt		
10mL....2 tsp. cinnamon	(5)	Stir flour and spices together.
2mL.....1/2 tsp. nutmeg	(6)	Add brown sugar and bread crumbs.
1mL.....1/4 tsp. cloves		
500mL...2 cups brown sugar	(7)	Mix together thoroughly.
1L ......4 cups soft bread crumbs	(8)	Add molasses or corn syrup along with eggs, which have been beaten until light.
500mL...2 cups light molasses **or** corn syrup		
5........5 well beaten eggs	(9)	Stir until well blended.

****

(10) Spoon the mixture into two well buttered bowls or moulds.
(11) Fill not more than 2/3 full.
(12) Cover bowl with heavy wax paper.
(13) Tie each bowl in a separate cloth.
(14) Place bowls on rack in kettle (large saucepan, dutch oven or canner).
(15) Fill kettle with water 2/3 up on bowls. Cover. Check water level occasionally. Water must be kept 2/3 up on bowls.
(16) Steam for 3 hours; adding water when necessary.

* Rewarm in same manner.
* Serve with Brown Sugar Sauce p. 156.

Bread Pudding

5........5 slices stale white bread
30mL....2 Tbsp. butter
125mL...1/2 cup seedless raisins
75mL....1/3 cup sugar
1mL.....1/4 tsp. salt
3........3 slightly beaten eggs
750mL...3 cups milk
1mL.....1/4 tsp. cinnamon
30mL....2 Tbsp. brown sugar
****

(1) Butter bread and cut into cubes.
(2) In a buttered casserole alternate layers of bread and raisins.
(3) Mix sugar, salt, eggs and milk.
(4) Pour over bread mixture. Let stand 10 minutes.
(5) Combine cinnamon and sugar and sprinkle over top of pudding.

(6) Bake just below centre in 160°C (325°F) oven for 25 minutes.

* Serves 4-6.

Fruit Cobbler

750mL...3 cups *berries
125mL...1/2 cup sugar
5mL.....1 tsp. cinnamon
15mL....1 Tbsp. butter or margarine
****

(1) Place berries into a 22x22cm. (9x9-inch) cake pan. Mix sugar and cinnamon together and sprinkle over berries. Dot with butter, set aside.

Batter

175mL...3/4 cup sugar
250mL...1 cup flour
2mL.....1/2 tsp. salt
10mL....2 tsp. baking powder
125mL...1/2 cup milk
1........1 slightly beaten egg
30mL....2 Tbsp. melted butter or margarine
2mL.....1/2 tsp. vanilla
****

(2) In a mixing bowl stir sugar, flour, salt and baking powder together.
(3) In another bowl blend milk, egg, butter and vanilla together. Add the milk mixture to the flour mixture, combine until moistened.
(4) Drop batter by spoonfuls evenly

across top of berries. (DO NOT STIR). Bake just above centre in 180°C (350°F) oven for 35 minutes or until the centre tests done.

* You may use various fruits in this recipe: Raspberries, strawberries, blueberries, saskatoons, rhubarb, etc. Just cover bottom of baking pan with water or juice, if berries are dry as in saskatoons or rhubarb.
* Delicious when served warm from oven with ice-cream or cream.

Yorkshire Pudding

2........2 eggs
5mL.....1 tsp. salt
250mL...1 cup flour
250mL...1 cup milk
.........Drippings*
****

(1) In blender beat eggs for 3 minutes.
(2) Add salt.
(3) Mix flour and milk together; add all at once to beaten eggs.

(4) Place .4cm. (1/8-inch) drippings in each muffin tin.
(5) Place in 200°C (400°F) oven until drippings smoke.
(6) Remove from oven. Pour batter into hot drippings; fill muffin tins to .5cm. (1/4-inch) from top (use a pitcher to pour).
(7) Bake just above centre in 200°C (400°F) oven for 15 minutes.
(8) Reduce oven heat to 150°C (300°F) for 25-30 minutes longer.
(9) Turn off oven heat; leave in oven until ready to serve.

* Drippings must be free of any water. If water has been added to roast do not use drippings. Use bacon drippings instead.

Brown Sugar Pudding

A quick and easy dessert is this self-saucing pudding...

250mL...1 cup flour
250mL...1 cup brown sugar
10mL....2 tsp. baking powder
.........Pinch of salt
250mL...1 cup raisins
250mL...1 cup milk
30mL....2 Tbsp. melted butter or
        margarine
****

(1) In a medium mixing bowl stir together flour, sugar, baking powder, salt and raisins. Stir in milk and 30mL (2 Tbsp.) butter. Blend well.
(2) Pour into a well buttered 20cm. (8-inch) pan. Set aside.

Syrup

250mL...1 cup brown sugar
15mL....1 Tbsp. butter or margarine
500mL...2 cups boiling water
5mL.....1 tsp. vanilla, nutmeg, **or** cinnamon
****

(1) Using same mixing bowl as above stir together sugar, butter, boiling water and vanilla, until sugar is dissolved.
(2) Pour over above ingredients.

** DO NOT STIR
(3) Bake just above center in 180°C (350°F) oven for 30 minutes.

* Makes 9 servings.

Christmas Pudding

5mL.....1 tsp. cinnamon
1mL.....1/4 tsp. nutmeg
1mL.....1/4 tsp. cloves
5mL.....1 tsp. allspice
2mL.....1/2 tsp. salt
250mL...1 cup flour
250mL...1 cup brown sugar
250mL...1 cup mixed peel
250mL...1 cup seedless raisins
250mL...1 cup chopped walnuts
250mL...1 cup suet
250mL...1 cup dry crushed bread
        crumbs
3........3 beaten eggs
125mL...1/2 cup sour milk
5mL.....1 tsp. baking soda (scant)
        (Dissolved in small
        amount of hot water)
        ****

(1) Mix spices, flour and sugar together.
(2) Stir in mixed peel, raisins, walnuts, suet and bread crumbs.
(3) Combine beaten eggs, sour milk and soda.
(4) Add to fruit mixture, mix together well.
(5) Pack into sterilized jars.
(6) Process for 3 hours.
*   Makes 2L (2 Qts.).
(7) To reheat, place a metal sealer top in bottom of saucepan. (This will prevent jar from breaking). Place jar of pudding on metal top.
(8) Fill sauce pan with warm water about 3/4 up on the jar.

(9) Place over low heat, simmer for 1 hour or until warm.
(10) Serve warm with following Brown Sugar Sauce and a dollop of whipping cream, if desired.

Brown Sugar Sauce:

250mL...1 cup brown sugar
50mL....1/4 cup flour
500mL...2 cups water
30mL....2 Tbsp. butter
5mL.....1 tsp. vanilla **or** dark rum
        to taste
        ****

(1) In a medium saucepan; mix sugar and flour together.
(2) Slowly add water, place over heat, bring to a boil, stirring constantly.
(3) Boil slowly for 5 minutes.

(4) Lower heat, just enough to keep warm.

Vanilla Pudding

75mL....1/3 cup cornstarch
125mL...1/2 cup sugar
1mL.....1/4 tsp. salt
750mL...3 cups milk
2........2 well beaten egg yolks
15mL....1 Tbsp. butter
5mL.....1 tsp. vanilla
****

(1) In a medium saucepan combine cornstarch, sugar, and salt. Gradually add milk, stir well.
(2) Over medium heat, bring mixture to a boil. Boil 2 minutes, stirring constantly to ensure even thickening.

(3) Cook slowly for 10 minutes. Stirring gently occasionally. Remove from heat.
(4) In a mixing bowl, stir half of the hot mixture into the egg yolks; return to hot mixture.
(5) Over medium heat bring mixture to a boil and boil 2 minutes stirring constantly, but gently. Remove from heat. Stir in butter and vanilla. Blend well.
(6) Pour into individual dessert bowls.

* Makes 4 servings.

Chocolate Pudding

75mL....1/3 cup cocoa
150mL...2/3 cup sugar
1/2mL...1/8 tsp. salt
45mL....3 Tbsp. cornstarch
500mL...2 cups milk
5mL.....1 tsp. vanilla
****

(1) Combine cocoa, sugar, salt, and cornstarch in the top of double boiler.
(2) Gradually add 1/4 cup of the milk and stir until blended. Add the rest of the milk

(3) Place over boiling water, bring to a boil stirring constantly for 2 minutes to ensure even thickening.
(4) Cover and cook slowly 10 minutes. Remove from heat, stir in vanilla. Pour into individual dessert bowls. Serve warm or cold with milk.

* These are very good in the lunch pail. Pour into plastic glasses. Cool completely before putting on lids.
* Makes 500mL (2 cups).

Lemon Sauce

125mL...1/2 cup sugar
35mL....2 Tbsp. + 1 tsp. corn-
        starch
........Pinch of salt
5mL.....1 tsp. grated lemon rind
375mL...1 1/2 cups water
15mL....1 Tbsp. butter
50mL....1/4 cup lemon juice
****

(1) In a medium saucepan stir together sugar, cornstarch, salt
and lemon rind.
(2) Gradually add water; stir continually and cook until mixture
is thick.
(3) Cover and cook 8 minutes, over
low heat. Stir occasionally.

(4) Remove from heat, stir in butter then lemon juice.
(5) Pour into glass container. Serve warm over heavy fruit puddings and
ginger bread, or cold over cheese cakes.

* Makes 375mL (1 1/2 cups).

Gingerbread

500mL...2 cups flour
2mL.....1/2 tsp. salt
2mL.....1/2 tsp. cinnamon
5mL.....1 tsp. baking powder
2mL.....1/2 tsp. ginger
2mL.....1/2 tsp. nutmeg
125mL...1/2 cup butter or margar-
        ine
250mL...1 cup brown sugar
125mL...1/2 cup molasses
150mL...2/3 cup boiling water
5mL.....1 tsp. baking soda
2........2 well beaten eggs
****

(1) Stir together flour, salt, baking
powder, nutmeg, cinnamon
and ginger. Set aside.
(2) Cream butter and sugar together, add molasses.
(3) Pour boiling water over soda,
stir and add to first mixture.
(4) Add flour and spices, then
eggs.
(5) Beat well. Pour into a well buttered wax paper lined 22x22cm.
(9x9-inch) cake pan.

(6) Bake just above center in 160°C (325°F) oven for 40 minutes or until
done.
(7) Let cool for 10 minutes in pan before removing to wire rack.
(8) Serve with whipped cream.

158

Squares

Brownies

Double chocolate... double delicious...

250mL...1 cup butter or margarine
125g.....4 oz. unsweetened chocolate
2........2 large eggs
250mL...1 cup sugar
250mL...1 cup brown sugar
5mL.....1 tsp. vanilla
1mL.....1/4 tsp. salt
5mL.....1 tsp. baking powder
250mL...1 cup flour
500mL...2 cups frozen mini marshmallows
250mL...1 cup chopped walnuts
250mL...1 cup semi-sweet chocolate chips **or**
125mL...1/2 cups chocolate chips &
125mL...1/2 cup chopped white chocolate
****

(1) Heat butter and 125g (4 oz.) of chocolate over hot water until melted. Cool slightly.
(2) In a large bowl cream together butter mixture with eggs, white and brown sugar. Beat vigorously until mixture is thick about 5 min.
(3) Stir in vanilla. Combine salt, baking powder and flour; gradually blend into creamed mixture.
(4) Fold in frozen marshmallows, walnuts, chocolate chips and white chocolate.
(5) Gently pour mixture into buttered 22x33cm. (9x13-inch) baking pan. Spread until smooth.

(6) Bake just above center in 180°C (350°F) oven for about 35 minutes.

* Brownies will feel soft but will firm up when cooled. When slightly cooled cut into squares. Allow to finish cooling in pan.
* Makes 24 squares.

Wheat Puffs

By popular request... again and again...

75mL....1/3 cup butter
125mL...1/2 cup syrup
250mL...1 cup brown sugar
30mL....2 Tbsp. cocoa
5mL.....1 tsp. vanilla
2L ......8 cups wheat puffs
****

(1) Melt butter in a large saucepan.
(2) Add syrup, sugar, cocoa and vanilla.
(3) When this mixture begins to bubble, remove from heat.
(4) Add wheat puffs. Mix well.

(5) Put in 22x33cm. (9x13-inch) pan. Press down with spoon.
(6) Let cool. Cut into squares.

Peanut Butter Squares

Absolutely delicious. . .

15mL. . . .1 Tbsp. butter
125mL. . .1/2 cup syrup
125mL. . .1/2 cup sugar
250mL. . .1 cup crunchy peanut
        butter
500mL. . .2 cups cornflakes
250mL. . .1 cup rice krispies
5mL. . . . .1 tsp. vanilla
****

(1) Dissolve over medium heat; butter, syrup and sugar.
(2) Remove from heat.
(3) Stir in peanut butter, cornflakes, rice krispies and vanilla.
(4) Pour into 22x22cm. (9x9-inch) square pan. Spread evenly.

Icing:

125mL. . .1/2 cup brown sugar
20mL. . . .4 tsp. cream
45mL. . . .3 Tbsp. butter
125mL. . .1/2 cup icing sugar
****

(1) Combine in medium saucepan, brown sugar, cream and butter.
(2) Bring to a boil and simmer gently for 3 minutes.

(3) Remove from heat. Cool a little and add icing sugar. Spread evenly.

Chocolate Logs

Very colourful. . .very tasty. . .a must at Christmas time. . .

250mL. . .1 cup sifted icing sugar
125mL. . .1/2 cup short sweetened
        coconut
250g. . . . .1/2 lb. coloured marsh-
        mallows cut into quart-
        ers
2. . . . . . . .2 squares (2 oz.) unsweet-
        ened chocolate
2. . . . . . . .2 squares (2 oz.) semi-
        sweet chocolate
30mL. . . .2 Tbsp. butter or margar-
        ine
1. . . . . . . .1 egg
. . . . .Long sweetened coconut
****

(1) In a medium mixing bowl, mix icing sugar, short coconut and marshmallows together. Set aside.
(2) In top of double boiler melt butter and chocolate together.
(3) Add egg, beat well. Cook a few minutes longer.
(4) Pour over sugar mixture. Blend well.
(5) Shape into a thick roll, on wax paper. Sprinkle all sides with long coconut. Roll tightly.
(6) Place on sheet of tin foil and roll tightly.

(7) Place in refrigerator. Slice when cold.

* Freezes well.

160

Coconut Bars

A tried and true recipe is this one. . . very delicious. . .

Base:

125mL. . .1/2 cup butter	(1) Cream butter, brown sugar and
125mL. . .1/2 cup brown sugar	flour together.
firmly packed	(2) Press firmly into a buttered
250mL. . .1 cup flour	20x30cm. (8x12-inch) pan.
*********	

(3) Bake just above centre in 160°C (325°F) oven for 20 minutes.

* Do not brown.

Topping:

250mL. . .1 cup brown sugar	(1) Stir together brown sugar,
firmly packed	flour, baking powder and salt.
30mL. . . .2 Tbsp. flour	Set aside.
2mL. . . . .1/2 tsp. baking powder	(2) Beat eggs and vanilla, stir in
1/2mL. . .1/8 tsp. salt	dry ingredients. Beat until light.
2. . . . . . . .2 eggs (beaten)	(3) Stir in walnuts just to blend.
5mL. . . . .1 tsp. vanilla	(4) Spread over partially baked
250mL. . .1 cup walnuts (chopped)	batter.
250mL. . .1 cup shredded coconut	(5) Sprinkle with coconut.
*********	

(6) Bake just above centre in 160°C (325°F) oven for 25 minutes or until meringue is browned.

* Cut into small bars while warm, cool in pan.

Hello Dolly Bars

Truly a winner. . .be sure and try these bars. . .

175mL. . .1/3 cup butter	(1) Melt butter, add crumbs, coco-
250mL. . .1 cup graham wafer	nut, sugar, vanilla and egg.
crumbs	(2) Press into 20x20cm. (8x8-inch)
15mL. . . .1 Tbsp. medium sweetened	pan.
coconut	(3) Sprinkle with chocolate chipits,
15mL. . . .1 Tbsp. sugar	then crushed walnuts.
5mL. . . . .1 tsp. vanilla	(4) Pour condensed milk over
1. . . . . . . .1 egg (beaten)	(Do not mix).
250mL. . .1 cup chocolate chipits	(5) Bake just above centre in 180°C
250mL. . .1 cup finely crushed	(350°F) oven for 30 minutes.
walnuts	
340mL. . .12 oz. sweetened condens-	
ed milk	
*********	

* Bar will be soft when warm; cut when cool.

Bran Muffins

So handy to have ready in the fridge...a real time saver on busy mornings...

500mL...2 cups all bran cereal	(1) Pour boiling water over all bran. Cool slightly.
500mL...2 cups boiling water	
1 1/4L ..5 cups flour	(2) Stir flour, soda and salt together thoroughly. Set aside.
45mL....3 Tbsp. baking soda	
15mL....1 Tbsp. salt	(3) Cream margarine and sugar.
250mL...1 cup shortening	(4) Add eggs then buttermilk.
250mL...1 cup brown sugar	(5) Add cooled bran mixture, add bran flakes, then flour mixture.
500mL...2 cups white sugar	
1L ......1 Qt. buttermilk	(6) Fold mixture till moist.
4........4 eggs	(7) Add raisins or dates.
1L ......4 cups bran flakes	(8) Fill well buttered or paper lined muffin tins 3/4 full.
500mL...2 cups raisins **or** chopped dates	
**********	(9) Bake just above centre in 200°C (400°F) oven for 25 minutes.

* Let stand for 5 minutes. Remove and place on wire rack to cool.
* Batter may be left in refrigerator and used as required.
* Keeps up to six weeks.
* Do not beat or mix again; just spoon into well buttered or paper lined muffin tins.
* Choose unsugared bran flakes.

Variations:

* Use one of these mixtures for a nice change...
  175mL...3/4 cup of orange filling, mocha sauce or date filling (see Icings).
* Line large muffin tins, fill almost half full of bran mixture, place 15mL (1 Tbsp.) of mocha sauce, orange filling or date filling on top of mixture. Place additional bran mixture on top of filling.
* Bake as instructed above.

Chocolate Muffins

The addition of bananas makes these muffins moist and adds flavour...

150mL...2/3 cup sugar
75mL....1/3 cup cocoa
500mL...2 cups flour
5mL.....1 tsp. salt
10mL....2 tsp. baking powder
1........1 beaten egg
250mL...1 cup mashed bananas
250mL...1 cup milk
75mL....1/3 cup salad oil
5mL.....1 tsp. vanilla
250mL...1 cup chopped walnuts
****

(1) In a mixing bowl stir sugar, cocoa, flour, salt and baking powder together. Set aside.
(2) In another bowl, combine egg, milk, bananas, oil and vanilla. Add all at once to dry ingredients; stirring just until moistened.
(3) Stir in nuts.
(4) Spoon mixture into 12 large paper lined muffin cups.

* Cups will look very full but not to worry, they won't run over.

(5) Bake just above centre in 225°C (425°F) oven for 20-25 minutes.
(6) Sprinkle with icing sugar.

* Makes 12.

Buttermilk Bran Muffins

375mL...1 1/2 cups 60% whole
        wheat flour
250mL...1 1/4 cups bran
250mL...1 cup firmly packed
        brown sugar
10mL....2 tsp. soda
5mL.....1 tsp. baking powder
2mL.....1/2 tsp. salt
250mL...1 cup raisins
125mL...1/2 cup oil
500mL...2 cups buttermilk
175mL...3/4 cup drained, crushed
        pineapple
2........2 slightly beaten eggs
750mL...3 cups all-bran cereal
****

(1) Combine whole wheat flour, bran, brown sugar, baking powder, soda and salt. Set aside.
(2) In a small bowl stir raisins and oil together. Set aside.
(3) Mix buttermilk, pineapple and eggs together. Set aside.
(4) In a medium bowl, combine all-bran cereal, buttermilk mixture, then the raisin and oil mixture.
(5) Add flour mixture stirring only until combined.
(6) Spoon mixture into well buttered or paper lined muffin tins.
(7) Bake just above center in 200°C (400°F) oven for 20 min. Let stand for 5 minutes.

(8) Remove muffins to wire rack to cool.

* For larger muffins, spoon batter into well buttered oven proof custard cups. Bake as above for 25 minutes.
* Makes 24 regular or 12 extra large muffins.

Graham Cracker Pineapple Squares

An elegant dessert to serve your guests...

First Layer:

250mL...1 cup graham wafer crumbs
125mL...1/2 cup brown sugar
37mL....2 1/2 Tbsp. butter
****

(1) Mix wafer crumbs, sugar and butter together.
(2) Press in 20x20cm. (8x8-inch) pan.

(3) Bake just above centre in 190°C (375°F) oven for 8 minutes. Cool.

Second Layer:

2........2 eggs
125mL...1/2 cup butter
325mL...1 1/3 cup icing sugar
****

(1) Mix eggs, butter and icing sugar together.
(2) Spread over first layer.

Third Layer:

250mL...1 cup whipping cream
1........1 can drained crushed pineapple 392g (14 oz.)
****

(1) Whip cream until stiff peaks form.
(2) Fold in crushed pineapple.
(3) Spread over second layer.

(4) Refrigerate for several hours.
(5) Cut into squares, serve in paper baking cups.

Rice Krispie Squares

By popular request...

50mL....1/4 cup butter
1L ......4 cups miniature marsh-mallows **or** 40 regular marshmallows
1 1/4L ..5 cups rice krispies
2mL.....1/2 tsp. vanilla
****

(1) In a 3L (3 Qt.) saucepan melt butter, add marshmallows.
(2) Cook over low heat, stirring constantly until marshmallows are melted.

(3) Remove from heat, stir in vanilla then rice krispies. Stir until well coated.
(4) Press into a buttered 22x33cm. (9x13-inch) pan.
(5) Cut into squares when cool.

164

Nanaimo Bars

Well known to all...loved by everyone...

500mL...2 cups graham wafer crumbs	(1) Mix wafer crumbs, walnuts and coconut together. Set aside.
250mL...1 cup coconut	(2) In the top of a double boiler, over hot water, place butter, sugar, cocoa, vanilla and egg.
125mL...1/2 cup chopped walnuts	
125mL...1/2 cup butter	
75mL....1/3 cup sugar	(3) Stir mixture until butter has melted and is the consistency of custard.
75mL....1/3 cup cocoa	
2mL.....1/2 tsp. vanilla	
1........1 beaten egg	(4) Remove from heat.

****

(5) Add crumb mixture to the cocoa mixture.
(6) Blend well, pack into unbuttered 22x22cm. (9x9-inch) pan.

* Spread with the following icing.

Icing:

30mL....2 Tbsp. vanilla custard powder	(1) Combine custard powder with milk.
45mL....3 Tbsp. milk	(2) Add butter.
75mL....1/3 cup butter	(3) Mix in icing sugar.
500mL...2 cups sifted icing sugar	(4) Spread over base, allow to set for 1/2 hour.
4........4 squares (4 oz.) melted semi-sweet chocolate	
30mL....2 Tbsp. butter or margarine	(5) Melt chocolate with 30mL (2 Tbsp.) butter, spread evenly.

****

Chocolate Squares

125mL...1/2 cup butter	(1) Cream butter and sugar together until well blended.
250mL...1 cup brown sugar	
2........2 well beaten eggs	(2) Add eggs, vanilla, then chocolate. If using cocoa, sift cocoa and flour together.
5mL.....1 tsp. vanilla	
45g......1 1/2 squares melted unsweetened chocolate **or** 3 Tbsp. cocoa	(3) Add flour. Stir in walnuts.
	(4) Pour into buttered 20x20cm. (8x8-inch) cake pan.
175mL...3/4 cup flour	(5) Bake just above centre in 180°C (350°F) oven for 25-30 minutes.
250mL...1 cup walnuts	

****

* Cool in pan.

165

Oh Henry Bars

Very rich chocolate bar flavour...

150mL...2/3 cups butter
250mL...1 cup brown sugar
1L ......4 cups quick rolled oats
125mL...1/2 cup corn syrup
........Dash salt
15mL....3 tsp. vanilla
250mL...1 cup chocolate chips
     (light)
150mL...2/3 cup peanut butter
425mL...1 3/4 cups coarsely crush-
     ed salted peanuts
****

(1) Cream butter and sugar.
(2) Add rolled oats, syrup, salt and vanilla.
(3) Press firmly into buttered 22x33 cm. (9x13-inch) cake pan.
(4) Bake just above centre in 190°C (375°F) oven for 15 minutes. Cool slightly.
(5) Melt chocolate chips and peanut butter in double boiler. Pour over base.

(6) Sprinkle with peanuts.
(7) Gently press, embedding peanuts slightly.
(8) Refrigerate.
(9) Cut into small squares when cool.

Raspberry or Rhubarb Slice

An attractive addition to your tray of goodies...

Base:

250mL...1 cup flour
30mL....2 Tbsp. icing sugar
........Few grains of salt
75mL....1/3 cup margarine
175mL...3/4 cup jam of your
     choice
****

(1) In a mixing bowl stir together flour, icing sugar and salt. Blend in margarine.
(2) Press into 20x20cm. (8x8-inch) pan.
(3) Spread bottom layer with jam.

Topping:

375mL...1 1/2 cup medium grind
     coconut
250mL...1 cup sugar (scant)
15mL....1 Tbsp. butter
1........1 beaten egg
5mL.....1 tsp. vanilla
****

(1) Combine coconut, sugar and butter. Mix well.
(2) Add egg and vanilla.
(3) Drop by tablespoon on top of jam base, spread carefully.
(4) Bake just above centre in a 180°C (350°F) oven for 25-30 minutes.

(5) Cool and cut into squares.

Lemon Slice

A light, delightful dessert...

Base:

250mL...1 cup graham wafer crumbs	(1) Mix crumbs, butter and brown sugar together well.
125mL...1/2 cup butter	(2) Press into 20x20cm. (8x8-inch) pan.
125mL...1/2 cup brown sugar	
*********	

(3) Bake just above centre in 180°C (350°F) oven for 10 minutes.

Filling:

1........1 lemon, grated rind and juice	(1) In a saucepan mix together lemon rind, lemon juice, sugar, beaten egg yolks and hot water.
175mL...3/4 cup sugar	
3........3 egg yolks (beaten)	(2) Cook until thick.
45mL....3 Tbsp. hot water	(3) Fold in beated egg whites.
3........3 egg whites (beaten)	(4) Pour over first mixture.
*********	

(5) Sprinkle top with dry wafer crumbs.
(6) Return to oven for 3 minutes.

Graham Gems

A delightful taste...easy to make old time muffins...

175mL...3/4 cup graham flour	(1) Stir together graham flour, white flour, soda and salt. Set aside.
125mL...1/2 cup white flour	
2mL.....1/2 tsp. baking soda	
2mL.....1/2 tsp. salt	(2) Cream together brown sugar and butter, stir in sour cream.
250mL...1 cup brown sugar	
125mL...1/2 cup butter	(3) Beat egg slightly, add to sugar butter mixture.
250mL...1 cup sour cream	
1........1 egg	(4) Add dry ingredients.
*********	

(5) Stir just enough to moisten flour.
(6) Fill well buttered or paper lined muffin tins 3/4 full.
(7) Bake just above centre in 220°C (425°F) oven for 15-20 minutes.

* Let stand 5 minutes. Remove and place on wire rack to cool.

Magic Lemon Squares

A delicate, lemon flavour sandwiched between a walnut-coconut crumb crust...

250mL...1 cup quick oats (uncooked)
250mL...1 cup flour
125mL...1/2 cup flaked coconut
125mL...1/2 cup coarsely chopped walnuts
125mL...1/2 cup firmly packed brown sugar
5mL.....1 tsp. baking powder
125mL...1/2 cup melted butter or margarine
1........1 can sweetened condensed milk
125mL...1/2 cup lemon juice
****

(1) In a medium bowl combine oats, flour, coconut, nuts, sugar, baking powder and butter. Stir to form a crumbly crust. Set aside.
(2) In another bowl combine sweetened condensed milk and lemon juice.
(3) Spread 1/2 of the crumb mixture (press quite lightly) into bottom of 22x22cm. (9x9-inch) pan.
(4) Spread sweetened condensed milk mixture on top and spread with remaining crumbs.

(5) Bake just above centre in 180°C (350°F) oven for 30-35 minutes or until light brown. Cool before cutting.

Cherry Cha Cha

An easy make ahead dessert... very colourful...

625mL...2 1/2 cups graham cracker crumbs
50mL....1/4 cup icing sugar
125mL...1/2 cup cooking oil
250mL...1 cup whipping cream (whipped)
1L ......4 cups miniature marshmallows
540mL...19 oz. can cherry pie filling
****

(1) In a mixing bowl combine cracker crumbs, icing sugar and cooking oil together.
(2) Press 2/3 of crumb mixture into a 22x33cm. (9x13-inch) pan (Save 1/3 for top of cake).
(3) Bake just above centre in 180°C (350°F) oven for 10 minutes. Cool completely.
(4) Stir whipped cream and marshmallows together.

(5) Spread half the cream mixture over the crumbs.
(6) Spread cherry pie filling over the cream.
(7) Spread remaining cream mixture over the pie filling.
(8) Sprinkle with the rest of the crumb mixture.
(9) Refrigerate overnight or all day.

Crunchy Spice Bars

These little bars have a crunchy, gingerbread taste...

125mL...1/2 cup sifted flour
1mL.....1/4 tsp. baking soda
1mL.....1/4 tsp. mace
1mL.....1/4 tsp. allspice
1mL.....1/4 tsp. salt
2mL.....1/2 tsp. cinnamon
1........1 beaten egg
175mL...3/4 cup brown sugar
45mL....3 Tbsp. melted butter or
         margarine
75mL....1/3 cup toasted sesame
         seeds*
****

(1) Stir together flour, baking soda, mace, allspice, salt and cinnamon. Set aside.
(2) Gradually add sugar to beaten egg. Mix well.
(3) Stir in butter, then spice mixture.
(4) Sprinkle half the sesame seeds over the bottom of the buttered 20x20cm. (8x8-inch) cake pan. Pour in batter carefully. Spread evenly.

(5) Sprinkle with remaining seeds.
(6) Bake just above centre in 180°C (350°F) oven for 20 minutes. Let cool. Cut into bars.

* To toast sesame seeds...spread seeds in a shallow pan. Place just above centre in 180°C (350°F) oven for 10 minutes.

Trifle

I'm sure you will find this dessert special...especially tasty, colourful and easy to prepare...

22cm ....9-inch sponge cake p. 177.
175mL...3/4 cup raspberry jam
125mL...1/2 cup sherry
1L ......4 cups prepared vanilla
         pudding
375mL...1 1/2 cups fresh rasp-
         berries or halved straw-
         berries. Frozen fruit
         may be used in off sea-
         son. If frozen, thaw,
         drain well and pre-
         sweeten.
375mL...1 1/2 cups whipping
         cream (whipped)
****

(1) Cut cake in half horizontally.
(2) Place bottom half of cake in a large glass bowl.
(3) Spread jam over bottom half of cake.
(4) Replace top half. Sprinkle with sherry and chill for four hours.
(6) Prepare pudding, chill until cool but not set.
(7) Without removing cake from bowl cut into serving pieces, pushing pieces slightly apart with the knife.

(8) Pour pudding over cake. Chill 4 hours or overnight.
(9) Just before serving top with berries, whipped cream and additional berries.

* Serves 8.

Cream Puffs

250mL...1 cup flour
5mL.....1 tsp. baking powder
2mL.....1/2 tsp. sugar
1/2mL...1/8 tsp. salt
250mL...1 cup water
125mL...1/2 cup butter
3........3 eggs unbeaten**
        ****

(1) Stir flour, baking powder, sugar and salt together. Set aside.
(2) Bring water and butter to a boil. Stir until butter is melted. Remove from heat.
(3) Stir in flour mixture all at once.
(4) Stirring vigorously, cook until the mixture forms a mass, leaving the sides of the pot clean. Cool for 5 minutes.
(5) Add eggs one at a time, beating well after each addition.
(6) Drop in mounds about size of an egg, well apart on a buttered cookie sheet.
(7) Bake just above centre in 220°C (425°F) oven for 15 minutes. Lower heat to 180°C (350°F) and bake until puffs are delicately browned, about 25 minutes for average size puffs, or 15 minutes for small puffs.
(8) Turn heat off, open oven door and allow puffs to dry 10 minutes. Remove from oven.
(9) Cool on wire rack.
(10) When cool make a slit in the side and fill with flavoured whipping cream (whipped).
(11) Dust with icing sugar.

* Makes 12 puffs.

Chocolate Eclairs

(1) Follow same recipe as above, instead of shaping into puffs, form into 12 10x2.5cm. (4x1-inch) bars on a buttered baking sheet.
(2) Bake just above centre in 200°C (400°F) oven for 40-50 minutes. Let stand in oven with door opened to cool.
(3) Split eclairs open on one side.
(4) Scoop out any soft centre dough, if any.
(5) Fill with cream filling, as in Coconut Cream Pie p. 147. Omit coconut. Use a pastry tube to fill eclairs.
(6) Ice with chocolate or mocha icing.

Cakes

Preparation Details for Fruit Cakes

Have these tasks done the day before you make your fruit cake...

Lining Cake Tins:
* Place cake tins on brown paper, trace bottoms, cut out size required. Measure sides and extend paper 2 1/2cm. (1-inch) higher than tins and 5cm. (2-inches) longer around tins to allow for overlapping of seams (straight strips).
* Having the 2 1/2cm. (1-inch) extension helps to keep the top of the cake from drying out.
* Butter cake tins, lay brown paper on flat surface and butter both sides. Margarine may be used in place of butter to grease brown paper.
* Line cake tins bottoms first making sure paper fits snugly in corners if square tins are used.
* To keep free from dust cover until ready to use.

* Wash raisins and currants. Strain through colander. Place single layer on towel to dry (use an old towel as fruit will stain). Leave overnight to dry. May be covered with absorbent paper.
* Cut glazed fruit, pineapple, chop mixed peel, if needed. Cut cherries in half. Keep covered with tight fitting lid to prevent drying out. Chop walnuts. Do not add until cake is mixed.
* Separate eggs while cold. Cover tightly. Do not beat until ready to use. Do not refrigerate.
* The day the cake is baked, add raisins, nuts and currants to the fruit mixture. Dredge (coat) with 375mL (1 1/2 cups) of measured flour.
* Let cakes remain in tins for 2 hours before removing.
* Cool completely before wrapping.
* Do not remove brown paper from cakes until ready to ice or serve.
* To store cakes: wrap in plastic wrap, then wrap securely again in tin foil.
* These cakes freeze well...they mellow while being stored...they will keep for a year or more in the freezer.
* Make sure the cakes are wrapped very well.
* Fruit cakes should be made at least 1 month before serving.

Dark Fruit Cake

*A rich, heavy, luscious fruit cake...use for wedding or Christmas cakes...
For Preparation Details see p. 171.*

10mL....2 tsp. cinnamon
1mL.....1/4 tsp. EACH of cloves,
       nutmeg and allspice
5mL.....1 tsp. mace and salt
5mL.....1 tsp. baking soda (dis-
       solved in 30mL (2
       Tbsp.) hot water
500mL...2 cups brown sugar
250mL...1 cup white sugar
500g.....1 lb. butter
10.......10 medium eggs
       (separated)
500g.....1 lb. currants
500g.....1 lb. sultana raisins
500g.....1 lb. seeded raisins
500g.....1 lb. walnuts
500g.....1 lb. mixed peel
250g.....1/2 lb. glazed fruit
250g.....1/2 lb. glazed pineapple
500g.....1 lb. red cherries (halved)
500g.....1 lb. green cherries
375mL...1 1/2 cups grape jelly
1125mL..4 1/2 cups flour (divided)
****

(1) Stir together cinnamon, cloves, nutmeg, allspice, mace and salt. Set aside.
(2) Cream butter, add sugar gradually. Blend well.
(3) Blend in spices, baking soda, grape jelly, beaten egg yolks and 750mL (3 cups) flour. (375mL (1 1/2 cups) flour reserved for coating fruit.)
(4) Pour over prepared fruit.
(5) Blend all together well.
(6) Whip egg whites until stiff but not dry.
(7) Mix whipped egg whites into fruit mixture. Blend well.
(8) Pour into well buttered brown paper lined cake tins.
* 2-20x20x9cm. (8x8x3 1/2-inch) 1-15x15x7 1/2cm. (6x6x3-inch) 1-10x10x5cm. (4x4x2-inch).
(9) Fill 2/3 full. Spread evenly.

(10) Bake just below centre in 140°C (275°F) oven for 4 hours for larger layer...3 hours for medium and 2 1/2 hours for small layer or until tests done when tested with a toothpick.
(11) Place on wire rack to cool in tins for 2 hours before removing.

* Makes approx. 5.90kg (13 lbs.).

Light Fruit Cake

Heavy with fruit. . . very colourful. . .
For Preparation Details see p. 171.

2mL.....1/2 tsp. salt
5mL.....1 tsp. baking powder
1125mL..4 1/2 cups flour
500g.....1 lb. butter
500mL...2 cups sugar
9........9 eggs
500mL...2 cups chopped walnuts
500mL...2 cups mixed peel
500mL...2 cups glazed red cherries
500mL...2 cups glazed green
          cherries
500mL...2 cups sultana raisins
1........1 rind and juice from 1
          lemon
          ****

(1)   Stir together salt, baking pow-
      der and 875mL (3 1/2 cups)
      flour. (Set aside 250mL (1 cup)
      flour for coating fruit.)
(2)   Cream butter, add sugar grad-
      ually.
(3)   Add eggs one at a time, beating
      well after each egg addition.
(4)   Blend in flour mixture. Then
      lemon juice and rind.
(5)   Pour over prepared fruit; blend
      all together well.
(6)   Pour into well buttered brown
      paper lined cake tins.

(7)   Bake just below centre in a 140°C (275°F) oven for 3-3 1/2 hours or un-
      til centre tests done when tested with a toothpick.

*   Place on wire rack. Let cool 2 hours in tins.

Zucchini Nut Loaf

Just a good, tasty loaf...freezes well...

250mL...1 cup grated raw, unpeel-
          ed zucchini
375mL...1 1/2 cups flour
7mL.....1 1/2 tsp. cinnamon
2mL.....1/2 tsp. pumpkin pie spice
2mL.....1/2 tsp. salt
2mL.....1/2 tsp. baking powder
1........1 egg
250mL...1 cup sugar
125mL...1/2 cup oil
7mL.....1 1/2 tsp. vanilla
125mL...1/2 cup chopped walnuts
          ****

(1)   Grate zucchini. Drain well.
      Measure 1 cup.
(2)   Stir flour, cinnamon, pumpkin
      pie spice, salt and baking pow-
      der together. Set aside.
(3)   Beat egg well, blend in sugar,
      zucchini, oil and vanilla.
(4)   Add flour mixture blending just
      until mixed.
(5)   Fold in walnuts.
(6)   Pour into a buttered, waxed
      paper lined 23x12x7cm. (9x5x3-
      inch) loaf pan.

(7)   Bake just above centre in 160°C (325°F) oven for 1-1 1/2 hours.
(8)   Let stand in baking pan for 20 minutes before removing to rack.
(9)   Wrap when completely cool.

Mocha Frosted Coffee Cake

The coffee gives a delightful, more pleasing flavour....

500mL...2 cups flour
10mL....2 tsp. cinnamon
5mL.....1 tsp. baking soda
2mL.....1/2 tsp. salt
5mL.....1 tsp. baking powder
500mL...2 cups brown sugar
250mL...1 cup margarine
2........2 beaten eggs
5mL.....1 tsp. vanilla
250mL...1 cup hot coffee
250mL...1 cup raisins
175mL...3/4 cup chopped walnuts
****

(1) Stir together flour, cinnamon, salt, baking soda and baking powder. Set aside.
(2) Cream sugar and margarine together until light and fluffy.
(3) Add eggs and vanilla.
(4) Add flour mixture alternately with hot coffee.
(5) Fold in raisins and walnuts.
(6) Pour into a buttered waxed paper lined 22x22cm. (9x9-inch) cake pan.

(7) Bake just above centre in 180°C (350°F) oven for 45 minutes.
(8) Cool and spread with icing.

Icing:

45mL....3 Tbsp. margarine
1mL.....1/4 tsp. maple flavouring
         or almond extract
45mL....3 Tbsp. hot coffee
5mL.....1 tsp. vanilla
500mL...2 cups icing sugar
........Few grains of salt.
****

(1) Cream margarine with flavouring, coffee and vanilla.
(2) Gradually add icing sugar (salt added) to a spreading consistency.

Spice Cake

This is a very tasty cake...sure to please...

500mL...2 cups flour
2mL.....1/2 tsp. salt
5mL.....1 tsp. baking powder
5mL.....1 tsp. baking soda
5mL.....1 tsp. cinnamon
2mL.....1/2 tsp. nutmeg
2mL.....1/2 tsp. allspice
250mL...1 cup brown sugar (firmly packed)
125mL...1/2 cup margarine
2........2 beaten eggs
175mL...3/4 cup sour milk **or** buttermilk
****

(1) Stir first 7 ingredients together. Set aside.
(2) Cream brown sugar and margarine together, add eggs.
(3) Add flour mixture alternately with sour milk.
(4) Pour batter into well buttered waxed paper lined 22x22cm. (9x9-inch) square baking pan.
(5) Bake just above centre in 180°C (350°F) oven for 40-45 minutes.
(6) Cool on wire rack.

174

Sour Cream Coffee Cake

You will probably make this time and time again...

375mL...1 3/4 cups flour
10mL....2 tsp. baking powder
250mL...1 cup sour cream
5mL.....1 tsp. baking soda
125mL...1/2 cup butter
250mL...1 cup sugar
2........2 well beaten eggs
5mL.....1 tsp. vanilla
****

(1) Stir together flour and baking powder. Set aside.
(2) Combine sour cream and baking soda in a bowl. Set aside.
(3) Cream butter and sugar together until light and fluffy.
(4) Add eggs then vanilla.
(5) Add flour mixture alternately with sour cream.
(6) Spread half of the batter into a buttered 22x22cm. (9x9-inch) cake pan (wax paper lined).

Topping:

50mL....1/4 cup brown sugar
15mL....1 Tbsp. cinnamon
30mL....2 Tbsp. finely chopped walnuts. Stir topping together. Set aside.
****

(7) Sprinkle with half of the topping mixture.
(8) Cover with remaining batter.
(9) Sprinkle with remainder of the topping mixture.

(10) Bake just above centre in 180°C (350°F) oven for 45-50 minutes.

Fluffy Banana Cake

This cake is light, unlike most banana cakes that are heavy...

2-3 ......2 large or 3 small bananas
500mL...2 cups flour
2mL.....1/2 tsp. baking powder
3mL.....3/4 tsp. baking soda
2mL.....1/2 tsp. salt
125mL...1/2 cup margarine
375mL...1 1/2 cups sugar
2........2 beaten eggs
5mL.....1 tsp. vanilla
50mL....1/4 cup buttermilk **or** sour milk
****

(1) Mash bananas to measure 250mL (1 cup). Set aside.
(2) Stir together flour, baking powder, baking soda and salt. Set aside.
(3) Cream margarine and sugar together, add eggs then vanilla and buttermilk.
(4) Add flour mixture alternately with mashed banana.
(5) Mix only enough to blend.

(6) Pour batter into two buttered, waxed paper lined 22cm. (9-inch) round layer cake pans.
(7) Bake just above centre in 180°C (350°F) oven for 30-35 minutes.
(8) Cool. Fill and top with whipped cream, or ice with butter icing.

Applesauce Cake

Old fashioned...good tasting...good keeping...

500mL...2 cups flour
2mL.....1/2 tsp. salt
5mL.....1 tsp. baking soda
5mL.....1 tsp. cinnamon
2mL.....1/2 tsp. cloves
2mL.....1/2 tsp. nutmeg
125mL...1/2 cup butter
250mL...1 cup sugar
2........2 beaten eggs
250mL...1 cup applesauce (thick)
175mL...3/4 cup raisins
125mL...1/2 chopped walnuts
****

(1) Stir together first 6 ingredients. Set aside.
(2) Cream butter and sugar together, add eggs.
(3) Add half the dry ingredients.
(4) Stir in applesauce, raisins and walnuts.
(5) Add dry ingredients.
(6) Pour batter into a well buttered, waxed paper lined 22x22cm. (9x9-inch) square baking pan.
(7) Bake just above centre in 180°C (350°F) oven for about 55 min.

(8) Let rest for 5 minutes. Place on a wire rack to cool.
(9) Ice with Caramel Icing.

Crumb Cake

This cake may be served while real warm...also delicious when cold...

500mL...2 cups flour
250mL...1 cup sugar
175mL...3/4 cup butter or margarine
5mL.....1 tsp. cinnamon
5mL.....1 tsp. cloves
5mL.....1 tsp. nutmeg
10mL....2 tsp. baking powder
1........1 beaten egg
250mL...1 cup sour milk
2mL.....1/2 tsp. baking soda (dissolved in milk)
125mL...1/2 cup raisins
****

(1) Blend together flour, sugar and butter (roll through hands until consistency of peas).
(2) Reserve 125mL (1/2 cup) crumbs for top of cake.
(3) Stir into the remaining crumbs, the spices, egg, sour milk, soda and raisins.
(4) Pour into a well buttered waxed paper lined 22x22cm. (9x9-inch) cake pan.
(5) Sprinkle reserved crumbs over top of cake.

(6) Bake just above centre in 180°C (350°F) oven for 35-40 minutes or until done. Let cool in pan.

* Double recipe if larger cake is desired. Pour into well buttered wax paper lined 22x33cm. (9x13-inch) pan. Bake for 55-60 minutes or until done in centre.

Sponge Cake

This is the cake I use when making strawberry shortcake or trifle...

300mL...1 1/4 cup cake flour
3mL.....3/4 tsp. baking powder
6........6 eggs (separated)
........Few grains of salt
2mL.....1/2 tsp. cream of tartar
300mL...1 1/4 cups fine sugar
30mL....2 Tbsp. cold water
5mL.....1 tsp. lemon **or** vanilla extract
****

(1) Sift flour and baking powder together several times. Set aside.
(2) Separate the eggs.
(3) On high speed of electric mixer, beat egg whites adding a pinch of salt.
(4) When foamy, add cream of tartar and beat until stiff while slowly adding 125mL (1/2 cup) of the sugar.
(5) Beat until stiff peaks form (12-15 minutes). Set aside.
(6) Beat egg yolks on high speed while slowly adding remaining sugar, cold water and flavouring (12-15 minutes).
(7) Sift half the flour mixture over egg yolks, add egg whites over top, sift remaining half of flour mixture over all.
(8) Combine all together by cutting and folding gently with a rubber spatula.
(9) Pour into an unbuttered 25cm. (10-inch) tube pan.

* Bake just below centre in 180°C (350°F) oven for 60 minutes.
* Do not under mix egg whites or the egg yolks.
* When folding egg white and dry mixture, fold gently, you do not want to force the air out of the mixture.
* Turn the cake upside down when you remove it from the oven. The cake must be kept above the surface of the table. An inverted metal funnel may be used to rest the pan on. Allow the cake to cool completely in the pan.
* To remove the cake from the pan, use a thin serrated edge knife. With a sawing motion loosen cake around side and centre tube. Tip cake out and loosen bottom.

Hazelnut Cake

This recipe comes from Germany. A long time family favorite. . . very impressive. . .

375g.....3/4 lb. hazelnuts	(1) Grind hazelnuts and almonds very fine. Set aside.
125g.....1/4 lb. peeled almonds	
325mL...1 1/3 cup sugar (divided)	(2) Beat egg whites until very stiff while slowly adding 125mL (1/2 cup) sugar; beat for 12-15 min.
5........5 egg whites	
5........5 egg yolks	
4........4 eggs	(3) Beat egg yolks and 4 eggs

****

together with the 175mL (3/4 cups) remaining sugar. Beat for 10-15 minutes.
(4) Add hazelnuts and almonds and blend until well mixed.
(5) Fold in egg whites by cutting and folding gently with rubber spatula.
(6) Pour into a 25cm. (10-inch) round, waxed paper lined, spring form pan.
(7) Bake just below centre in 180°C (350°F) oven for 55-60 minutes.
(8) Let cool in pan for 20 minutes; gently loosen sides and cool on wire rack.

* Ice with Lemon Icing or Chocolate Coffee Icing.
* For maximum results with this cake, do not under mix the egg whites or the egg yolks. It is the air that is beat into the eggs that makes it rise.
* When folding in egg whites fold gently as you do not want to force the air out of the mixture.
* The cake pan will be full of mixture but not to worry it will not run over.

Angel Food Cake

375mL...1 1/2 cups flour	(1) Stir together flour and 260mL (1 cup + 2 Tbsp.) sugar. Set aside.
260mL...1 cup plus 2 Tbsp. sugar	
500mL...2 cups egg whites (approx. 14 large egg whites)	
	(2) In a large bowl beat egg whites; gradually adding cream of tartar, salt and vanilla until foamy.
10mL....2 tsp. cream of tartar	
2mL.....1/2 tsp. salt	
10mL....2 tsp. vanilla	
300mL...1 1/4 cup sugar	(3) Gradually add 300mL (1 1/4 cups) sugar. Whip until stiff peaks form, about 10 minutes.

****

(4) Sift about half of the sugar and flour mixture over the batter.
(5) Fold it in gently and quickly with a rubber spatula. Sift remaining half of the flour mixture and fold in gently.
(6) Pour batter into an unbuttered 125cm. (10-inch) tube pan.
(7) Cut through with a knife to remove any large air pockets.
(8) Bake just below center in a 180°C (350°F) oven for 1 hour to 1 hour 10 min. or until cake looks cracked and dried.

* Do not under mix. **Do not under bake.
* All utensils must be free from grease.

178

Chocolate Angel Food Cake

235mL...1 cup less 1 Tbsp. cake
flour
260mL...1 cup plus 2 Tbsp. sugar
50mL....1/4 cup cocoa
7mL.....1 1/2 tsp. vanilla

(1) Sift cake flour, 260mL (1 cup plus 2 Tbsp.) sugar and cocoa together. Do this 3 times.

** Mix the same as Angel Food Cake omitting 7mL (1/2 tsp.) vanilla, and exchange 375mL (1 1/2 cups) flour with 235mL (1 cup less 1 Tbsp.) cake flour.

* Turn the pan upside down when you remove it from the oven.
* The cake must be kept above the surface of the table. An inverted metal funnel may be used to rest the pan on.
* Allow the cake to cool completely in the pan.
* To remove cake from pan, use a thin serrated edged knife. With a sawing motion loosen cake around side and centre tube. Tip cake out and loosen the bottom of the cake.

Carrot Cake

Ah! The best in the west, north, east, or south...

500mL...2 cups flour
10mL....2 tsp. cinnamon
10mL....2 tsp. baking soda
5mL.....1 tsp. salt
3........3 eggs
300mL...1 1/4 cups oil
500mL...2 cups white sugar
10mL....2 tsp. vanilla
500mL...2 cups coconut
250mL...1 cup crushed pineapple
including juice
500mL...2 cups grated carrots
****

(1) Stir together flour, cinnamon, salt and baking soda. Set aside.
(2) Beat eggs, add oil then sugar.
(3) Stir in vanilla. Add flour mixture.
(4) Blend well, add coconut, pineapple, juice and carrots.
(5) Pour into buttered waxed paper lined 22x33cm. (9x13-inch) pan.
(6) Bake just above centre in 180°C (350°F) oven for 50 minutes or until done.

(7) Let set in pan 10 min. before removing to rack.

Icing:

50mL....1/4 cup butter
125g.....1-4 oz. pkg. cream cheese
375mL...1 3/4 cups icing sugar
5mL.....1 tsp. vanilla
****

(1) Cream butter and cheese together. Add vanilla then the icing sugar.
(2) Blend well, spread over cake.

179

Black Forest Cake

The fanciest birthday cake in town...

2........2 baked 22cm. (9-inch) round Sour Cream Chocolate Cakes p. ☞ 181
75mL....1/3 cup cherry brandy
175mL...3/4 cup cherries
250mL...1 cup cherry pie filling (divided)
1........1-500mL container of Nutri-whip topping
3........3 squares (3 oz.) Bakers semi-sweet chocolate (grated)
.........Maraschino cherries
****

(1) Cut each cake layer into two parts (horizontally).
(2) Brush cut surfaces with cherry brandy.
* To Assemble Cake:
(3) Spread bottom layer with half of cherry pie filling.
(4) Set second layer on top.
(5) Spread with 250mL (1 cup) whipped topping.
(6) Set third layer on top, spread with balance of cherry pie filling.

(7) Top with fourth layer.
(8) Cover entire cake with remaining whipped topping. Reserve some topping for decorating the top of the cake.
(9) Garnish sides of cake with grated chocolate.
(10) Set approx. 7-9 maraschino cherries on top.
(11) Using an icing bag, with a star tip, decorate the top of the cake with swirls.
(12) Apply a fancy design around the top outer edge of the cake.

Boiled Raisin Cake

Use a gentle hand when mixing and spreading...very tasty...

300mL...1 1/4 cups raisins
250mL...1 cup brown sugar
2mL.....1/2 tsp. cinnamon
2mL.....1/2 tsp. nutmeg
1mL.....1/4 tsp. cloves **or** mace
1mL.....1/4 tsp. salt
300mL...1 1/4 cups water
50mL....1/4 cup butter
2mL.....1/2 tsp. vanilla
375mL...1 1/2 cups flour
3mL.....3/4 tsp. baking powder
3mL.....3/4 tsp. baking soda
****

(1) Combine raisins, sugar, spices, salt and water in a covered saucepan and bring to boiling point.
(2) Boil 3 minutes, remove from heat, add butter and cool.
(3) When cool, add vanilla.
(4) Sift flour, baking powder and soda together, four times.
(5) Stir into raisin mixture gently and quickly until batter is blended.
* Do not over mix.

(6) Spread carefully into well buttered 22x22cm. (9-inch) square baking pan.
(7) Bake just above centre in 180°C (350°F) oven for 60-70 minutes.
(8) Allow cake to set in pan for 25 minutes before removing.
(9) Ice with a butter icing.

Sour Cream Chocolate Cake

A large cake, birthday size...

125mL...1/2 cup butter	(1) Cream butter gradually add
550mL...2 1/4 cups brown sugar	sugar, then almond paste. Beat
(firmly packed)	well.
125mL...1/2 cup almond paste	(2) Add eggs one at a time, beat
(Opt.)	well after each addition.
3........3 eggs	(3) Add vanilla and chocolate.
7mL.....1 1/2 tsp. vanilla	(4) Sift together flour, baking soda,
3........3 squares (3 oz.) melted	and salt.
unsweetened chocolate	(5) Alternately blend in flour mix-
550mL...2 1/4 cups cake flour	ture and sour cream.
10mL....2 tsp. baking soda	(6) Add boiling water, blend well.
2mL.....1/2 tsp. salt	* Batter will be thin.
250mL...1 cup sour cream	(7) Pour into two 22cm. (9-inch)
250mL...1 cup boiling water	round prepared layer cake pans.

****

(8) Bake just above centre in 180°C (350°F) oven for 35-40 minutes or until cakes test done by inserting a wooden toothpick in the centre of the cake. If it comes out clean, cake is done.
(9) Cool in pans for 10 minutes before removing from pans to racks.

* Line bottom of pans with buttered wax paper (butter both sides). Do not butter sides of pan. The cake will have something to cling to as it rises.

Thrifty Cupcakes

These cupcakes are plain; so go ahead and goop them up for the birthday parties...

300mL...1 1/4 cups sifted cake	(1) Stir together flour, salt, and
2mL.....1/2 tsp. salt	baking powder. Set aside.
11mL....2 1/4 tsp. baking powder	(2) Cream margarine and sugar to-
75mL....1/3 cup margarine	gether. Add egg then vanilla.
150mL...2/3 cup sugar	(3) Add half the dry ingredients,
1........1 beaten egg	stir in milk, add remaining dry
5mL.....1 tsp. vanilla	ingredients. Blend together thor-
125mL...1/2 cup milk	oughly.

****

(4) Butter muffin tins well or line with paper liners.
(5) Fill muffin tins 3/4 full.
(6) Bake just above centre in 190°C (375°F) oven for 15 minutes or until golden brown.
(7) Remove from oven. Let rest 5 minutes before removing from tins.
(8) Cool on wire rack.

* Makes 1 dozen large cupcakes.

Date Nut Bread

Just the handiest loaf to have around... keeps well, freezes well, very moist...

500mL...2 cups sugar
1........1 egg
15mL....1 Tbsp. butter
375mL...1 1/2 cups boiling water
675mL...2 3/4 cups flour
10mL....2 tsp. baking soda
2mL.....1/2 tsp. salt
500g.....1 lb. coarsely chopped
           dates
250mL...1 cup chopped walnuts
2mL.....1 tsp. vanilla
****

(1) Chop dates coarsely and pour boiling water to just cover. Drain and reserve liquid.
(2) Beat egg with sugar, stir in boiling water (use reserved liquid add boiling water to 375mL (1 1/2 cups) with butter added).
(3) Sift flour, soda and salt together, add to egg mixture.
(4) Add dates, nuts and vanilla.

(5) Stir all together,
(6) Pour into two buttered, lined loaf tins.
(7) Bake just below centre in 180°C (325°F) oven for 1 1/2 hours.

* Line loaf tins with parchment paper large enough to project 2cm. (1/2-3/4-inch) over edge of tin (ends do not need lining).
* If parchment paper is not available, use waxed paper (buttered on both sides). Wax paper should be even with top of pans.
* Do not remove paper until loaf is served. Leave paper on to freeze.
* Let loaf stand in baking tin for 20 minutes before removing onto racks.
* Wrap when completely cooled.

Date Orange Cake

A moist, very delicious cake...

250mL...1 cup white sugar
125mL...1/2 cup butter
1........1 beaten egg
15mL....1 Tbsp. grated orange rind
500mL...2 cups flour
5mL.....1 tsp. baking soda
5mL.....1 tsp. baking powder
125mL...1/2 cup sour milk
250mL...1 cup chopped dates
****

(1) Cream sugar and butter until light and creamy.
(2) Beat in egg then orange rind.
(3) Sift flour, baking soda, and baking powder together.
(4) Add flour mixture alternately with sour milk. Blend well.
(5) Stir in dates.
(6) Pour into buttered waxed paper lined 22x22cm. (9x9-inch) cake pan.

Icing:

125mL...1/2 cup sugar
.........Juice of 1 orange
****

(7) Bake just above centre in 180°C (350°F) for 30 minutes or until cake tests done.

(8) Pour orange icing over cake while warm.

182

Matrimonial Cake

An old favorite that soon disappears from the lot...

Date Filling:

250mL...1 cup boiling water	(1) In a medium saucepan bring water and sugar to a boil.
125mL...1/2 cup brown sugar	
500mL...2 cups chopped dates	(2) Lower heat, add dates, cook 5 min. Stir occasionally.
1mL.....1/4 tsp. lemon juice	
*********	(3) Remove from heat, stir in lemon juice. Cool.

Rolled Oat Mixture:

175mL...3/4 cup butter	(4) Cream butter and sugar together.
250mL...1 cup brown sugar	
375mL...1 1/2 cups flour	(5) Blend in flour, salt and rolled oats.
1mL.....1/4 tsp. salt	
425mL...1 3/4 cups rolled oats	(6) Dissolve baking soda in the water and stir into mixture. Mix well.
5mL.....1 tsp. baking soda	
30mL....2 Tbsp. water	
*********	

(7) Press half of this mixture into the bottom of a 22x22cm. (9x9-inch) pan.
(8) Spread date filling on top.
(9) Crumble remaining half of rolled oat mixture over the dates, press gently.

* Bake just above centre in 180°C (350°F) oven for 30-40 minutes.
* Cool. Cut into squares.

Wacky Chocolate Cake

Saves time...saves dirty dishes...enjoyed by all... What's so wacky about it?...

375mL...1 1/2 cups flour	(1) In a 20x20cm. (8x8-inch) baking pan, stir together flour, sugar, baking soda, baking powder, cocoa and salt.
250mL...1 cup sugar	
5mL.....1 tsp. baking soda	
5mL.....1 tsp. baking powder	
45mL....3 Tbsp. cocoa	(2) Make three wells in dry ingredients in well one put in vinegar; in well two put oil and in well three put vanilla.
2mL.....1/2 tsp. salt	
15mL....1 Tbsp. vinegar	
75mL....1/3 cup oil	
5mL.....1 Tbsp. vanilla	(3) Pour coffee over all and mix well.
250mL...1 cup warm coffee	
*********	

(4) Bake just above centre in 180°C (350°F) oven for 30-40 minutes or until centre tests done.

Chocolate Chip Cupcakes

Hold on, they're going to shoot for the heart...

125mL...1/2 cup margarine
250mL...1 cup brown sugar
2........2 beaten eggs
5mL.....1 tsp. vanilla
500mL...2 cups flour
10mL....2 tsp. baking powder
2mL.....1/2 tsp. salt
125mL...1/2 cup milk
250mL...1 cup chocolate chips
****

(1) Cream margarine and brown sugar together.
(2) Add eggs and vanilla, beat well.
(3) Mix dry ingredients together.
(4) Add dry ingredients to above mixture, alternately with milk.
(5) Stir in chocolate chips.
(6) Butter muffin tins well or line with paper liners.

(7) Fill muffin tins 3/4 full.
(8) Bake just above centre in a 180°C (350°F) oven for 20-25 minutes.
(9) Remove from oven. Let rest in tins for 5 minutes before removing.

* Cool on wire rack.
* For chocolate, Chocolate Chip Cupcakes, use the same recipe as above but deduct 50mL (1/4 cup) white flour and add 50mL (1/4 cup) cocoa.
* Makes 12 cupcakes.

Fudge Cake

A very thin cake dough...a delightful taste.

425mL...1 3/4 cups flour
2mL.....1/2 tsp. salt
10mL....2 tsp. cream of tartar
5mL.....1 tsp. baking soda
125mL...1/2 cup butter
375mL...1 1/2 cups sugar
2........2 eggs, separated
2........2 squares (2 oz.) melted
         unsweetened chocolate
5mL.....1 tsp. vanilla
125mL...1/2 cup milk
125mL...1/2 cup boiling water
****

(1) Stir flour, salt, cream of tartar and baking soda together. Set aside.
(2) Cream butter and sugar together until light and fluffy.
(3) Beat egg yolks, add to butter mixture.
(4) Mix in melted chocolate and vanilla.
(5) Add dry ingredients alternately with milk, beginning and ending with dry ingredients.

(6) Add boiling water, then fold in stiffly beaten egg whites.
(7) Pour batter into two buttered, wax paper lined 22cm. (9-inch) round layer cake tins.
(8) Bake just above centre in 180°C (350°F) oven for 20 minutes or until cake tests done when inserted toothpick comes out clean.

* Do not open oven door until cake is 3/4 done.

184

Chocolate Oatmeal Cake

A moist cake, with a good old fashioned flavour...a good keeper...

470mL...1 7/8 cups boiling water
325mL...1 1/2 cups rolled oats
550mL...2 1/4 cups flour
3mL.....3/4 tsp. salt
11mL....2 1/4 tsp. baking powder
6mL.....1 1/4 tsp. baking soda
175mL...3/4 cup butter
5mL.....1 tsp. vanilla
375mL...1 1/2 cups brown sugar
3........3 eggs
3........3 squares (3 oz.) melted
        unsweetened chocolate
        ****

(1)   Pour boiling water over rolled oats and set aside to cool.
(2)   Mix flour, salt, baking powder and baking soda together thoroughly. Set aside.
(3)   Cream butter until soft and creamy. Add vanilla while creaming.
(4)   Gradually add sugar and beat until fluffy.
(5)   Beat eggs until foamy and add gradually to butter-sugar mixture.

(6)   Add chocolate, blend in well.
(7)   Add dry ingredients and rolled oats mixture, alternately to the butter-egg mixture. Beginning and ending with dry ingredients.
(8)   Stir gently and quickly until batter is well blended, but do not over mix.
(9)   Spread carefully into a well buttered wax paper lined 25x25cm. (10x10-inch) cake pan.
(10)   Bake just above centre in a 180°C (350°F) oven for 45-50 minutes.
(11)   Allow cake to set for 25 minutes before removing from pan to rack.
(12)   Cool and spread with Butter Icing or your favorite icing.

Cream Cake

This old recipe is moist and has a good flavour...excellent for birthday cake...

300mL...1 1/4 cup flour
10mL....2 tsp. baking powder
2mL.....1/2 tsp. salt
250mL...1 cup sugar
250mL...1 cup cream
2........2 well beaten eggs
5mL.....1 tsp. vanilla
        ****

(1)   Stir together flour, baking powder and salt. Set aside.
(2)   Combine sugar and cream together well.
(3)   Add eggs, then vanilla. Set aside.

(4)   In a mixing bowl, add dry ingredients alternately with liquid, beginning and ending with flour. Stir until blended.
(5)   Pour into buttered wax paper lined 22x22cm. (9x9-inch) cake pan.
(6)   Bake just above centre in 160°C (325°F) oven for 30 minutes.
(7)   Let stand in pan 5 minutes before removing to wire rack to cool.

*   Double recipe if larger cake is desired. Pour into 22x33cm. (9x13-inch) cake pan. Bake for 50-55 minutes.

Devil's Food Chocolate Cake

This makes a large cake...

750mL...3 cups flour
7mL.....1 1/2 tsp. baking soda
250mL...1 cup vegetable shortening
500mL...2 cups firmly packed
        brown sugar
5mL.....1 tsp. salt
10mL....2 tsp. vanilla
4........4 squares (4 oz.) melted
        unsweetened chocolate
5........5 eggs
425mL...1 3/4 cups milk plus 2
        Tbsp. vinegar **or** 1 3/4
        cups buttermilk
        ****

(1) Stir flour and baking soda together. Set aside.
(2) Cream shortening until light and fluffy.
(3) Gradually stir in brown sugar, salt, and vanilla.
(4) Put chocolate into a bowl or top of double boiler and melt over hot water.
(5) Stir melted chocolate into shortening and sugar mixture.
(6) Beat in eggs one at a time. Beat until smooth after each addition.

(7) Stir in 1/3 cup of the flour, then 1/2 of the milk, 1/3 of the flour, remaining milk and then the remaining flour.

* Beat until smooth after each addition and scrape sides of bowl and spoon often during mixing.
* If using an electric beater add ingredients using low speed and then beat at medium speed.

(8) Pour batter into 3 buttered waxed paper lined 22cm. (9-inch) layer cake pans (do not butter sides of pan).
(9) Spread batter evenly in pans, pushing batter so it is slightly lower in the centre.
(10) Bake just above center in a 180°C (350°F) oven for 20-25 minutes or until cake tests done.

* Let set in pans for 5 minutes. Loosen edge of cake with a sharp knife. Put cake rack on pans and turn upside down. Cool.
* Ice with your favorite icing.

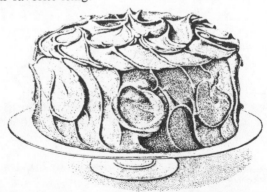

Marble Cake

This old recipe has an interesting appearance...also boasts real cake appeal...

325mL...1 1/3 cup flour	(1) Stir together flour, baking powder and salt. Set aside.
10mL....2 tsp. baking powder	
2mL.....1/2 tsp. salt	(2) In a cup measure combine milk and vanilla. Set aside.
150mL...2/3 cup milk	
2mL.....1/2 tsp. vanilla	(3) Cream butter, sugar and egg together until fluffy.
75mL....1/3 cup butter or margarine	
250mL...1 cup sugar	(4) Add flour mixture alternately with milk. Stir each addition in well before adding more (starting and ending with flour).
1........1 egg	
1........1 square (1 oz.) melted unsweetened chocolate	
5mL.....1 tsp. grated orange rind	(5) Divide batter into 2 equal parts.

****

(6) Stir 30g (1 oz.) melted chocolate, into one half of the batter and 5mL (1 tsp.) grated orange rind into other half of batter.

(7) Drop chocolate and white batters alternately (checkerboard fashion) by large spoonfuls into well buttered waxed paper lined 22x22cm. (9x9-inch) pan.

* Leave as is for a checkerboard appearance or run a knife back and forth in a few places to give a marble effect.

(8) Bake just above centre in 180°C (350°F) oven for 25-30 minutes or until a toothpick stuck in centre comes out clean.

Topping:

(1) Spread hot cake with 10mL (2 tsp.) soft butter.

(2) Combine 75mL (1/3 cup) brown sugar and 2mL (1/2 tsp.) cinnamon and sprinkle evenly over the butter.

(3) Return cake to oven for 5 minutes or until sugar has melted a little.

(4) Cool in pan.

Pineapple Upside-Down Cake

Simply spectacular!

50mL....1/4 cup butter or margarine
250mL...1 cup firmly packed
brown sugar
540mL...1-19 oz. can sliced pineapple
10.......10 maraschino cherries,
drained
500mL...2 cups flour
15mL....1 Tbsp. baking powder
2mL.....1/2 tsp. salt
250mL...1 cup sugar
125mL...1/2 cup butter
5mL.....1 tsp. lemon extract
5mL.....1 tsp. vanilla
250mL...1 cup milk
3........3 egg whites
30mL....2 Tbsp. sugar
****

(1) Place 30mL (2 Tbsp.) of the
butter in each of the 2-20cm.
(8-inch) round cake pans.
(2) Heat pan until butter is melted.
(3) Blend half of the brown sugar
with the melted butter in each
pan. Spread mixture evenly over
bottom of the cake pans.
(4) Drain pineapple, reserve juice
for other use. Arrange pineapple slices over the brown
sugar mixture in each pan.
Place a cherry in the centre of
each pineapple slice. Set aside.
(5) Combine flour, baking powder
and salt. Set aside.
(6) In a mixing bowl blend 125mL
(1/2 cup) butter with 250mL

(1 cup) sugar. Stir in lemon extract and the vanilla.
(7) Add dry ingredients alternately with the milk. Beat egg whites until stiff.
Add 30mL (2 Tbsp.) sugar, fold into cake mixture.
(8) Pour 1/2 of batter over pineapple slices in both pans. Spread evenly.
(9) Bake just above centre in 180°C (350°F) oven for 35 minutes or until
done.

* Cool on wire racks, when cool place one layer on top of the other.
* Ice with whipping cream.

Lemon Cheese Cake

Incredibly delicious...

Part One

250mL...1 cup white sugar	(1) Cream sugar, vanilla, cheese
10mL....2 tsp. vanilla	and lemon juice until smooth.
250g.....8 oz. cream cheese	(2) Chill 1/2 hour in refrigerator.
10mL....2 tsp lemon juice.	

****

Part Two

500mL...2 cups graham wafer	(1) Mix crumbs, sugar and butter
crumbs	together. Save 175mL (3/4 cup)
125mL...1/2 cup white sugar	for top.
50mL....1/4 cup butter	(2) Pat crumbs in large pie plate
	and bake in 180°C (350°F)
	oven for 5 min. Cool.

****

Part Three

170g.....1 pkg. lemon jello	(1) Combine jello and water.
250mL...1 cup hot water	(2) Cool; but do not let set.

****

Part Four

385mL...1 large can evaporated	(1) Whip until stiff, add lemon
milk (well chilled)	juice.
2-3 ......2-3 drops of lemon juice	(2) Add cooled jello to whipped
	milk, then the cheese mixture.

****

(3) Whip all together thoroughly and pour into prepared graham pie shell.
(4) Sprinkle reserved crumbs on top.
(5) Refrigerate until set.

Jelly Roll

Makes a pleasing dessert when served with ice-cream

250mL...1 cup flour
7mL.....1 1/2 tsp. baking powder
3........3 eggs
250mL...1 cup sugar
1/2mL...1/8 tsp. salt
75mL....1/3 cup milk
2mL.....1/2 tsp. lemon **or** vanilla
175mL...3/4 cup raspberry jam **or**
         lemon filling
         ****

(1) Sift flour and baking powder together. Set aside.
(2) Separate the eggs.
(3) Beat egg whites adding salt. When foamy gradually add half of the sugar.
(4) Beat until stiff peaks form. Set aside.
(5) Beat the egg yolks until thick and lemon coloured. Add remaining sugar gradually. Add milk and flavouring.
(6) Sift half the flour mixture over egg yolks. Add beaten egg whites over top.
(7) Sift remaining half of flour mixture over all.
(8) Combine all together by cutting and folding gently with rubber spatula.
(9) Pour into a well buttered waxed paper lined 25x35cm. (10x14-inch) jelly roll pan or cookie sheet.
(10) Bake just above centre in 180°C (350°F) oven for 12 minutes or until it tests done.
(11) Turn at once onto a towel dusted with icing sugar. Peel off wax paper. Trim crisp edges if any.
(12) Spread immediately with jam or cooled lemon pie filling. With the help of the towel roll at once. Work quickly or it will crack.
(13) Leave wrapped until cold.

Saving Maraschino Juice

* Cover glazed cherries with juice left over from maraschino cherries. Let set 2 days. When glazed cherries are used up, repeat with new glazed cherries and add 1mL (1/4 tsp.) of almond extract.

Icings

Marshmallow Icing

2........2 egg whites
1........1 cup golden syrup
8........8 diced marshallows
****

(1) Beat egg whites with syrup in a double boiler over hot water until thick and fluffy.

(2) Add marshallows, beat until melted.
(3) Remove from stove, beat until icing holds peaks.
(4) Spread.

Lemon Icing

50mL....1/4 cup margarine
15mL....1 Tbsp. grated lemon peel
2mL.....1/2 tsp. salt
750mL...3 cups sifted icing sugar
15mL....1 Tbsp. lemon juice
45mL....3 Tbsp. hot water
........Yellow food colouring,
        as desired
****

(1) Combine margarine, lemon peel, salt, food colouring and 250mL (1 cup) of sugar.
(2) Add lemon juice, water and the remaining sugar alternatively.
(3) Mix until smooth.
(4) Add sugar or water as necessary for good spreading consistency.

* Enough to ice two 22cm. (9-inch) layers or one 22x33cm. (9x13-inch) cake.

Butter Icing

50mL....1/4 cup butter or margar-
         ine
500mL...2 cups icing sugar
2mL.....1/2 tsp. vanilla
45mL....3 Tbsp. milk **or** cream
****

(1) Cream butter until soft then gradually add sugar. Blend well.
(2) Add vanilla.
(3) Thin with milk, a small amount at a time, until of right consistency to spread.

* Ices one 20x20cm. (8x8-inch) cake.

Mocha Icing (Coffee)

50mL....1/4 cup butter or margarine
125mL...1/2 cup + 2 Tbsp. brewed coffee
250g.....8 oz. (8 squares) unsweetened chocolate
500mL...2 cups icing sugar
****

(1) In a saucepan heat butter and
125mL (1/2 cup) brewed coffee
(very hot). Reserve 30mL (2
Tbsp.) of brewed coffee.
(2) Add chocolate and stir constantly. Remove from heat just
before the chocolate has finished melting.

(3) Beat until smooth.
(4) Cool until just warm.
(5) Stir in icing sugar. Add enough coffee to make a smooth workable icing.

* Enough to ice a 22cm. (9-inch) layer cake.

Quick Caramel Icing

250mL...1 cup brown sugar firmly
packed
1/2mL...1/8 tsp. salt
30mL....2 Tbsp. margarine
75mL....1/3 cup milk
5mL.....1 tsp. vanilla
15mL....1 Tbsp. cream
****

(1) In a medium saucepan combine
sugar, salt, margarine and milk.
(2) Cook, stirring until dissolved.
Then cook without stirring, to a
soft ball stage 112°C (234°F).
(3) Cook to lukewarm. Beat until it
begins to thicken. Add vanilla
and cream.

(4) Continue beating until spreading consistency.
(5) Beat in a small amount of icing sugar, if needed. Quickly spread on
cake.
(6) Sprinkle with chopped nut meats.

* Enough to ice a 22x22cm. (9x9-inch) cake.

Easy Fudge Icing

And easy it is...easy to make...easy to spread...

3........3 squares (3 oz.) unsweetened chocolate
50mL....1/4 cup margarine
500mL...2 cups icing sugar
1/2mL...1/8 tsp. salt
5mL.....1 tsp. vanilla
75mL....1/3 cup hot milk **or** cream
****

(1) In top of double boiler melt
chocolate and margarine.
(2) In separate bowl blend together
icing sugar, salt, vanilla and
milk.
(3) Add chocolate mixture, beat
until thick enough to spread.

(4) More icing sugar or cream may be added to give desired consistency.

* Enough to ice a 22cm. (9-inch) layer cake.

Cream Cheese Icing

Omit chocolate from recipe if you prefer it without...

50mL....1/4 cup butter
125g.....4 oz. cream cheese
2........2 squares (2 oz.) unsweetened chocolate
5mL.....1 tsp. vanilla
500mL...2 cups icing sugar
****

(1) Cream butter and cream cheese together.
(2) Melt chocolate and add to butter mixture.
(3) Add vanilla, mix well.
(4) Blend in icing sugar.
(5) Beat until fluffy.

Royal Icing

This is the traditional icing used in cones for decorative effects...
Also used to ice heavy fruit cakes, such as wedding cakes...

2........2 egg whites
1mL.....1/4 tsp. cream of tartar
875mL...3 1/2 cups icing sugar
2-3 ......2-3 drops flavouring,
white vanilla **or** almond
extract
2mL.....1/2 tsp. glycerine
****

(1) Beat egg whites until foamy.
(2) Add cream of tartar.
(3) Gradually add sifted icing sugar, flavouring and glycerine.
(4) Beat until it is a good consistency to spread, add more icing sugar, if needed. This icing becomes very hard when dry.

(5) Cover with a damp cloth until ready to use. The addition of glycerine weakens the strength of the icing. Therefore do not add glycerine when heavy fruit cakes are going to be tiered.

* Do not add glycerine when making decorations.
* Store left over icing in refrigerator. Keep well covered.
* Beat icing very well when taken from the fridge.
* The sawing motion of an electric knife is preferred when cutting through the hard icing on fruit cakes. Other types of knives seem to crumble and crack hard icing.

Favorite Chocolate Icing

Just a simple icing, enjoyed by all...

125mL...1/2 cup butter or margarine
125mL...1/2 cup cocoa
1mL.....1/4 tsp. salt
75mL....1/3 cup milk
7mL.....1 1/2 tsp. vanilla
875mL...3 1/2 cups icing sugar

(1) Combine melted butter, cocoa and salt.
(2) Add milk and vanilla.
(3) Stir in sugar in three parts.
(4) Mix until smooth.
(5) Add sugar or milk to spreading consistency.

* Makes enough to ice a 22cm. (9-inch) layer cake.

Luscious Lemon Icing

This is a creamy, smooth icing... with a tangy taste.

1........1 envelope lemon pie
        filling
125mL...1/2 cup sugar
220mL...1 cup less 2 Tbsp. water
2........2 slightly beaten egg yolks
15mL....1 Tbsp. butter
250mL...1 cup whipping cream
30mL....2 Tbsp. icing sugar
****

(1) In a medium saucepan stir pie filling and sugar together.
(2) Gradually add the water, then the egg yolks.
(3) Over medium heat, bring mixture to a boil, stirring constantly to ensure even thickening. Boil 1 minute.
(4) Remove from heat; stir in butter. Cool thoroughly.
(5) Fold gently with a knife now and then while cooling, to keep surface from getting hard as well as to let the steam escape.
(6) Whip cream, add icing sugar gradually. Blend lemon filling and whipped cream together well.
(7) Spread over cake of your choice.

* Exceptionally good on angel food cake.
* Makes 500mL (2 cups) of icing.

Date Filling

Filling for cookies, etc....

500mL...2 cups cut up dates
50mL....1/4 cup water
50mL....1/4 cup finely chopped
        walnuts (Opt.)
30mL....2 Tbsp. brown sugar
        (Opt.)
****

(1) In a saucepan combine dates, water and sugar.
(2) Cook slowly, stirring often until thickened. Cool
(3) Add nuts, spread.

Orange Filling

A splendid orange flavour... filling for cookies, etc....

50mL....1/4 cup cornstarch
2mL.....1/2 tsp. salt
250mL...1 cup sugar
250mL...1 cup orange juice
30mL....2 Tbsp. butter
30mL....2 Tbsp. grated orange rind
30mL....2 Tbsp. lemon juice
****

(1) In a saucepan combine cornstarch, salt and sugar.
(2) Slowly stir in orange juice.
(3) Bring to a boil stirring constantly.
(4) Boil 1 minute. Remove from heat.

(5) Blend in butter, orange rind and lemon juice. Chill.

* Makes 375mL (1 1/2 cups).

194

Lemon Filling

175mL...3/4 cup sugar
75mL....1/3 cup cornstarch
1mL.....1/4 tsp. salt
5mL.....1 tsp. grated lemon rind
375mL...1 1/2 cups water
2........2 beaten egg yolks
15mL....1 Tbsp. butter
90mL....6 Tbsp. lemon juice
****

(1) In a double boiler stir together sugar, cornstarch, salt, and grated lemon rind.
(2) Gradually add water; stir continually and cook until mixture thickens (about 12 min.).
(3) Cover and cook 10 minutes more. Stir occasionally. Remove from heat.

(4) Pour half of the mixture over beaten egg yolks, beat and return to mixture in double boiler. Cook and stir gently 5 minutes more.
(5) Remove from heat. Stir in butter and lemon juice. Cool, stir gently twice to let steam escape.

* Use in pre-cooked pie or tart shells, spread between cakes or spread on jelly roll before rolling.
* Makes 500mL (2 cups).

Strawberry Glaze

Ideal over angel food cake, sponge cake, cheese cake, or puddings...

1L ......4 cups fresh or frozen
          strawberries
30mL....2 Tbsp. cornstarch
125mL...1/2 cup sugar
30mL....2 Tbsp. lemon juice
****

(1) If fresh fruit is used mash some of the berries to create 175mL (3/4 cup) of juice; reserve juice. If frozen fruit is used drain and reserve juice.

(2) In a saucepan mix cornstarch with small amount of juice to make a paste. Add remaining juice, sugar and lemon juice. Bring to a boil and stir until thickened. Simmer 5 minutes.
(3) Gently fold in strawberries, pour into sterilized jar. Cool and refrigerate.

* Makes 750mL (3 cups).
* Raspberry glaze is done the same as above.
* Harder fruits as blueberries, etc. take longer to cook. Add the berries the same time as the sugar. Cook until fruit is tender.

Chocolate Sauce

250mL...1 cup evaporated milk
50mL....1/4 cup powdered sugar
10mL....2 tsp. cocoa
        ****

(1) Heat milk in double boiler.
(2) Cook for 5 minutes, cool.
(3) Set in refrigerator, chill thoroughly.

(4) Whip like cream until stiff.
(5) Add powdered sugar and cocoa.

Mocha Sauce

You will find this recipe to be excellent... use wherever a good chocolate flavour is required...

125mL...1/2 cup water
45mL....3 Tbsp. instant coffee
30mL....2 Tbsp. butter
125mL...1/2 cup firmly packed
        brown sugar
250mL...1 cup semi-sweet chocolate
        chips
5mL.....1 tsp. vanilla
        ****

(1) In a small saucepan combine water, coffee, butter, and sugar. Bring to a boil, then boil for 3 min. Stirring constantly.
(2) Remove from heat, pour into blender, add chocolate chips and vanilla. Mix for 1 minute. Pour into sterilized jar and refrigerate.

* Makes 300mL (1 1/4 cups).
* Warm slightly and stir, use over ice cream or desserts.
* If a mint flavor is required, exchange half of the semi-sweet chocolate chips with mint flavored chocolate chips.

Cookies

Date Oatmeal Cookies

Chewy, tasty and full bodied...

125mL...1/2 cup margarine	(1) Cream together margarine and sugar, then add eggs.
250mL...1 cup sugar	
3........3 eggs	(2) Sift together flour, baking powder, salt, baking soda, cinnamon and allspice.
375mL...1 1/2 cups flour	
5mL.....1 tsp. baking powder	
2mL.....1/2 tsp. salt	(3) Add dry ingredients to creamed mixture alternately with milk; starting and ending with dry ingredients.
5mL.....1 tsp. baking soda	
5mL.....1 tsp. cinnamon	
2mL.....1/2 tsp. allspice	
125mL...1/2 cup milk	(4) Stir in rolled oats, dates, coconut and nuts, if desired.
500mL...2 cups rolled oats	
250mL...1 cup chopped dates	(5) Drop by teaspoon onto buttered cookie sheet.
125mL...1/2 cup coconut	
125mL...1/2 cup nuts (Opt.)	(6) Bake just above centre in 180°C (350°F) oven for 10-12 minutes.
*********	

(7) Cool on wire rack.

Coconut Macaroons

Gone with the wind...

2........2 egg whites	(1) Beat egg whites until stiff and stand in peaks.
150mL...2/3 cup sugar	
2mL.....1/2 tsp. vanilla	(2) Add sugar and vanilla.
500mL...2 cups coconut	(3) Beat for 1 minute more.
*********	

(4) Fold in coconut until moistened.
(5) Drop from teaspoon onto prepared cookie sheet (see note).
(6) Bake just above centre in 140°C (275°F) oven for 20 minutes or until just faintly browned.
(7) Turn heat off, open door, leave in oven 10 minutes.

* **Note:** The cookie sheet must be sprayed very well with *Pam. If Pam cannot be used, substitute by lining ungreased cookie sheet with parchment paper. If the macaroons stick to the paper, lay the paper on a cold wet cloth, just until they can be lifted off easily.
* Pam contains a pure vegetable product in a spray can.

Chocolate Drop Cookies

Easy to make...easier to eat...

125mL...1/2 cup butter or margarine
250mL...1 cup sugar
2........2 beaten eggs
3........3 squares (3 oz.) melted chocolate
2mL.....1/2 tsp. vanilla
375mL...1 1/2 cups flour
15mL....1 Tbsp. baking powder
2mL.....1/2 tsp. salt
125mL...1/2 cup milk
175mL...3/4 cup raisins
175mL...3/4 cup nuts
****

(1) Cream butter and sugar together until well blended.
(2) Add eggs, chocolate, and vanilla.
(3) Sift flour, baking powder and salt together, add alternately with milk.
(4) Gently and quickly stir in raisins and nuts.
(5) Drop by teaspoon onto well buttered cookie sheet.
(6) Bake just above centre in 190°C (375°F) oven for approx. 10-12 minutes.

(7) Cool on wire rack.

Sugar Ginger Snaps

You'll have a desperado love for these... "I guarantee it"...

375mL...1 1/2 cups white sugar
250mL...1 cup butter or margarine
2........2 beaten eggs
250mL...1 cup molasses
15mL....1 Tbsp. baking soda
10mL....2 tsp. baking powder
15mL....1 Tbsp. ginger
1L ......4 cups flour
5mL.....1 tsp. nutmeg
5mL.....1 tsp. cinnamon
5mL.....1 tsp. cloves
5mL.....1 tsp. allspice
****

(1) Cream sugar and butter together.
(2) Add eggs, then molasses.
(3) Sift baking soda, baking powder, ginger, flour, nutmeg, cinnamon, cloves and allspice together.
(4) Stir into molasses mixture.
(5) Roll dough into small balls.
(6) Dip top in white sugar.
(7) Place them on a buttered cookie sheet. Do not press down.

(8) Bake just above centre in 180°C (350°F) oven for approx. 15 min.
(9) They crack on top when done.
(10) Cool on wire rack.

Spiced Oatmeal Cookies

A treat in the lunch box or whenever...

125mL...1/2 cup butter or margar- ine	(1) Cream butter, sugar and syrup until well blended.
300mL...1 1/4 cups sugar	(2) Add egg and rolled oats.
50mL....1/4 cup syrup	(3) Sift dry ingredients together,
1........1 egg	gradually add to above mixture.
300mL...1 1/4 cups rolled oats	(4) Roll dough into balls and place
300mL...1 1/4 cups flour	on buttered cookie sheet.
2mL.....1/2 tsp. salt	(5) Press with wet fork.
5mL.....1 tsp. baking soda	(6) Bake just above centre in 180°C
2mL.....1/2 tsp. ginger	(350°F) oven for 10-12 minutes
2mL.....1/2 tsp. cinnamon	or until light brown.
*********	(7) Cool on wire rack.

Shortbread

When only the best will do...

750mL...3 cups flour	(1) Sift together flour, rice flour
250mL...1 cup rice flour	and berry sugar.
250mL...1 cup berry sugar	(2) Add butter and mix in well.
500g.....1 lb. butter (no substitute)	(3) Wrap in waxed paper, place in
*********	fridge until chilled.

(4) Roll out on pastry sheet to .83cm. (1/3-inch) thickness.
(5) Cut with a cookie cutter. Do not sprinkle with flour when rolling.
(6) Place on ungreased cookie sheet.
(7) Make designs on top of cookie, or prick with a fork.
(8) Cookie press may be used instead of rolling.
(9) Bake just above centre in 150°C (300°F) oven until faintly browned.

* Use shiny cookie sheets. Dark cookie sheets absorb heat and cookies may be too brown on the bottom.
* The slightest amount of water in the shortbread will give it a sandy texture; therefore, have utensils and hands dry. Do not wet fork if piercing.
* If using butter from the farm, make sure all water is removed.
* When rolling shortbread, work gently.
* If rolling pin sticks, usually a rub with your hand is all that is required.
* There is no need to turn dough over as you roll it.
* Roll it out, cut it and then lift it out with a spatula and place it onto cookie sheet.
* Makes 5 1/2 doz. 5cm. (2-inch) cookies.

Peanut Butter Cookies

A good textured cookie with a pleasant flavour of peanut butter...

250mL...1 cup flour
2mL.....1/2 tsp. baking soda
1mL.....1/4 tsp. salt
125mL...1/2 cup butter or margarine
250mL...1 cup brown sugar
1........1 unbeaten egg
125mL...1/2 cup peanut butter
2mL.....1/2 tsp. vanilla
****

(1) Stir together flour, baking soda and salt. Set aside.
(2) Cream butter and sugar together.
(3) Stir in egg.
(4) Add peanut butter and vanilla.
(5) Add flour mixture. Blend well.
(6) Drop from teaspoon onto buttered cookie sheet.

(7) Press with a wet fork.
(8) Bake just above centre in 180°C (350°F) oven 15-20 minutes.
(9) Cool on wire rack.

Chocolate Chip Cookies

Just an excellent basic cookie recipe...good all by itself, or add your choice of whatever...

500mL...2 cups butter
500mL...2 cups shortening
500mL...2 cups brown sugar
500mL...2 cups white sugar
4........4 eggs
15mL....1 Tbsp. vanilla
20mL....4 tsp. cream of tartar
20mL....4 tsp. baking soda
2L ......8 cups flour
350g.....12 oz. pk. chocolate chips
250mL...1 cup walnuts
****

(1) Cream butter, shortening, white sugar and brown sugar together.
(2) Add eggs, then vanilla, mix well.
(3) Sift cream of tartar and baking soda with 1L (4 cups) of flour.
(4) Add to the butter mixture.
(5) Stir in additional 1L (4 cups) of flour, then add chocolate chips and walnuts.

(6) Roll dough into balls, place on a greased cookie sheet. Press with a wet fork (flatten well).
(7) Bake just above centre in 180°C (350°F) oven for 10 minutes or until slightly browned. Do not overbake.
(8) Cool on wire rack.

* Reduce ingredients by half if smaller amount is required.

Chocolate Chip Oatmeal Cookies

Double chocolate and the almond flavour, makes these cookies scrumptious...

500mL...2 cups rolled oats
500mL...2 cups flour
1mL.....1/4 tsp. salt
125mL...1/2 cup coconut
250mL...1 cup brown sugar
250mL...1 cup margarine
1mL.....1/4 tsp. vanilla
1mL.....1/4 tsp. almond extract
2mL.....1/2 tsp. baking soda
30mL....2 Tbsp. boiling water
150mL...2/3 cup chopped white
          chocolate
350g.....1 1/2 cups semi-sweet
          chocolate chips
          ****

(1) Stir together rolled oats, flour, salt and coconut. Set aside.
(2) Cream brown sugar and margarine, add vanilla and almond extract.
(3) Dissolve baking soda in boiling water, add to sugar mixture.
(4) Mix in dry ingredients, white chocolate, then chocolate chips.
(5) Blend well. Roll in 2.5cm. (1-inch) balls, flatten slightly in hands. Add droplets of water if needed to form into balls.
(6) Place on buttered cookie sheet.

(7) Bake just above centre in 180°C (350°F) oven for 15-20 minutes.
(8) Place on wire rack or brown paper to cool.

* Makes 5 dozen cookies.

Jumbo Oatmeal Cookies

Made especially for the cookie monster...

250mL...1 cup butter or margarine
375mL...1 1/2 cups brown sugar
          firmly packed
2........2 eggs
5mL.....1 tsp. vanilla
375mL...1 1/2 cups flour
10mL....2 tsp. baking soda
5mL.....1 tsp. salt
625mL...2 1/2 cups oats
500mL...2 cups Bakers semi-sweet
          chocolate chips
250mL...1 cup raisins
          ****

(1) Cream together sugar and butter until well blended.
(2) Beat in eggs, then vanilla.
(3) Sift together flour, baking soda and salt. Add to butter mixture.
(4) Stir in rolled oats. Mix well.
(5) Stir in chocolate chips and raisins.
(6) Drop dough in 50mL (1/4 cup) mounds 7.5cm. (3-inch) apart onto buttered cookie sheet.
(7) Flatten each cookie into 6cm. (2 1/2-inch) circle with wet fork.

(8) Bake just above centre in 180°C (350°F) oven for approx. 20 minutes.
(9) Cool on pans 5 minutes; finish cooling on racks.

* Makes approx. 25 cookies.

Filled Oatmeal Cookies

From days of yore, and they still want more...

500mL...2 cups flour
2mL.....1/2 tsp. salt
125mL...1/2 cup shortening
125mL...1/2 cup butter
250mL...1 cup brown sugar
5mL.....1 tsp. vanilla
5mL.....1 tsp. baking soda
      (dissolved)
50mL....1/4 cup boiling water
500mL...2 cups rolled oats
    ****

(1) Stir together flour and salt, set aside.
(2) Cream shortening and butter together.
(3) Gradually add sugar, then vanilla.
(4) Dissolve soda in water, add to creamed mixture.
(5) Add flour mixture and rolled oats. Stir well.

(6) Roll dough thin .05cm. (1/4-inch) cut with 5cm. (2-inch) cookie cutter.
(7) Place on buttered cookie sheet.
(8) Bake just above centre in 180°C (350°F) preheated oven for 20 minutes.
(9) Cool on rack. Then sandwich two cookies together with Date or Orange Filling.

* Date Filling or Orange Filling, p. 194.

Monster Cookies

There is no flour in this recipe...believe it or not...

500mL...2 cups brown sugar
      firmly packed
500mL...2 cups white sugar
250mL...1 cup butter or margarine
6........6 eggs
10mL....2 tsp. white syrup
10mL....2 tsp. vanilla
20mL....4 tsp. baking soda
375mL...1 1/2 cups peanut butter
250mL...1 cup smarties
375mL...1 1/2 cups chocolate chips
2L ......9 cups oatmeal
    ****

(1) Cream together brown sugar, white sugar and butter.
(2) Beat in eggs, three at a time.
(3) Add syrup, vanilla and baking soda.
(4) Stir in peanut butter, smarties, chocolate chips and oatmeal. Mix together well.
(5) Roll into balls, place on a buttered cookie sheet. Press with wet fork.
(6) Bake just above centre in 180°C (350°F) oven 10-12 minutes.

* Dough will be kind of sticky.
* Drop cookie mixture onto work surface by teaspoon. Let stand for 5 minutes, then roll into balls.
* Rinse hands under water when they get too sticky.

Dad's Cookies

Mom likes them...kids like them...none left for Dad...

250mL...1 cup white sugar	(1) Cream together sugar and but-
125mL...1/2 cup brown sugar	ter until well blended.
250mL...1 cup butter or margarine	(2) Add egg, and vanilla.
1........1 beaten egg	(3) Stir in oats and coconut.
5mL.....1 tsp. vanilla	(4) Sift together flour, baking pow-
300mL...1 1/4 cups rolled oats	der and soda. Stir into butter
175mL...3/4 cup coconut	mixture.
375mL...1 1/2 cups flour	(5) Roll into 2.5cm. (1-inch) balls,
5mL.....1 tsp. baking powder	place on buttered cookie sheet.
5mL.....1 tsp. baking soda	(6) Press with a wet fork.

(7) Bake just above centre in 180°C (350°F) oven for 12 minutes or until lightly browned.

* Cool on wire rack.

Quick, Crisp Sugar Cookies

Disappearing cookies...now you see them...now you don't...

125mL...1/2 cup butter or margar- ine	(1) Cream together butter and sugar until well blended.
250mL...1 cup sugar	(2) Add eggs, vanilla or nutmeg.
2........2 eggs, beaten	(3) Sift together flour, baking soda,
5mL.....1 tsp. vanilla **or** nutmeg	baking powder and salt.
15mL....1 Tbsp. milk	(4) Add to butter mixture.
550mL...2 1/4 cups flour	(5) Wrap in wax paper and chill.
2mL.....1/2 tsp. baking soda	(6) Roll out on floured board to
5mL.....1 tsp. baking powder	.03cm. (1/8-inch) thickness.
2mL.....1/2 tsp. salt	(7) Sprinkle with sugar, cut with
*********	cookie cutter.

(8) Place on buttered cookie sheets.
(9) Bake just above centre in 220°C (425°F) oven for 10 minutes, or until slightly browned.

* Cool on wire rack.
* Approx. 4 dozen.

Fruit Jumbles

A classic recipe still favoured today...

375mL...1 1/2 cups brown sugar
125mL...1/2 cup butter or margar-
        ine
3........3 eggs
5mL.....1 tsp. baking soda (dis-
        solved in hot water)
5mL.....1 tsp. vanilla
500mL...2 cups flour
500g.....1 lb. chopped dates
115g.....1/4 lb. walnuts
      ****

(1) Cream sugar and butter together.
(2) Add eggs, baking soda and
vanilla.
(3) Stir in flour, add dates and
walnuts.
(4) Drop by teaspoon onto a greased cookie sheet, about 5cm.
(2-inches) apart.
(5) Bake just above centre in 180°C
(350°F) oven for approx. 12
min. or until browned.

(6) Cool on wire rack.

Jams

Raspberry Jam

1L ......4 cups raspberries
1L ......4 cups sugar
****

(1) Place raspberries in flat bottom saucepan.

(2) Mash with potato masher.
(3) Heat until tumbling boil is reached.
(4) Boil for 2 minutes. Add sugar. Stir well.
(5) Bring back to boil. Boil 2 minutes, stirring constantly.
(6) Remove from heat. Beat with rotary beater, or wire whip for 4 minutes.
(7) Pour into sterilized jars and seal.

* Yields 1 1/2L (6 cups).

Citrus Marmalade

2........2 oranges
2........2 grapefruit
2........2 lemons
.........Water
.........Sugar
****

(1) Wash and squeeze juice from fruit, remove seeds.
(2) Put all skins and pulp through medium blade of food chopper. Add to juice.

(3) Measure juice and pulp, add same amount of boiling water. Let stand for 24 hours.
(4) Boil slowly for 20 minutes. Let stand another 24 hours.
(5) In a 6L (6 Qt.) heavy kettle bring 1L (4 cups) of citrus mixture to a boil and boil for 30 minutes uncovered. Add 1L (4 cups) of sugar.
(6) Over medium high heat bring to a boil and boil until it reaches the jelling stage.
(7) Pour into sterilized jars and seal.
(8) Repeat from #5 until mixture is all cooked. **Do not attempt to make a larger amount at one time. Mixture needs room to boil and could easily run over.

* Makes 6-500mL (6 pints) jars.
* To test for doneness; lift spoonful up over pan, letting fall off the spoon. You will notice if not ready it will run off spoon, most freely and look thin. When done three drops will come together and fall off spoon. **Do not boil too hard or too long as this will darken your marmalade — you will learn by doing.

205

Zucchini Jam

Different and delicious...

1L ......4 cups coarsely shredded zucchini
500mL...2 cups water
125mL...1/2 cup fresh lime juice
1........1 pkg. Certo
1 1/4L ..5 cups sugar
45mL....3 Tbsp. grated lime peel
****

(1) In a 6L (6 Qt.) saucepan combine zucchini, water and lime juice.
(2) Bring to a boil and boil gently for 10 minutes. Stir in sugar and lime peel. Return to boil.
(3) Stir in Certo.

(4) Return to hard rolling boil. Boil 2 minutes.
(5) Remove from heat.
(6) Stir for 5 minutes.
(7) Seal in jars.

* Makes 1 1/2L (6 cups).

Peach Jam

1L ......4 cups fully ripe peaches
50mL....1/4 cup lemon juice
1 1/4L ..5 cups sugar
5mL.....1 tsp. cinnamon
1/2......1/2 bottle Certo
****

(1) Remove peel and pit from peaches.
(2) In a large saucepan place peaches, lemon juice, sugar and cinnamon. Mix well.

(3) Place over high heat, bring to a rolling boil. Boil hard for 1 min., stir constantly.
(4) Remove from heat. Immediately stir in Certo.
(5) Skim off foam with metal spoon.
(6) Stir gently for 4 minutes.
(7) Seal in sterilized jars.

* Makes 1L (4 cups)

Applesauce

The way we like it...on the chunky side...

1 1/4L ..5 lbs. tart apples	(1)	Peel, core and cut apples into approx. 2cm. (3/4-inch) chunks.
125mL...1/2 cup water		
500mL...2 cups sugar	(2)	Measure 3L (3 Qts.) of chunked apples into a large heavy saucepan.

****

(3) Add water. Bring to a boil. Reduce heat. Cover. Simmer for 15 minutes.
(4) Add sugar while stirring gently.
(5) Cover and cook slowly until chunks are just tender. Gently turn chunks over occasionally. Rough stirring will make applesauce mushy.
(6) Pour into sterilized sealers, seal with snap lids. Process in hot water bath for 10 minutes.

*   Makes 2L (2 Qts.).
*   Serve with pork, beef, ice-cream, etc.

Blackberry or Grape Jelly #1

2.27kg ...5 lbs. blackberries **or** grapes	(1)	Stem and wash fruit.
250mL...1 cup water	(2)	In a large heavy dutch oven bring fruit and water to a boil. Reduce heat and simmer for 25 minutes covered.
1 1/2L ..6 cups sugar (approx.)		
1........1 bottle Certo		

****

(3) Mash fruit twice with a potato masher while simmering.
(4) Place in a jelly bag and let drip several hours.
(5) In a 1 1/2L-2L (6-8 Qt.) heavy dutch oven bring 1L (4 cups) juice and 1L (4 cups) sugar to a boil. Boil hard for 2 minutes, stirring constantly.
(6) Add 1/2 bottle Certo. Bring to a full rolling boil and boil for 2 minutes, stirring constantly.
(7) Let stand for 1 minute. Skim off foam with a metal spoon.
(8) Pour into sterilized jars. Let cool.
(9) Repeat procedure until all juice is made into jelly. (Use 250mL (1 cup) sugar to 250mL (1 cup) juice).

*   Cover with paraffin wax when cooled and set.
*   Jelly will boil over if pot is not large enough. Watch closely.
*   Wipe inside top of jelly jar with a damp cloth before applying wax.
*   Makes 1 1/2L (6 cups).

Grape Jelly #2

Stretching the budget in this one...very flavourful...

2.27kg...5 lbs. concord grapes
875mL...3 1/2 cups water
2........2 pkgs. unsweetened grape
        Kool-Aid powder
2L ......9 cups sugar (approx.)
1........1 bottle Certo
****

(1) Stem and wash grapes.
(2) In a heavy 6L (6 Qt.) dutch oven bring grapes and water to a boil, covered. Reduce heat and simmer covered for 25 min.
(3) Mash grapes twice with a potato masher, while simmering.

(4) Place in a jelly bag and let drip several hours.
(5) In a 6L (6 Qt.) dutch oven bring 1L (4 1/2 cups) of grape juice, 1 pkg. grape Kool-Aid powder (mix powder with small amount of juice), 1L (4 1/2 cups) sugar together.
(6) Over high heat bring to a boil and boil for 4 minutes. Add 1/2 bottle Certo.
(7) Bring to a rolling boil. Boil for 2 minutes; stirring constantly.
(8) Remove from heat. Let stand 1 minute.
(9) Skim off foam with a metal spoon. Pour into sterilized jars. Let cool.

* Repeat procedure until all grape juice is made into jelly. (Use 250mL (1 cup) sugar to 250mL (1 cup) juice).
* Cover with paraffin wax when cooled and set.
* Makes 2 3/4L (11 cups) approx.
* Jelly will boil over if pot is not large enough. Watch closely.
* Wipe inside top of jelly jar with a damp cloth before applying wax.

Raspberry Sauce

Not quite as sweet as jam...very tasty...

750mL...3 cups raspberries
375mL...1 1/2 cups sugar
30mL....2 Tbsp. cornstarch
****

(1) In a heavy saucepan bring the raspberries to a boil.
(2) Stir together sugar and cornstarch.

(3) Add to raspberries. Return to boil.
(4) Reduce heat, simmer for 10 minutes. Stir gently and frequently.

* Serve over ice-cream, in milk shakes, cereal, etc.

Strawberry Jam

1 1/4L ..5 cups whole, ripe strawberries
1 1/4L ..5 cups sugar
2mL.....1/2 tsp. butter
30mL....2 Tbsp. lemon juice
1/2......1/2 bottle Certo
****

(1) Wash berries remove stems. Place them in a bowl. Cut some berries to release juice (cut all berries, if large).

(2) Stir in the sugar (some sugar crystals will remain). Cover and let stand overnight.

(3) In the morning stir well, transfer into a large, heavy dutch oven, add butter. Over medium heat stir mixture until all sugar crystals are dissolved. Bring to a boil without stirring for 10 minutes. With a wooden spoon move mixture around gently once or twice. Keep heat down low enough to just keep mixture at a gentle boil.

(4) Gently stir in lemon juice, then Certo. Remove from heat. Skim off foam, pour into sterilized jars. Cover with paraffin wax when cooled and set.

Pickles

Yellow Bean Pickles

2.72kg . . .6 lbs. yellow beans	(1) String beans, cut into 2.5cm.
2mL. . . . .1/2 tsp. salt	(1-inch) lengths. In a saucepan
2L . . . . . .8 cups sugar	boil beans with salt added until
500mL. . .2 cups flour	tender. Drain well. Set aside.
10mL. . . .2 tsp. turmeric	(2) Stir together dry ingredients.
125mL. . .1/2 cup mustard (dry)	(3) Add vinegar slowly. Mix to-
15mL. . . .1 Tbsp. celery seed	gether well.
3L . . . . . .3 Qts. vinegar	(4) Boil gently 10 minutes.

****

(5) Add beans, heat through thoroughly.
(6) Pack in sterilized jars. Seal while hot.

Million Dollar Pickles

These pickles resemble bread and butter pickles...

1. . . . . . . .1 red pepper	(1) Remove seeds from peppers.
4L . . . . . .4 Qts. thinly sliced	Cut into pieces.
cucumbers	(2) Place cucumbers and peppers
2. . . . . . . .2 green peppers	into a stone crock.
227mL. . .1 scant cup salt	(3) Sprinkle with salt.

****

(4) Cover with water; let stand
overnight.

Syrup:

1L. . . . . 4 cups Sugar
1L . . . . . .1 Qt. vinegar	(5) In the morning drain well and
5mL. . . . .1 tsp. turmeric	prepare syrup.
5mL. . . . .1 tsp. celery seed	(6) In a large saucepan, blend
2mL. . . . .1/2 tsp. mustard seed	syrup ingredients together.
30mL. . . .2 Tbsp. pickling spice	(7) Bring to a boil. Add cucumbers

****

and peppers. Cook for 20 min.

(8) Pack in sterilized jars. Seal while hot.

* Do not use metal container when soaking vegetables overnight.

Thousand Island Relish

8........8 large cukes
12.......12 large onions
1........1 large cauliflower
2........2 red peppers
2........2 green peppers
125mL...1/2 cup pickling salt
1 1/4L ..5 cups water
****

(1) Wash and wipe cukes, do not peel.
(2) Peel onions, wash cauliflower.
(3) Remove seeds from peppers.
(4) Put all vegetables through coarse blade of food grinder.
(5) Sprinkle with 125mL (1/2 cup) salt.

(6) Add 1 1/4L (5 cups) water. Let stand 1 hour. Drain well.

Dressing:

1 1/4L ..5 cups vinegar
750mL...3 cups water (divided)
1 1/2L ..6 cups sugar
15mL....1 Tbsp. mustard seed
15mL....1 Tbsp. celery seed
15mL....1 Tbsp. turmeric
175mL...3/4 cup flour
90mL....6 Tbsp. mustard (dry)
****

(7) Heat vinegar, 250mL (1 cup) water, sugar, mustard seed and celery seed.
(8) Mix turmeric, flour and mustard together. Slowly add remaining 500mL (2 cups) of water. Blend until all lumps are smooth. Pour into vinegar mixture.

(9) Cook 3 minutes. Add vegetables, cook 20 minutes.
(10) Seal in jars.

* If vegetables are not drained well, relish will be too runny.
* Makes approx. 3L (12 pints).

Beet Pickles

500g.....1 lb. small beets
1L ......1 Qt. vinegar
500mL...2 cups sugar
6mL.....1 1/4 Tbsp. pickling spice
****

(1) Wash beets. *Do not peel. Leave 3cm. (1 1/2-inch) stems.
(2) In a saucepan boil beets in a small amount of water until tender. *Do not over cook.

(3) Drain, rinse with cold water.
(4) Remove skins, slice or leave whole if very small; pack in sterilized jars.
(5) In a saucepan, bring vinegar, sugar and pickling spice to a boil. Boil slowly for 5 minutes.
(6) Pour syrup over beets. Insert a knife and move beets around to get rid of any air bubbles.
(7) Seal while hot.

* Beets retain colour and vitamins, if left unpeeled while boiling.
* Syrup enough for 1 3/4L (7 pints).

212

Green Tomato Pickles

30.......30 medium green tomatoes	(1) Slice green tomatoes, cut onions
6........6 large onions	into pieces.
125mL...1/2 cup salt	(2) Place tomatoes and onions into
*********	a stone crock.
	(3) Sprinkle with salt. Let stand
	overnight.

Syrup:

750mL...3 cups vinegar	(4) In the morning drain and rinse
625mL...2 1/2 cups brown sugar	well. Drain well.
5mL.....1 tsp. cloves	(5) Heat vinegar, add sugar and
5mL.....1 tsp. allspice	spices. Bring to a boil.
5mL.....1 tsp. celery seed	(6) Add tomatoes and onions.
5mL.....1 tsp. mustard seed	(7) Cook slowly, stirring often
*********	1 1/2 hours. If not sweet

enough, add more sugar. If tomatoes are very green, pickles will be bitter.

(8) Pack into sterilized jars. Seal while hot.

* Do not use a metal container when soaking vegetables overnight.

Dill Pickles

So simple...sooo good...

8-10cm ..3-4-inch pickling cucumb-	(1) Scrub cucumbers, leave whole.
ers	Do not cut ends off. Do not
........Dill weed	pierce.
........Garlic cloves	(2) Pack cucumbers into jars. *Fill
*********	3/4 full.
	(3) Cut garlic cloves in half. Add
	to jars (approx. 4 pieces).
	(4) Place one or two heads of dill
	in each jar. Some stock may be
	used also.

Brine:

1 1/2L ..6 cups water	(5) Bring water, vinegar and pick-
75mL....1/3 cup vinegar	ling salt to a boil. Cool slightly.
75mL....1/3 cup pickling salt	(6) Pour over cucumbers; making
*********	sure cucumbers are covered
	with brine. Seal with hot lids.

* Approx. 625mL (2 1/2 cups) of brine to fill 1L (1 Qt.) jar.

Hamburger Sauce

A must with hamburger...use as a sandwich spread also...

12.......12 large to medium green tomatoes	(1)	Put green tomatoes through medium blade of meat grinder.
6........6 medium onions	(2)	Strain through colander.
2........2 large red pepper	(3)	Save juice, in case your sand-
2........2 large green peppers		wich spread is too thick.
750mL...3 cups sugar	(4)	Grind onions, red and green
15mL....1 Tbsp. salt		peppers.
250mL...1 cup water	(5)	Put drained tomatoes and vege-
175mL...3/4 cup flour		tables into large saucepan.
250mL...1 cup vinegar	(6)	Add sugar, salt and water.
250mL...1 cup water		Cook 10 minutes.
1L ......1 Qt. Miracle Whip salad dressing	(7)	Mix flour, vinegar and water together, add to vegetables.
170mL...6 oz. prepared mustard	(8)	Cook 10 minutes longer.

****

(9) Remove from heat. Add Miracle Whip and prepared mustard. Stir together very well.
(10) Put into sterilized jars and seal.
(11) Put into hot water bath and process for 20 minutes.

* Makes eight 500mL (pint) jars.

Mint Chutney

This is delicious served with cold meat...

1kg .....2 lbs. ripe tomatoes	(1)	Chop tomatoes, apples, pep-
1kg .....2 lbs. tart apples		pers, onions and mint. Add
3........3 large sweet peppers		raisins.
6........6 small onions	(2)	Scald vinegar, add sugar, salt
125mL...1/2 cup mint leaves		and mustard. Let cool.
1........1 small hot pepper (Opt.)	(3)	Add the chopped ingredients.
250mL...1 cup seedless raisins	(4)	Mix thoroughly. Pack cold into
750mL...3 cups vinegar		sterilized jars.
750mL...3 cups sugar	(5)	Seal with hot lids.
30mL....2 Tbsp. salt	(6)	Let stand 10 days before using.
30mL....2 Tbsp. mustard (dry)		

****

214

Royal Anne Specialty

The combined ingredients give this relish a taste tempting tangy treat...
A prize winning recipe...

3.18kg...7 lbs. green tomatoes	(1) Chunk green tomatoes and
3........3 large onions	onions. *Place in a stone crock.
150mL...2/3 cup pickling salt	(2) Sprinkle with pickling salt. Let
2 1/2L ..10 cups brown sugar	stand overnight.
10mL....2 tsp. cayenne pepper	(3) In the morning drain, rinse,
5mL.....1 tsp. cinnamon	drain well and combine with the
4.7mL...4/5 tsp. cloves	rest of ingredients, except flour
4.7mL...4/5 tsp. allspice	and 125mL (1/2 cup) vinegar.
650mL...2 2/3 cups vinegar	(4) Boil gently for 30 minutes.
(divided)	(5) Mix flour with 125mL (1/2 cup)
45mL....3 Tbsp. curry powder	vinegar to make a paste. Add
2........2 cloves garlic	gradually to pickles, cook until
175mL...3/4 cup flour	thick.

****

(6) Pack in sterilized jars. Seal while hot.

* Makes approx. ten 500mL (pint) jars.
* Do not use metal container when soaking vegetables overnight.

Pickled Onions

So nice to have on hand at party time or whenever...

2.27kg...5 lbs. silver skin onions	(1) Peel onions, sprinkle with salt
250mL...1 cup pickling salt	and cover with boiling water.
1L ......4 cups sugar	(2) Leave for 24 hours. Drain. Re-
1L ......1 Qt. white vinegar	serve liquid. Rinse.
30mL....2 Tbsp. mixed whole pick-	(3) Reheat reserved liquid to boil-
ling spice	ing point; pour over onions.

****

(4) Repeat this process for 3 days. On the fourth day drain liquid off and
     rinse thoroughly.
(5) Bring sugar, vinegar and spices (tied in a bag) to a boil; pour over
     onions. Leave for 24 hours.
(6) Drain off liquid and reheat. Pour over onions again.
(7) Repeat this process for 3 days.
(8) On the fourth day drain off liquid and bring to a boil.
(9) Place onions in hot sterilized jars. Cover with hot syrup. Seal
     immediately.

* Makes three 500mL (pint) jars.

Sweet Mixed Pickles

You won't be disappointed in these pickles...
Every bit as good as the purchased ones...

3.18kg...7 lbs. pickling cucumbers
1kg .....2 lbs. silver skin onions
1kg .....2 lb. head of cauliflower
****

(1) Cut cucumbers into 1-2cm. (1/2-3/4-inch) slices.
(2) Pour boiling water over silver skin onions for easy removal of skins.
(3) Remove core from cauliflower, section into serving pieces.

Brine:

3L ......12 cups water
375mL...1 1/2 cups pickling salt
****

(4) Place in crock (non metal).
(5) Cover with brine.
(6) Mix water with salt until salt is dissolved. *Do not boil.

Solution:

1L ......1 Qt. vinegar
2L ......2 Qts. water
30mL....6 tsp. alum
****

(7) Let stand for 5 days.
(8) Drain, cover with solution.
(9) In a large kettle heat vinegar, water and 30mL (6 tsp.) alum to boiling. Add vegetables. Let get real hot. Let stand for 1 day.
(10) Drain, throw away solution.

Syrup:

2L ......2 Qts. vinegar
5mL.....1 tsp. turmeric
125mL...1/2 cup pickling spice
         (tied in a bag)
2L ......8 cups white sugar
****

(11) In saucepan heat vinegar, tumeric, pickling spice and sugar. Bring to a boil.
(12) Pour over pickles. Let stand overnight.

(13) Drain; reheat syrup to a boil, pour over pickles. Let stand overnight. Repeat this process the next day.
(14) On the last day, preheat syrup, add 5mL (1 tsp.) soda to each 4 litres (1 gallon) of syrup. Skim off foam to leave syrup clear.
(15) Place pickles in sterilized jars.
(16) Cover with syrup and seal.

* Syrup will foam up when soda is added.
* Vegetables must be covered at all times with brine, solution or syrup.
* Store in a cool, dark place.
* Makes 9L (9 Qt.) jars.

Tomato Ketchup

8L ......8 Qts. ripe tomatoes
500mL...2 cups chopped onions
50mL....1/4 cup salt
500mL...2 cups vinegar
500mL...2 cups sugar
125mL...1/2 cup pickling spice tied
       loosely in a bag
      ****

(1) Wash tomatoes. *Do not peel. Cut into small pieces.
(2) Add onions and cook until soft.
(3) Strain and mash through a sieve.
(4) Add salt, sugar, pickling spice and vinegar.

(5) Cook slowly until thick. About 2 hours.
(6) Remove spices. Seal in sterilized jars.

* If mixture and spices are left to simmer longer you could end up with chili.

Ice-Cream Pail Pickles

2kg .....4 lbs. thinly sliced
      cucumbers.
1kg .....2 lbs. sliced onions **or**
      small silver skin onions
1........1 green pepper
500g.....1 lb. head cauliflower
      (Opt.)
      ****

(1) Wash and slice cucumbers.
(2) Slice onions, if large. Leave silver skin onions whole.
(3) Seed green pepper, cut into strips.
(4) Remove excess core and outer leaves from cauliflower, section flowerettes into serving pieces.
(5) Place vegetables into an ice-cream pail.

Syrup:

1 1/2L ..6 cups sugar
750mL...3 cups vinegar
30mL....2 Tbsp. pickling salt
15mL....3 tsp. celery salt
15mL....3 tsp. mustard seed
15mL....3 tsp. tumeric
      ****

(6) Mix together, but do not boil: sugar, vinegar, salt, celery salt, mustard seed and tumeric.
(7) Pour over vegetables. Store in refrigerator.
(8) Stir first 2 days. Keeps indefinitely.

(9) Vegetables must be completely covered with syrup.

* This amount of syrup should cover 3L (3 Qts.) of vegetables.

Chili Sauce

Very good served with cold beef...

12.......12 large ripe tomatoes	(1)	Peel and core tomatoes.
2........2 large onions	(2)	Chop onions (fine).
5mL.....1 tsp. salt	(3)	Put into large saucepan.
250mL...1 cup brown sugar	(4)	Add rest of ingredients.
5mL.....1 tsp. cinnamon	(5)	Cook slowly till thick; stir
5mL.....1 tsp. cloves		often.
1mL.....1/4 tsp. cayenne pepper	(6)	Pack in sterilized jars.
675mL...1 1/2 cups vinegar	(7)	Seal while hot.

****

Candy

Peanut Brittle

This brittle will surely satisfy the sweet tooth in your family...

500mL...2 cups white sugar
250mL...1 cup brown sugar
125mL...1/2 cup corn syrup
125mL...1/2 cup water
.........Dash of salt
50mL....1/4 cup butter or margarine
500mL...2 cups peanuts (roasted)
5mL.....1 tsp. baking soda
****

(1) Have ready 2 buttered cookie sheets.
(2) In heavy 3L (3 Qt.) saucepan combine white sugar, brown sugar, water, corn syrup and salt.
(3) Cook and stir until the sugar is dissolved.
(4) When the mixture boils, stir in the butter.

(5) Cook without stirring to 110°C (230°F).
(6) Cook and stir to 149°C (300°F).
(7) Remove from heat, stir in soda, mix well.
(8) Quickly stir in peanuts, spread evenly onto buttered cookie sheets.
(9) Immediately stretch mixture, using two forks, take care as candy is very hot.

* Brittle should be thin.
* When cool, break into serving pieces.

Brazil Slab

The ultimate for all chocolate lovers...a cut above the others...

500g.....1 lb. milk chocolate
170g.....6 oz. coarsely cracked Brazil nuts
****

(1) Coarsely crack Brazil nuts. Set aside.
(2) Partially melt chocolate over water.

(3) Remove from heat.
(4) Continue stirring until chocolate is melted.
(5) Stir in Brazil nuts. Spread on waxed paper lined 22x22cm. (9x9-inch) pan.
(6) Chill until chocolate is firm.
(7) Break into pieces.
(8) Store in cool place.

* Makes approx. 625g (1 1/4 lbs.).

Chocolate Fudge

Tempting...luscious fudge... Could be named Beginners Fudge, with...professional results...

500mL...2 cups sugar	(1) In a heavy 3L (3 Qt.) saucepan mix together sugar, butter, canned milk, marshmallows and salt.
50mL....1/4 cup butter	
16.......16 large marshamallows	
175mL...3/4 cup canned milk	
1mL.....1/4 tsp. salt	(2) Over medium heat cook until mixture is bubbling all over top. Stir constantly. Continue to cook for 5 minutes.
250mL...1 cup chocolate chipits	
5mL.....1 tsp. vanilla	
250mL...1 cup chopped walnuts	

****

(3) Remove from heat.
(4) Stir in chipits until melted.
(5) Stir in vanilla and nuts.
(6) Spread in buttered 20cm. (8-inch) square pan.
(7) Cool and cut into 36 square pieces.

* **Important:** Watch heat closely while stirring to prevent scorching.
* For Caramel Fudge, simply exchange caramel chipits in place of chocolate.

Maple Walnut Fudge

Not for reducers...but cheaters allowed...

750mL...3 cups brown sugar	(1) In a heavy 3L (3 Qt.) saucepan mix together sugar, milk, maple syrup and marshmallows.
250mL...1 cup evaporated milk	
6........6 large marshmallows	
75mL....1/3 cup maple syrup **or** corn syrup	(2) Over medium heat and stirring constantly, bring to a boil. Boil until soft ball stage 116°C (240°F) on candy thermometer.
16mL....1 1/4 Tbsp. butter	
3mL.....3/4 tsp. vanilla	
125mL...1/2 cup chopped walnuts	(3) Remove from heat.

****

(4) Add butter and vanilla.
(5) Beat until it starts to sugar.
(6) Quickly add 125mL (1/2 cup) chopped walnuts.
(7) Spread in a 20cm. (8-inch) square buttered pan.
(8) Cut into squares when near cool.

* **Important:** Watch heat closely to prevent scorching.

Caramels

250mL...1 cup butter
550mL...2 1/4 cups brown sugar
        (packed)
250mL...1 cup light corn syrup
398mL...14 oz. can sweetened con-
        densed milk
5mL.....1 tsp. vanilla

****

(1) In a heavy 3L (3 Qt.) saucepan melt butter, add corn syrup, sugar, and salt. Combine well.
(2) Gradually add condensed milk, stirring constantly.
(3) Cook and stir over medium heat to 120°C (245°F), firm ball stage.

(4) Remove from heat. Stir in vanilla.
(5) Pour into well buttered 22x22cm. (9x9-inch) square pan.
(6) Cut into 2.5cm. (1-inch) squares when cooled.
(7) Wrap pieces individually in clear plastic. 72-7.4x10cm. (3x4-inch) clear plastic wraps required.

Chocolate Caramels

(1) Cut up 2 squares 50g (2 oz.) unsweetened chocolate.
(2) Add to condensed milk.
(3) Prepare as above.
(4) Store wrapped caramels in air tight container in a cool place.

Chocolate Treats

500mL...2 cups semi-sweet choco-
        late chips
175mL...3/4 cup raw oatmeal
175mL...3/4 cup wheat germ
30mL....2 Tbsp. peanut butter
125mL...1/2 cup raisins
125mL...1/2 cup shredded unsweet-
        ened coconut
****

(1) In top of double boiler melt chocolate chips, stirring often.
(2) Add remaining ingredients and mix well.
(3) Drop by a teaspoon onto a buttered cookie sheet.
(4) Refrigerate until hard.

Serves 8.

Albino Almond Bark

500g.....1 lb. white chocolate
170g.....6 oz. coarsely cracked
blanched toasted
almonds
****

(1) Coarsely crack almonds. Set aside.
(2) Partially melt chocolate over hot water.

(3) Remove from heat, continue stirring until chocolate is completely melted.
(4) Stir in almonds. Spread in single layer in waxed paper lined 22x33cm. (9x13-inch) pan.
(5) Chill until chocolate is firm.
(6) Break into pieces. Store in cool place.

* Bakers semi-sweet chocolate could be used in place of white chocolate, with very good results.
* Add 125mL (1/2 cup) raisins to above mixture for variation, reduce almonds by 125mL (1/2 cup).

222

Miscellaneous

Mixed Breakfast Cereal

This is the taste so many love...the best way to start your day...

250mL...1 cup cracked wheat
125mL...1/2 cup cracked rye
45mL....3 Tbsp. flax seed
****

(1) Mix these three ingredients together.
(2) Store in covered container.

* When preparing to cook cereal mix three parts water with one part mix.

2 Servings:	6 Servings:
250mL...1 cup water	750mL...3 cups water
1mL.....1/4 tsp. salt	3mL.....3/4 tsp. salt
75mL....1/3 cup mixed cereal	250mL...1 cup mixed cereal
*********	*********

(1) Bring water and salt to a boil, slowly add mixed cereal, stirring vigorously. Cover.
(2) Reduce heat to low, cook slowly for 15-20 minutes, longer if you prefer.
(3) Stir occasionally to keep from settling to the bottom.
(4) Serve hot with milk, white or brown sugar.

* When making porridge, add 1-2mL (1/4-1/2 tsp.) of butter.
* This will make clean up easier.

Iced Tea

1 1/2L ..6 cups boiling water
2........2 tea bags (dark)
125mL...1/2 cup sugar (approx.)
****

(1) Pour boiling water over tea
bags. Let steep 8-10 minutes.
(2) Remove tea bags. Stir in sugar
until dissolved.

(3) Pour into a glass bottle, add several ice cubes. Refrigerate. Serve well
chilled.
(4) Add lemon juice to taste, if desired.

* Makes 1.5mL (6 cups).

Granola

You will find this simple granola flavourful and easy to chew...

500mL...2 cups whole wheat flour
2 1/2L ..6 cups rolled oats
250mL...1 cup coconut
250mL...1 cup wheat germ
125mL...1/2 cup water
250mL...1 cup oil
250mL...1 cup honey **or** corn syrup
10mL....2 tsp. vanilla
10mL....2 tsp. salt
****

(1) In a large mixing bowl combine whole wheat flour, rolled oats, coconut and wheat germ together. Set aside.
(2) Blend water, oil, honey, vanilla and salt together. Add to dry ingredients and mix thoroughly.
(3) Spread out on 2 greased cookie sheets.

(4) Bake in 120°C (250°F) oven for 1 hour, stirring occasionally.
(5) After granola is removed from the oven you may stir in nuts, raisins, dried fruit, dates or figs.
(6) Store in a covered container in the refrigerator.

Sesame Granola

1L ......4 cups rolled oats
250mL...1 cup finely chopped nuts
3mL.....3/4 tsp. salt
125mL...1/2 cup coconut
125mL...1/2 cup sesame seeds
5mL.....1 tsp. cinnamon
125mL...1/2 cup honey
75mL....1/3 cup vegetable oil
2mL.....1/2 tsp. vanilla
250mL...1 cup finely cut dried
         dried apples
****

(1) In a large mixing bowl combine nuts, rolled oats, salt, coconut, sesame seeds and cinnamon. Set aside.
(2) Blend honey, oil and vanilla together. Add to dry ingredients and mix thoroughly.
(3) Spread on 2 greased cookie sheets.
(4) Bake in 150°C (300°F) oven for 20-25 minutes.
(5) Stir occasionally.

(6) After granola is removed from the oven, add 250mL (1 cup) dried apples.
(7) Cool, then store in tightly covered container in the refrigerator.

Mock Almond Paste

This will double as a marzipan paste...
Use on heavy fruit cakes...dip in chocolate...

1........1 medium sized baked or
         boiled sweet potato
1........1 egg yolk
1mL.....1/4 tsp. salt
1kg .....2 lbs. sifted icing sugar
         (more or less)
15mL....1 Tbsp. almond flavouring
****

(1) Bake potato until tender.
(2) Peel and mash well. Add un-beaten egg yolk and salt.
(3) Work in almond extract, then icing sugar to a smooth stiff paste.
(4) Place in plastic bag.

(5) Turn twister on tight to seal out all air.
(6) Store in refrigerator for four days.
(7) Turn out on work surface, sprinkled with icing sugar and knead.
(8) Roll to desired thickness, sprinkle with icing sugar, as needed.

* Makes 1.14kg. (2 1/2 lbs.).
* Mock marzipan can be frozen.
* Do not use yams as they are orange in colour.

Chocolate Mix

6........6 squares (6 oz.) unsweet-
         ened chocolate
250mL...1 cup water
150mL...2/3 cup sugar
250mL...1 cup whipping cream*
2........2 dashes EACH salt and
         cinnamon
5mL.....1 tsp. vanilla
****

(1) Melt chocolate over hot water until almost melted. Remove from heat and beat smooth.
(2) Bring water and sugar to boil, stir until sugar is dissolved, making a syrup.
(3) Simmer 3 minutes. Remove from heat, let cool to warm.

(4) Place chocolate, syrup, cream, cinnamon, salt, and vanilla into blender and mix for 1 minute. Store in sterilized jar and refrigerate.

* Makes 625mL (2 1/2 cups).
* Place 1/4 cup chocolate mix into a 250mL (8 oz.) mug, fill mug with milk.
* If hot chocolate is desired, place mug into microwave oven on high for 40 seconds. Add 1-2 marshmallows.
* Try it in your thermos.
* Evaporated milk can be used in place of whipping cream, if desired.

Bouquet Garni

This is the blend of herbs we enjoy in our soups...

2mL.....1/2 tsp. dried savory
leaves
2mL.....1/2 tsp. dried marjoram
leaves
1mL.....1/4 tsp. dried parsley
flakes
1mL.....1/4 tsp. dried thyme
leaves
1mL.....1/4 tsp. dried tarragon
leaves
1mL.....1/4 tsp. dried basil leaves
****

(1) Combine all ingredients together, store in moisture free bottle.
(2) Use by small amounts in soups, add to desired tastes.

Butter Mincemeat

Just the way you like it...

10.......10 medium grated cooking
apples
.68kg....1 1/2 lbs. seedless raisins
(cut)
.68kg....1 1/2 lbs. dark sultanas
(cut)
.68kg. ...1 1/2 lbs. currants
.........Juice and rind of 2 large
oranges and 1 lemon
finely chopped
50mL....1/4 cup mixed peel
5mL.....1 tsp. EACH cinnamon,
nutmeg and salt
2mL.....1/2 tsp. EACH cloves and
mace
750mL...3 cups brown sugar
375mL...1 1/2 cups sweet cider
juice
.23kg....1/2 lb. butter
300mL...1 1/4 cup rye whiskey **or**
dark rum (Opt.)
****

(1) Mix all the ingredients together in a large saucepan.
(2) Place over low heat, stirring often until completely blended and butter is melted.
(3) Remove from heat, stir in rye whiskey.
(4) Bottle in sterilized jars.
(5) Store in cool dark place.
* Rye whiskey may be stirred in just prior to baking, if desired. 50mL (1/4 cup) rye whiskey to each 1L (4 cups) of mincemeat.

Slush

750mL...3 cups sugar
1 1/2L ..6 cups water
1.36L....48 oz. can pineapple **or** grapefruit juice
355mL...12 1/2 oz. can frozen lemon juice concentrate
355mL...12 1/2 oz. can frozen orange juice concentrate
........Lemon lime soda
****

(1) In a saucepan combine sugar and water.
(2) Heat and stir until sugar is dissolved.
(3) Bring to a full, rolling boil.
(4) Remove from heat and chill.
(5) Mix in pineapple juice, undiluted orange and lemon juices.
(6) Pour into containers and freeze.

(7) To serve, half-fill tall glasses with lemon lime soda. Spoon in frozen mixture to fill glasses.
(8) Serve with spoons and straws.

* Makes 4L (16 cups).

Traditional Eggnog

The way Grandma made it...

6........6 large eggs, separated
1mL.....1/4 tsp. salt
150mL...2/3 cup sugar, divided
625mL...2 1/2 cups light cream
500mL...2 cups milk
300mL...1 1/4 cups whipped cream
........Nutmeg
........Rum **or** rye
****

(1) In a mixer beat egg whites and salt until frothy throughout.
(2) Gradually add 75mL (1/3 cup) of the sugar, continue beating until stiff peaks form.
(3) In another bowl beat egg yolks until light.
(4) Gradually add remaining sugar, beat until thick and lemon coloured.

(5) Very slowly add light cream and milk, beating constantly.
(6) Whip cream until softly stiff; beat egg whites until stiff.
(7) Gently fold whipped cream and meringue into egg cream mixture. Chill thoroughly.
(8) Mix 30mL (1 oz.) rum or rye to each 250mL (8 oz.) glass of eggnog.
(9) Sprinkle with nutmeg.

* Makes 12 servings.

Lemonade Mix

Digging down deep for this one...very good...

1L ......4 cups water	(1) In a saucepan bring water to a
1L ......4 cups sugar	boil.
45mL....3 Tbsp. cream of tartar	(2) Add sugar and stir until dis-
45mL....3 Tbsp. citric acid	solved.
15mL....1 Tbsp. epsom salts	(3) Remove from heat; stir in
.........White of 1 egg	cream of tartar, citric acid, ep-
425mL...1 3/4 cups lemon juice	som salt and lemon rind.
(approx. 4 lemons)	(4) When cool, add lemon juice.
.........Grated rind of 2 lemons	(5) Beat egg with a fork until
*********	foamy, add to lemonade mix-
	ture.

(6) Strain, store in refrigerator.
(7) To serve, mix 250mL (1 cup) of lemonade mixture with 750mL (3 cups) water. Serve cold.
(8) Makes 2L (8 cups) mix. Diluted makes 1L (32 oz.).

* This lemonade may be frozen before mixed with water. If frozen freeze in 250 or 500mL (1 or 2 cup) portions. Label portion sizes.

Frosty Fruit Flavoured Drink

Cool and refreshing...ideal for those warm, summer days or whenever...

1........1 egg	(1) Place all ingredients into a
2mL.....1/2 tsp. vanilla	blender.
45mL....3 Tbsp. sugar	(2) Blend at high speed approx. 3-5
30mL....2 Tbsp. skim milk powder	seconds.
500mL...2 cups prepared, frozen	(3) Serve at once in tall glass
orange juice	with straw.
6........6 ice cubes	
*********	

* Makes 625mL (2 1/2 cups).

Variation:

40mL....1 1/2 oz. Grand Marnier
      mixed with
250mL...1 cup flavoured drink
      above
    ****

228

Deep Fat Batter

Use for vegetables, meat or fish...as in fish and chips...

125mL...1/2 cup flour
125mL...1/2 cup cornstarch
15mL....3 tsp. baking powder
5mL.....1 tsp. dry mustard
1mL.....1/4 tsp. salt
150mL...2/3 cup milk (or more)
1........1 beaten egg
.........Oil for deep frying
****

(1) Stir flour, cornstarch, baking powder, salt and mustard together.
(2) In a mixing bowl combine milk and egg.
(3) Mix well.
(4) Pat cleaned vegetables, meat or fish dry with paper towel. Coat with batter and deep fry in hot oil.

Nuts and Bolts

1........1 small pkg. Cheerios
1........1 pkg. pretzel sticks
1kg .....2 lbs. mixed nuts
500g.....1 lb. pecans
175mL...3/4 cup butter
1/2mL...1/8 tsp. cayenne
15mL....1 Tbsp. seasoning salt
30mL....2 Tbsp. smoked salt
5mL.....1 tsp. marjoram
5mL.....1 tsp. savory
2mL.....1/2 tsp. onion powder
2mL.....1/2 tsp. garlic powder

(1) Mix Cheerios, pretzel sticks, mixed nuts and pecans together.
(2) Melt butter, add flavouring, pour over Cheerio mixture.
(3) Stir the mixture until all cereal and nuts are well coated.
(4) Bake in 120°C (250°F) oven for 45 minutes, stirring gently every 15 minutes.
(5) Cool on brown paper.
(6) Store in air tight container.

* Wheat Chex and Rice Chex may be added, if available.

Spickle Spackle/Nuts & Bolts

A favorite for years...

750mL...3 cups shreddies
175mL...3/4 cup salted peanuts
250mL...1 cup thin pretzel sticks
75mL....1/3 cup butter or margarine
15mL....1 Tbsp. worcestershire sauce
2mL.....1/2 tsp. celery salt
5mL.....1 tsp. onion salt
500mL...2 cups Cherrios
****

(1) Mix shreddies, peanuts, Cherrios and pretzels together on cookie sheets.
(2) Melt butter, add worcestershire sauce, celery salt and onion salt; Mix well.
(3) Pour butter mixture over cereal mix, stirring the mixture until all cereal is coated.
(4) Bake in 150°C (300°F) oven 35-40 minutes, stirring every 10 minutes.

(5) Cool on brown paper.
(6) Store in air tight container.

Antipasto

750mL...3 cups diced cauliflower
50mL....1/4 cup olive oil
398mL...1-14 oz. tin ripe olives
375mL...1-12 oz. jar pickled onions
250mL...1 cup green olives
284mL...1-10 oz. can mushrooms
1........1 large green pepper
128mL...1-4 1/2 oz. jar pimento
1L ......2-15 oz. bottles ketchup
375mL...1 1/2 cups hot ketchup
750mL...3 cups mixed pickles
50g......1 tin anchovies (chopped)
396g.....2-7 oz. tins solid white
            tuna
226g.....2-4 oz. tins small shrimps
        ****

(1) Chop all ingredients to the texture of very coarse relish. DO NOT USE BLENDER.
(2) In a large saucepan combine cauliflower, olive oil, ripe olives, onions and green olives. Cook 10 minutes. Keep heat low. Stir constantly.
(3) Add mushrooms, green pepper, pimento, ketchup, hot ketchup and mixed pickles.
(4) Over medium low heat, simmer 10 minutes, stirring often.
(5) Drain fish. Pour boiling water over to rinse. Flake tuna with a fork. Chop anchovies. Add to hot mixture. Stir in well.

(6) Pour into sterilized jars and seal. Process in hot water bath 10 minutes or freeze.

* If freezing, fill jars 3/4 full. Leave room for expansion.
* Makes approx. 3L (6 pints).
* Serve on crackers.

Sweetened Whipped Cream

With tips for success...

250mL...1 cup whipping cream
30mL....2 Tbsp. powdered sugar
2mL.....1/2 tsp. vanilla
        ****

(1) In a mixing bowl, beat cream until soft peaks form.
(2) Blend in sugar and vanilla, beat until stiff peaks form.

Tips:

* Chill bowl and beaters well in refrigerator. Cream should be well chilled. Beat with electric mixer or rotary beater. Add powdered sugar and vanilla after cream reaches soft peak stage. Beat until stiff peaks form and cream is still glossy. *Do not over beat or cream can begin to turn to butter. If cream starts to turn to butter, beat in a few tablespoons of cream or evaporated milk.

230

Sweetened Condensed Milk

So easy to make...so economical...
Use in all your favorite recipes...when called for...

30mL....2 Tbsp. butter or margar-
           ine
250mL...1 cup sugar
125mL...1/2 cup boiling water
500mL...2 cups skim milk powder
.........Pinch of salt
        ****

(1) In blender beat butter, sugar and water until smooth.
(2) Add skim milk powder.
(3) Beat until thick. Add salt.
(4) Pour into sterilized jar.
(5) Store in refrigerator.

* Makes 375mL (1 1/2 cups).

Buttermilk

125mL...1/2 cup buttermilk
1L ......4 cups fresh milk
        ****

(1) Leave 125mL (1/2 cup) commercial or homemade buttermilk in bottom of its container.

(2) Fill with milk, leaving 1.5-2.5cm. (1/2-1-inch) head space.
(3) Close container and shake well.
(4) Let sit in warm place for 10 days.
(5) Refrigerate when slightly thickened.

Perfect Eggs Everytime

Forget the worry, forget the fuss, perfect eggs everytime...
Boiled, poached, scrambled, fried or separated...

* Your timer is your key word for boiled eggs just as you like them.
* In my attempt to explain how to have perfect eggs everytime, I will give you an example how I achieve this task.
* This must be remembered: pot size, amount of water used, whether water is cold or hot, eggs from the refrigerator or room temperature.
* I will give you my chart. If it does not work for you, make up your own chart then time and time again repeating the same steps you will achieve perfect results. (This may take a few go arounds.)
* I must stress that when the buzzer sounds, you must remove them from the heat and immediately pour off boiling water, rinse with cold water, to stop them from cooking more.
* For best results, soft-boiled eggs should be served immediately. If they are not served immediately wrap them in a tea towel. Eggs will become a bit harder when wrapped in a towel.

Hard Boiled Eggs

* For perfectly centered yolks in cooked egg, roll egg horizontally two or three times in the same direction before cooking. No need to worry about over or under cooking. No need to worry about peeling boiled eggs. This method is fool proof on eggs as soon as they are one day old.
* If eggs are boiled the same day they are laid they will not peel easily. If you must boil eggs the same day as they are laid, chill them in cold water until all animal heat is out. Boil, cool, then cut them in half with a knife; using a spoon scoop egg out of their shells. At all times inspect carefully and remove any egg shells.
* Place 2 eggs into saucepan, cover with 625mL (2 1/2 cups) cold water, place pot on burner, turn burner on high; set timer for 14 minutes. Remove from heat, let set in hot water 10 minutes. Immediately rinse under plenty of cold water to stop eggs from cooking. The eggs will be tender with no grey rings.
* For easy shelling, gently (but hard enough to crack egg shells) roll the eggs back and forth in the pan containing a little cold water. The water will run into the cracks, which will help in shelling the eggs. Peel the eggs at this point, before they get cold. The egg is flexible when warm and can easily be peeled. After you peel each egg rinse it under cold water to remove any egg shells. Place the peeled and rinsed egg on a tea towel to dry. (Paper towel sometimes sticks to the peeled egg). Cool uncovered. Cover and refrigerate.

Separating Eggs

* Practice is your key word in separating eggs.
* Try separating eggs when you are going to make scrambled eggs, cakes or cookies; when it doesn't matter if you make a mistake.
* Eggs will separate easier if they are chilled. To separate the white of an egg from the yolk: place three bowls on the counter — one for egg whites, one for egg yolks and the middle one for working over. Place an egg in left hand (if you are right handed) using a knife tap the centre of the egg halfway around the circumference, tapping it just hard enough to break the shell. Working over the centre bowl, hold the egg in both hands, with one end of the egg down, pull egg shell apart. The yolk and part of the egg white will remain in the bottom half of the egg shell. Tip egg yolk back and forth between the two egg shell halves, letting the egg white flow into the bowl below. Place egg yolks in one bowl, place egg whites in the other bowl. Repeat separating additional eggs in this manner.
* If you make a mistake by letting some of the egg yolk accidently get into the egg white, you can set it aside and use it in future baking and you won't ruin more than one egg white. If any fat from the yolks get into the egg whites they will not whip properly.

To Whip Egg Whites (Meringue)

* It must be remembered all utensils must be free of any grease.
* To get the most volume out of your egg whites, whip them at room temperature.
* A good idea is to separate them when chilled, then let them come to room temperature before you whip them.
* The addition of cream of tartar acts as a stabilizer. You may add 5mL (1 tsp.) cream of tartar for every cup of whites. You can expect 2 1/2-4 times the volume you start out with.
* Tube pans are used for baking whipped egg whites, as the tube in the centre helps support the egg white mixture as it rises while baking. *Do not grease tube pan.
* If you do not add sugar to egg whites they will be tough after they are baked.

Soft Meringue

Used to top pies, tarts, etc. with cooked fillings...

For 20cm. (8-inch) pie

2........2 egg whites	(1) Beat egg whites with cream of tartar until foamy.
1/2mL...1/8 tsp. cream of tartar	
50mL....1/4 cup sugar	(2) Gradually add sugar and flavouring.
1mL.....1/4 tsp. vanilla (Opt.)	

2........2 egg whites
1/2mL...1/8 tsp. cream of tartar
50mL....1/4 cup sugar
1mL.....1/4 tsp. vanilla (Opt.)
****

For 22cm. (9-inch) pie

3........3 egg whites
1mL.....1/4 tsp. cream of tartar
75mL....1/3 cup sugar
1mL.....1/4 tsp. vanilla (Opt.)
****

(1) Beat egg whites with cream of tartar until foamy.
(2) Gradually add sugar and flavouring.
(3) Continue beating until stiff and sugar is completely dissolved.
(4) Rub a small amount of mixture between fingers. If you feel sugar crystals the mixture has not been beaten enough.
* If sugar is not completely dissolved there will be beads of syrup on the surface of the baked meringue.

(5) Pile meringue on top of cooked pie.
(6) Spread it evenly, making sure the meringue is sealed to the edge of the crust.
(7) Using a spatula tap top of meringue lifting it up, foaming peaks that curl over slightly.
(8) Bake just above centre in 180°C (350°F) oven for 8-10 minutes or until peaks are delicately browned. Cool pies in a draft-free place to avoid shrinkage of meringue.

* Always fold heavy mixture into beaten egg whites, rather than whites into mixture, as less air is forced out of whites in the process.

Boiled Egg Chart (For Extra Large Size)

Soft Boiled Eggs (Cold Start)

2 . . . . . . .2 refrigerated eggs
625mL. . .2 1/2 cups cold water
. . . . .Cold burner
. . . . .Time from start to finish
        13 minutes
        ****

(1) Place eggs in saucepan, cover with water.
(2) Place on burner, turn burner on.
(3) Set timer on for 13 minutes.

(4) When buzzer sounds immediately remove from heat. Pour off boiling water and rinse under cold water.

Soft Boiled Eggs (Hot Start)

625mL. . .2 1/2 cups water
2 . . . . . . .2 refrigerated eggs
. . . . .Time from start to finish
        cold egg 7 minutes
        ****

(1) Bring water to boil in saucepan.
(2) Pierce the large end of the egg shells with a pin, rinse under cold water. This will help prevent it from cracking when placed in the hot water.

(3) Lower eggs into boiling water with a spoon. Set timer. When buzzer sounds remove from heat, pour off boiling water, rinse under cold water. Serve immediately. If eggs are at room temperature, 4 minutes cooking time is sufficient.

Poached Eggs

* Butter the frying pan lightly. Add about 3.5cm. (1 1/2-inch) of water.
* A few drops of lemon juice or vinegar, keeps the eggs from spreading; it also keeps aluminum pans from discolouring.
* Bring to a boil, slip the eggs into the boiling water, reduce heat and let cook for 3-5 minutes (until the top of the egg is cooked).

Fried Eggs

* In a frying pan heat 5mL (1 tsp.) butter or margarine until hot and bubbly. Break and drop eggs into hot fat.
* Sprinkle with salt & pepper. Cover. Reduce heat immediately. Cook until desired doneness.
* A few drops of water may be added to frying pan to hasten cooking the top of the egg. Do not overcook.

Scrambled Eggs

Kountry Koop style...

6........6 strips bacon
30mL....2 Tbsp. butter or margarine
6........6 eggs
.........Salt & pepper
****

(1)　In a cold frying pan, place strips of bacon.
(2)　Turn burner on to medium high.
(3)　Cook bacon until crisp, turning once.

(4)　Place two thicknesses of paper towel onto a warm platter.
(5)　Transfer cooked bacon onto paper towel. Set aside. (This will help reduce some of the fat from the bacon).
(6)　Break the bacon into 1-2.5cm. (1/2-3/4-inch) pieces when cooled.
(7)　Drain fat from the frying pan.
(8)　Melt butter in the same frying pan, until hot enough to sizzle.
(9)　Break eggs into hot butter.
(10)　Cut through egg yolks with a knife. Do not stir, sprinkle with salt & pepper.
(11)　Scatter bacon pieces over the eggs. Cook over low heat just until they begin to set on the bottom.
(12)　Lift eggs to let uncooked part run underneath (do not stir) and continue to cook in this way until all egg is cooked through, but the mixture is still moist.
(13)　Remove from heat, turn gently and serve immediately.

*　To keep bacon from sticking start with a cold frying pan.

Devilled Eggs

6........6 hard boiled eggs
50mL....1/4 cup salad dressing
15mL....1 Tbsp. chopped green onion
1mL.....1/4 tsp. salt
1/2mL...1/8 tsp. pepper
.........Paprika
****

(1)　Using a sharp knife cut eggs in half lengthwise.
(2)　Remove yolks from the whites.
(3)　Using a fork mash yolks and mix in salad dressing, onions, salt & pepper.
(4)　Replace yolk mixture into egg white halves. Sprinkle with paprika.

235

Super Omelette

30mL....2 tsp. butter or margarine
250mL...1 cup chopped mushrooms
30mL....2 Tbsp. diced green pepper (Opt.)
30mL....2 Tbsp. diced onion
175mL...3/4 cup cooked diced ham
4........4 large eggs
30mL....2 Tbsp. water
.........Sprinkle with salt & pepper
50mL....1/4 cup grated cheddar cheese
****

(1) In a 25cm. (10-inch) frying pan melt 5mL (1 tsp.) butter, add mushrooms, pepper, onion and ham.
(2) Cook until vegetables are crisp tender and the ham is warmed through.
(3) Transfer mixture to warmed bowl. Keep warm.
(4) Using a whisk, in another bowl beat together eggs, water, salt & pepper.

(5) In the same frying pan heat remaining 5mL (1 tsp.) butter until hot and bubbly.
(6) Add egg mixture to the frying pan and start to stir immediately with the back of a fork; keeping cooked portions loose in the bottom of the pan. While the eggs are still creamy spread evenly in the pan and immediately sprinkle ham mixture onto half of the omelette.
(7) Cook until the bottom of the omelette is slightly browned.
(8) Slip spatula under the unfilled side of the omelette and fold it over filling.
(9) Sprinkle with grated cheese, remove from heat, cover. Let stand until cheese is partially melted, about 1 minute. Transfer onto heated platter. Serve immediately.

* Serves 2.

Party Cheese Ball

250g.....8 oz. cream cheese
750mL...3 cups grated cheddar cheese
50mL....1/4 cup sour cream
50mL....1/4 cup finely chopped green onions
.........Dash EACH of worcestershire sauce and tabasco sauce
.........Parsley Sprigs
****

(1) Soften cream cheese.
(2) Add remaining ingredients.
(3) Blend together.
(4) Moisten hands and mould into a ball.
(5) Garnish with parsley sprigs.
(6) Cover with plastic wrap.
(7) Chill in refrigerator for 6 hours.
(8) Serve with crackers.

Peanut Butter

1kg .....2 lbs. shelled peanuts   (1)   Warm peanuts and put through
         *********   fine blade of food grinder.

(2)   Transfer 50mL (1/4 cup) of ground peanuts into blender.
(3)   Process until butter begins to form around blades.
(4)   Stop the blender and push peanuts down into blender blades. Do not
     scrape the butter from the blades.

*   Add small amount 30mL (2 Tbsp.) peanuts at a time.
*   Remove the peanut butter from the blender after 250mL (1 cup) has been
    processed and start a new batch.
*   Do not scrape butter away from the blades as this will help process the
    next batch.
*   If peanuts are raw, spread them single layer onto a cookie sheet. Roast
    them just above center in 160-180°C (325-350°F) oven for 10-40 minutes
    until lightly toasted.

Canned Fruit

*   Outside of raspberries or strawberries, most fruits can be canned in a
    syrup made up of 750mL (3 cups) water to 250mL (1 cup) sugar. The
    amount of liquid will depend on what type of fruit is being canned.
*   Bring water and sugar to a boil, stirring until sugar is dissolved. Cover
    and set aside until cool.
*   When jars are packed with fruit (leaving 2.5cm. (1-inch) head space) cover
    with syrup. Seal jars according to directions on canning lids.
*   Process for 20 minutes in canner following the manufacturers instructions.
*   Due to individual tastes, sugar may be increased or decreased.
*   Pears do not need as much sugar; 3-1 is sufficient.
*   Crab apples and rhubarb require more sugar. Therefore 2 water to 1 sugar
    is needed. Process for 30 minutes.
*   Raspberries and strawberries are most tasty with a syrup made up of
    625mL (2 1/2 cups) water to 250mL (1 cup) of sugar. Process for only 10
    minutes.
*   Pour boiling water over peaches, skins can be peeled off easily.
*   To keep pears from turning dark, have ready a bowl of cold salted water
    30mL (2 Tbsp.) salt dissolved in 3L (12 cups) cold water). Peel and core
    pear and immerse in salted water immediately until ready to pack into jars
    and cover with syrup.

Sprouting Method of Mung Beans/Bean Sprouts

Sprouted Mung Beans are what you enjoy in many Chinese dishes as well as salads...

75mL....1/3 cup Mung Beans
****

(1) Rinse Mung Beans well, discard any stones.

Utensils Needed:

1........1 clean cloth
1........1 colander
1........1 pie plate
1........1 bath towel
****

(2) Soak beans in water overnight.
(3) Drain and place beans in a colander lined with a clean cloth.
(4) Fold edges of cloth down loosely over the beans.

(5) Run water through everything.
(6) Set colander in a pie plate to catch drips.
(7) Place in a warm place. Cover with a bath towel (this will keep light out).
(8) Two times a day for 3-4 days pour several litres (quarts) of tepid water through the colander, cloth and all. Replace towel.
(9) Sprouts are ready to eat on the fourth day, or sooner, if they are 3.5cm. (1 1/2-inches).
(10) Remove them from the cloth and place in a covered container. Refrigerate. Do not cut off all circulation of air. Open lid daily. Rinse if sprouts are drying.

* Yields approx. 1L (4 cups).
* The green hulls are good to eat. If you prefer to remove them, rinse fully grown sprouts in a bowl overflowing with warm water. Gently rub them between your hands. The hulls will rise to the top, tip bowl and hulls will be discarded as water flows out of the bowl.

Alfalfa Sprouts

This is one project the youngsters take interest in...

30mL....2 Tbsp. alfalfa seeds
.........Warm water
****

(1) Place alfalfa seeds in canning jar, cover with water. Soak overnight. Drain.

Utensils Needed:

1L ......1 Qt. canning jar with screw top lid
1........1 cheese cloth
1........1 bath towel
****

(2) Cover jar with cheese cloth then screw on ring.
(3) Place jar on its side in a warm place.

(4) Cover with bath towel (this will keep the light out).
(5) Three times a day, run water in, swish beans and pour off water.
     Replace towel. Repeat each day until seeds have sprouted.
(6) Set jar on its side in a sunny window to develop deep green colour as
     sprouts lengthen.
(7) Rinse regularly. Do not let them get dry. Refrigerate when sprouts reach
     desired length after 3 or 4 days.

*   Use in salads or sandwiches.
*   Store the mature sprouts loosely in containers. Open jar daily. Do not cut
     off all circulation of air. Remember sprouts are alive and should be
     handled carefully.

Sprouted Wheat Kernels

Sprouted wheat has a sweet taste...

250mL...1 cup wheat kernels
.........Warm water
****

(1) Place wheat kernels in canning
     jar, cover with water, soak
     overnight.

Utensils Needed:

1L ......1 Qt. wide mouth canning
          jar with screw top lid
1........1 cheese cloth
1........1 bath towel
****

(2) Drain. Cover jar with cheese
     cloth, then screw on lid.
(3) Place jar on its side. Cover
     with bath towel (this will keep
     out the light).

(4) Twice a day, run water into jar. Swish kernels and pour off water.
     *Replace towel.
(5) Keep in a warm place.
(6) When the sprouts are the same length as the grain .6cm (1/4-inch), rinse
     and drain well.
(7) Spread the sprouts on 2 ungreased cookie sheets.
(8) Dry in a 38°C (100°F) oven (no hotter) for 8 hours or until sprouts are
     crunchy.
(9) Store in a dry, air tight container. Keep refrigerated.

*   Add 50mL (1/4 cup) to flour when making a batch of brown bread.

Hints

Food and You

If you are working hard to pay off that mortgage and paying other bills, maybe a few tips about saving on food is the answer to some of your problems...

*   Be a wise shopper, stop and compare prices, stop and compare ingredients.
*   For an example, read the ingredients on a package of lemon pie filling. What is that stuff in there? Now read on, you add your own eggs, sugar and butter. What are you paying for? Cornstarch, salt and lemon flavour. Surprised? I was.
*   As a homemaker, the number one concern on your list, should be to have around you and your family, food that is going to keep your body supplied with the nutrients to keep you healthy.
*   To know what you are eating, good solid food not food that is full of preservatives and goodness knows what else. For taste and nutrition, nothing compares with good home cooking.
*   By using the recipes in this book, I'm hopeful that you will enjoy them as we have over the years. The old saying, practice makes perfect is a very true statement when it comes to cooking, as you will get better and better.
*   There is a wonderful world of food that we are blessed with. As you get acquainted with different foods and how to prepare them you will find it a very rewarding part of your life.
*   May I express the importance of planning. Fresh foods are unequaled. But not all of us have food so close at hand, therefore, freezing and preserving are what comes next.
*   Plan your meal with compassion and in advance. Not last minute what will I have for dinner with only an hour or less to prepare. Not much time to hurry a cut of meat, thaw it out and cook it the way it should be. The microwave oven helps "Oh get that meat on the defrost, will I have time".
*   Try to plan your meals a week in advance, as you do your grocery shopping purchase only enough perishable foods to be used that week. Have preserved and frozen extras for unexpected guests.
*   Take a few minutes to think of hospitals, restaurants, caterers, also if you could, imagine farm wives at harvest time. They prepared three meals plus lunches each day. This all was done from one farm house kitchen.
*   To me, this was planning at its best. When at least a dozen men (I mean, hungry men) sat down to a table of piping hot, scrumptious victuals, in-

240

cluding rich desserts. This planning was not done in one day as foods then were made from scratch.

* Remember, no fridge, no electricity and on coal and wood stoves. These foods are still on the top of everyone's list for taste.
* Food planning and preparing should not be difficult today. With interest you will be able to come through with flying colours.
* When you have company, try not to worry. Yes, you want your meal to be tasty and well presented, but this will come with practice.
* It is all very interesting and rewarding.
* Remember you are serving friends not paying customers. You have invited them over to enjoy their company. They are not there to pick holes in your mistakes. If they are that type, maybe next time you could be more selective in who you invite, someone who is worthy of your efforts. But let it be advised that a lot can be learned through criticism (if you can shun off the embarrassment).
* So relax and enjoy. You're not out to win blue ribbons to start with.
* May I emphasize again, plan what you are having and work accordingly. Having things prepared a day in advance (or even longer, like frozen casseroles, soups and desserts) all make entertaining a pleasure.
* Get the men to do the dishes, then you're smiling as you sit back with your hot coffee. Did I hear somebody grumble or was that laughter?

Utensils

Besides all the large appliances in your kitchen, it is imporant to have your smaller utensils at hand. . .

Kitchen Scales: You will find many uses for them.

Wire Whip: When choosing a wire whip make sure it is the size to fit your hand. I once bought a wire whip but gave it away to a gentleman as it was too large for me to use. Also, do not choose a whip with a plastic handle. The food gets trapped in the handle and will haunt you when it dries up and falls out into your mixture.

Metal Spatula: For icing cakes, choose one with square tip. This is a must when icing the sides of the cake. A rounded tip will not come in close enough to the cake bottom.

Cannisters: Glass containers are my preference. They hold 4 litres (4 Qts.) of supplies each. This is a good size for biscuit mix, bran, powdered milk, rice, etc. They measure 14cm. (5 1/2-inches) across the top. This is one feature I do enjoy, as I can dip my measuring cup right in. They have a glass lid with a knob on the top, heavy enough to keep air tight. Being glass you can easily see what you have inside. You can decorate them with decals, or wrap any wrapping paper around them to match your kitchen decor. Cut instructions off the package and put inside with the ingredients so you will know how to prepare them. If you are worried about chipping the top, wrap the inner part of the lid with 2cm. (3/4-inch) masking tape. It is quite unnoticeable.

Shaker: Use to shake whipping cream when only a small amount is needed, shake puddings, gravies, etc.

Funnels: Use to fill the small salad oil bottle you have close by. Filling salt & pepper shakers. Handy for adding sugar, juice mixes, etc. into bottles.

Assemble Ingredients:
* It is very important to read through the recipe you have decided to use. Reread it until it is familiar to you.
* Check list of ingredients and see if you have the necessary items, spices, butter, cake pans, cookie sheets, etc.
* Set everything you will need onto the counter, as you use each item place it apart from the others. Then there is no guess work.
* As you use your spices replace the top onto the bottle. Spices and herbs will retain their flavour a long time if this is done faithfully.

Knowing Your Oven

* Learning about your oven is very important.
* Ovens vary somewhat, therefore, the instructions in this book is only a guide, that works out best in most ovens. As you use your oven you will become more familiar as to which rack position works best for you.
* Place oven racks in the position you want them before you preheat your oven. My oven takes 12 minutes to preheat to 180°C (350°F). Check your timing so you don't have it on too long and waste electricity, but in time to have it ready when needed. All recipes in this book required a preheated oven for proper baking time.
* Do not overcrowd your oven. If heat cannot circulate to all parts of the oven the baking will not cook evenly and your baking will burn on the bottom.
* Leave a 5cm. (2-inch) margin between pans and the wall of the oven.
* You can use two top racks while making cookies; exchange cookie sheets half way through the baking time.

Diagram:

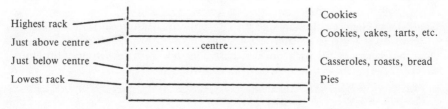

Highest rack	Cookies
	Cookies, cakes, tarts, etc.
Just above centre	centre
Just below centre	Casseroles, roasts, bread
Lowest rack	Pies

242

* Keep parsley in a glass of water, place on window sill, clip off with sharp scissors when needed.
* Chop parsley fine, place in a cottage cheese or any plastic container with a tight fitting lid. Freeze. Spoon out as needed, return container to freezer.
* Soak lemons in hot water for 15 minutes before squeezing. You will yield just about twice the amount.
* To perk up limp celery, cut into serving pieces, place in cold water and small amount of sugar.
* Extreme temperature change will cause dishes to crack. Never set hot dishes on a cold surface.
* After removing food from pots or pans, add hot not cold water for soaking prior to cleaning. Do this immediately after they are emptied. It makes washing time so much easier.
* To frost cold drink glasses, dampen the edge of each glass, place any flavour of jelly powder onto a plate. Dip in dampened glass to coat the rim. This is good with milk shakes, cold drinks, etc.
* Set out two 15cm. (6-inch) plates, put lemon juice on one and granulated sugar on the other. Dip a mug in the lemon juice then into the sugar. This is good with hot coffees.
* Keep empty coffee cans. Use them to dump cigarette ashes in; cover with its own lid. There is no need to worry about catching on fire. Empty coffee tins are also good for discarding hot fat. Or better yet, you can bake bread in well greased coffee tins.
* Melt wax in a metal container with a spout on it. Use to pour wax when sealing jams and jellies. Place jars of jams and jellies on paper towel when sealing with wax. Drips of wax if any rest on the towel not on the counter.
* To save precious time on wash day sort clothes the night before you wash. Put soap and dry clothes (first load) into machine, start machine when you rise in the morning. One load done while you get husband off to work. Load machine with second load, another load done while you get kids off to school.

Baking Soda

I am quite sure most everyone from time to time has read the many ways baking soda can be used. I would like to convey some ideas that I have used successfully, with no worry of scratching the surface...

* Make a paste of soda and water.
* With a soft cloth, you can wipe clean both coffee and tea stains from china cups, mugs, tea pots, and stainless steel cutlery.
* Ideal for cleaning the chrome on toasters, toaster ovens, and tea kettles.
* To clean the inside of thermos bottles, place 30mL (2 Tbsp.) baking soda in the thermos, fill with boiling water, let set for a few hours and rinse.
* Use soda paste to remove odours from hands.
* For a soothing, refreshing bath, add 125mL (1/2 cup) of baking soda to the bath water.

* To relieve sunburn discomfort, rub with apple cider vinegar or, a paste of baking soda and water.

* To clean out molasses carton: set carton in a bowl of hot water for about 5 minutes or until in liquid form. Cut off the top part of the carton and scrape clean with a spatula.

* If your juice container measures 2 1/2 litres (10 cups) and you only require 1 1/2 litres (6 cups) for your mix, mark the outside with adhesive tape. You won't have to measure each time, you will just have to fill to tape line.

* Freeze meat in small amounts. Have meat sliced to suit recipes before freezing, e.g., stir-fry, stew, hamburger patties, diced pork, etc. Partially frozen meat can be easily cut into paper thin slices or cubes to whatever size you require.

* Q-tips, toothpicks and toothbrushes are very handy tools for cleaning hard to get at places. For example, they are very helpful in cleaning around the blades of the blender or knife next to the handle; as well as can opener cutters or the telephone dial.

* To peel onions without tears, set a fan nearby to blow fumes away from you. If you are only doing a small amount, simply blow as you prepare.

* To keep cheese from graining when frozen; wrap it in tin foil, freeze. Remove from freezer, place in fridge to thaw in tin foil before unwrapping.

* Butter bottom of cake pan. Cover bottom of cake pan with wax paper, butter wax paper. Do not butter sides of cake pan. This will give the cake something to cling to as it rises.

* Cut an empty Nestle Quick carton in half, use the bottom part to store Kool-Aid or other small envelopes. Ideal to set bottle of oil in after using. Helps keep shelf clean. Cut off larger cartons like cold cereal boxes and use them to store spaghetti mix and other packages.

* Use Band-Aids to protect your thumb and index finger when grating cheese, nutmeg, etc.

* Set aside a new rubber spatula, using only when whipping and folding egg whites. It will remain free of grease which is very important when using for egg whites. Wrap it in plastic or a sandwich bag when not in use.

* Use colouring in paste form for icings, as paste will not water down your mixture. Use clean toothpicks when adding colouring paste as it must be kept clean.

* Before measuring molasses, honey and other syrup, oil cup with cooking oil. Dusting cup with flour works as well.

* Slicing cheese made easy: use 1m (3-ft.) of ordinary sewing thread, wrap around both hands with thread held taut between both index fingers. You will be able to slice cheese any thickness you prefer.

* Cheese should be very cold when grating.

* Icing cakes: mix together a very thin icing, using water and icing sugar. Spread on cake to set crumbs. Let harden then ice as usual. If colouring is used the crumb base should be coloured also.

* Keep all small lids in one cupboard or drawer, you will then know exactly where to find them.

* It also saves time when you have one place to store rubber gloves, wax applicators, vacuum attachments, etc., and returning them when you're finished; saves you from hunting for them the next time.
* Do not put sharp knives or other sharp objects in your dish water.
* Coat the inside of a gelatine mould with a slight amount of salad oil or salad dressing for easy removal.
* Rub a small amount of oil on a warm cast iron fry pan after each washing; this prevents rusting.
* To remove skins from tomatoes and peaches plunge them in very hot water.

Metric Conversions

Standard Metric Measure — Spoons

Standard Metric Measure	Spoons
1 millilitre	1/4 tsp.
2 millilitres	1/2 tsp.
5 millilitres	1 tsp.
10 millilitres	2 tsp.
15 millilitres	1 Tbsp.

Cups

50 millilitres	1/4 cup
75 millilitres	1/3 cup
125 millilitres	1/2 cup
150 millilitres	2/3 cup
175 millilitres	3/4 cup
250 millilitres	1 cup
1000 millilitres	4 1/3 cups

Weight — Ounces

Weight	Ounces
30 grams	1 oz.
55 grams	2 oz.
85 grams	3 oz.
125 grams	4 oz.
140 grams	5 oz.
170 grams	6 oz.
200 grams	7 oz.
250 grams	8 oz.
500 grams	16 oz.
1000 grams	32 oz.

Oven Temperature

Celsius	Fahrenheit
140°	275°
150°	300°
160°	325°
180°	350°
190°	375°
200°	400°
220°	425°
230°	450°

Baking Pans

20x20cm., 2L	8x8-inch
22x22cm., 2.5L	9x9-inch
22x33cm., 4L	9x13-inch
25x38cm., 4.5L	10x15-inch
20x5cm., 2L	8x2 round
22x5cm., 2.5L	9x2 round
20x10x7cm., 1.5L	8x4x3 loaf
23x12x7cm., 2L	9x5x3 loaf

Equivalent Chart

3 tsp . . . . = 1 Tbsp. (15mL)
2 Tbsp. . . . . = 1/8 cup (30mL)
4 Tbsp. . . . . = 1/4 cup (50mL)
8 Tbsp. . . . . = 1/2 cup (125mL)
16 Tbsp. . . . . = 1 cup (250mL)
5 Tbsp. + 1 tsp. . . . . = 1/3 cup (75mL)
12 Tbsp. . . . . = 3/4 cup (175mL)
4 oz. = 1/2 cup liquid (125mL)
8 oz. = 1 cup liquid (250mL)
16 oz. . . . . = 1 lb. (500g)
1 oz. . . . . = 2 Tbsp. fat **or** liquid
                                             (30g)
2 cups. . . . . = 1 pint (pt.) (500mL)
2 pints . . . . = 1 quart (qt.) (1L)
5/8 cup . . . . = 1/2 cup + 2 Tbsp.
                                             (155mL)
7/8 cup . . . . = 3/4 cup + 2 Tbsp.
                                             (205mL)
1 jigger. . . . . = 1 1/2 oz. (or 3 Tbsp.)
                                             (45mL)
1 lb. butter . . . . = 2 cups or 4 sticks
                                             (500g)
1 lb. granulated sugar . . . . = 2 cups (500g)
1 lb. icing sugar . . . . = 2 2/3 cups (500g)
1 lb. brown sugar . . . . = 2 2/3 cups (500g)
1 lb. all purpose flour . . . . = 4 cups sifted (500g)
1 lb. cake flour . . . . = 4 1/2 cups sifted (500g)
1 lb. whole wheat flour . . . . . = 3 1/2 cups unsifted
                                             (500g)
8-10 egg whites . . . . = 1 cup (250mL)
12-14 egg yolks. . . . . = 1 cup (250mL)
1 cup (250mL) unwhipped . . . = 2 cups whipped
   cream   (500mL)
1 lb. shredded cheddar cheese = 4 cups (500g)
1/4 lb. crumbled bleu cheese. = 1 cup (125g)
1 lemon . . . . = 3 Tbsp. juice approx.
                                             (45mL)
1 orange. . . . . = 1/3 cup juice approx.
                                             (75mL)

Substitutions for a Missing Ingredient

1 sq. (1 oz.) (30g) chocolate .	= 3 Tbsp. (45mL) cocoa + 1 Tbsp. (15mL) butter
1 Tbsp. (15mL) cornstarch **or** tapioca for thickening	= 2 Tbsp. (30mL) flour
1 cup (250mL) sifted all purpose flour	= 1 cup (250mL) + 2 Tbsp. (30mL) sifted cake flour
1cup (250mL) sifted cake .... flour	= 1 cup (250mL) minus 2 Tbsp. (30mL) sifted all purpose flour
1 tsp. (5mL) baking powder .	= 1/4 tsp. (1mL) soda + 1/2 tsp. (2mL) cream of tartar
1 cup (250mL) sour milk	= 1 Tbsp. (15mL) lemon juice **or** white vinegar; fill cup with sweet milk
1 cup (250mL) sweet milk ...	= 1 cup (250mL) sour milk **or** buttermilk + 1/2 tsp. (2mL) soda
3/4 cup (175mL) cracker .... crumbs	= 1 cup (250mL) bread crumbs
1 cup (250mL) heavy sour ... cream	= 1/3 cup (75mL) butter + 2/3 cup (150mL) milk in any sour milk recipe.
1 tsp. (5mL) dried herbs.....	= 1 Tbsp. (15mL) fresh herbs
1 cake compressed yeast.....	= 1 pkg. active dry yeast **or** 1 Tbsp. (15mL) active dry yeast
1 Tbsp. (15mL) instant onion rehydrated	= 1 small fresh onion
1 Tbsp. (15mL) prepared .... mustard	= 1 tsp. (5mL) dry mustard
1/8 tsp. (1/2mL) garlic...... powder	= 1 small pressed clove
1 lb. (500g) whole dates	= 1 1/2 cups (375mL) pitted dates
3 medium bananas..........	= 1 cup (125mL) mashed
3 cup (750mL) cornflakes....	= 1 cup (250mL) crushed
10 miniature marshmallows ..	= 1 lge. marshmallow
1 lge. egg.................	= 1/4 cup (50mL)

Index

253

The Bride's Choice Cook Book
Classic Collection

Name ....

Address ....

City ....

Province/State .... Postal Code/Zip ....

Please send .... copies of:
The Bride's Choice Cook Book at $14.95 per copy plus $2.00 for postage and handling.

Cheque or money order enclosed for $.........
Payable to: Kountry Koop Kitchen Ltd.
        21314 - 80th Avenue, R.R. #11
        Langley, B.C.
        V3A 6Y3

      Price subject to change.

....

The Bride's Choice Cook Book
Classic Collection

Name ....

Address ....

City ....

Province/State .... Postal Code/Zip ....

Please send .... copies of:
The Bride's Choice Cook Book at $14.95 per copy plus $2.00 for postage and handling.

Cheque or money order enclosed for $.........
Payable to: Kountry Koop Kitchen Ltd.
        21314 - 80th Avenue, R.R. #11
        Langley, B.C.
        V3A 6Y3

      Price subject to change.